GLOBAL ISLAMOPHOBIA

Global Connections

Series Editor: Robert Holton, Trinity College, Dublin

Global Connections builds on the multi-dimensional and continuously expanding interest in Globalization. The main objective of the series is to focus on 'connectedness' and provide readable case studies across a broad range of areas such as social and cultural life, economic, political and technological activities.

The series aims to move beyond abstract generalities and stereotypes: 'Global' is considered in the broadest sense of the word, embracing connections between different nations, regions and localities, including activities that are trans-national, and trans-local in scope; 'Connections' refers to movements of people, ideas, resources, and all forms of communication as well as the opportunities and constraints faced in making, engaging with, and sometimes resisting globalization.

The series is interdisciplinary in focus and publishes monographs and collections of essays by new and established scholars. It fills a niche in the market for books that make the study of globalization more concrete and accessible.

Also published in this series:

Global Islamophobia
Muslims and Moral Panic in the West

Edited by

GEORGE MORGAN
University of Western Sydney, Australia

SCOTT POYNTING
Manchester Metropolitan University, UK

ASHGATE

Published by
Ashgate Publishing Limited
Wey Court East
Union Road
Farnham, Surrey
GU9 7PT England

Ashgate Publishing Company
110 Cherry Street
Suite 3-1
Burlington, VT 05401-3818
USA

www.ashgate.com

British Library Cataloguing in Publication Data
Global Islamophobia : Muslims and moral panic in the West. – (Global connections)
1. Islamophobia. – Europe, Western. – Case studies. 2. Islamophobia. – Cross-cultural studies. 3. Moral panics. – Europe, Western. – Case studies. 4. Moral panics. – Cross-cultural studies. I. Series II. Morgan, George. III. Poynting, Scott.
305.6'9704–dc23

Library of Congress Cataloging-in-Publication Data
Global Islamophobia : Muslims and moral panic in the West / [edited] by George Morgan and Scott Poynting.
    p. cm. – (Global connections)
    Includes index.
    ISBN 978-1-4094-3119-0 (hardcover : alk. paper) – ISBN 978-1-4094-3120-6 (ebook) 1. Islamophobia. 2. Moral panics. 3. Islam – 21st century. 4. Muslims – Non-Muslim countries. I. Morgan, George. II. Poynting, Scott.
    BP52.G56 2011
    305.6'97091821–dc23   2011046422

ISBN   9781409431190 (hbk)
ISBN   9781409431206 (ebk)

Reprinted 2013

Printed and bound in Great Britain
by MPG PRINTGROUP

Contents

Notes on Contributors

Ryan J. Al-Natour is a doctoral candidate at the Institute for Culture and Society, University of Western Sydney.

Scott A. Bonn is Assistant Professor of Sociology at Drew University in Madison, New Jersey.

Bruce M.Z. Cohen is Senior Lecturer in the Department of Sociology at the University of Auckland.

Bruno Cousin is Assistant Professor of Sociology at the University of Lille 1.

Selda Dagistanli is Lecturer in Criminology at the School of Social Sciences, University of Western Sydney.

Kevin M. Dunn is Professor of Human Geography and Urban Studies at the School of Social Sciences and Psychology, University of Western Sydney.

Joanna Gilmore is a PhD candidate and Graduate Teaching Assistant in the School of Law, University of Manchester.

Kiran Grewal is a Lecturer in human rights and socio-legal studies at the University of Sydney.

Alanna Kamp is a PhD Candidate at the School of Social Sciences and Psychology, University of Western Sydney.

Joanne Massey is Senior Lecturer in Criminology, Manchester Metropolitan University.

Anneke Meyer is Senior Lecturer in Cultural Studies and Criminology, Manchester Metropolitan University.

George Morgan is Senior Lecturer in the School of Humanities and Communication and the Institute for Culture and Society, University of Western Sydney

Catharina Muhamad-Brandner is a Professional Teaching Fellow in the Department of Sociology, University of Auckland.

Diana Mulinari is Professor at the Centre of Gender Studies, Lund University.

Anders Neergaard is Associate Professor at REMESO - Institute for Research on Migration, Ethnicity and Society, Linköping University.

Greg Noble is Associate Professor at the Institute for Culture and Society, University of Western Sydney.

Francis Pakes is Reader in Comparative Criminology, Institute of Criminal Justice Studies, University of Portsmouth.

Scott Poynting is Professor in Sociology, Manchester Metropolitan University

Rajinder Singh Tatla is an Honours graduate in Criminology and Sociology from Manchester Metropolitan University.

Tommaso Vitale is Associate Professor of Sociology at Sciences Po, Paris (Centre d'études européennes).

Michael Welch is Professor, Criminal Justice Program, Rutgers University and Visiting Professor, Faculty of Law, University of Sydney.

Foreword

Michael Welch

Ten years after the attacks of 11 September 2001, we continue to witness the scapegoating of Islamic individuals, groups, and even nations accused of supporting terrorism (Welch 2006a, 2009). In March 2011, for instance, a series of US Congressional hearings began, aimed at investigating the supposed radicalization of American Muslims. Facing intense criticism that the panel was a bigoted show trial and would serve little purpose other than reinforce stereotypes that Muslims are somehow prone to political violence, Representative Peter King, the chairman of the House Homeland Security Committee, defended his platform. 'Al Qaeda is recruiting from the Muslim community,' said King (Shane 2011: 4). Opponents of the hearings countered by accusing King of pushing forward an inquisition rather than attempting to decipher the intricacies of terrorist plots. 'This hearing is not focusing on the acts of a criminal fringe but is broad-brushing an entire community,' remarked Alejandro J. Beutel, policy analyst at the Muslim Public Affairs Council in Washington (Shane 2011: 5).

Congressman King's hearings are emblematic of other campaigns geared at marginalizing Muslims, especially as America stepped closer to the ten-year anniversary of 9/11. In 2010, news organizations around the world gave close coverage to the controversy over the so-called 'Ground Zero Mosque.' Although its sponsors stress that the venue was planned to serve as an interfaith centre for followers of many religions, negative − even hostile − reaction to the 'mosque' gained momentum: some polls indicated that 71 per cent of Americans opposed the centre (Abdel-Fattah 2010: 9). Many commentators reiterated a common sentiment that Ground Zero is a sacred site, despite the fact that strip clubs with nude dancers surround the neighbourhood. When that observation was pointed out, one critic of the 'mosque' responded: 'The terrorists were not strippers' (Abdel-Fattah 2010: 9). Here, an all too familiar calculus persists: Muslims equal terrorists.

Such demonization in a post-9/11 world also resonates in personal testimonies of other self-appointed terrorist detectors, among them is Brigitte Gabriel. A potent public speaker, she lectures a circuit of hundreds of churches, synagogues, and conference rooms, as well as taking centre stage at a Tea Party convention in fall of 2010. According to Gabriel, 'America has been infiltrated on all levels by radicals who wish to harm America. They have infiltrated us at the CIA, at the FBI, at the Pentagon, at the State Department. They are being radicalized in radical mosques in our cities and communities within the United States' (Goodstein 2011: 2). Gabriel has built an aggressive network of activists committed to challenging Islam within American society. Her group, *ACT! for America* claims 155,000 members in 500 chapters across the country. Through *ACT!*, Gabriel advances a theme contained in her 2008 book titled: *Because They Hate: A Survivor of Islamic Terror Warns America*. She writes: 'In the Muslim world, extreme is mainstream.' She goes on to purport there is a 'cancer' infecting the world: 'The cancer is called Islamofascism. This ideology is coming out of one source: The Koran' (quoted in Goodstein 2011: 4). Amid the various events scheduled for the 10-year anniversary of 9/11, *ACT!* is organizing what it calls 'Open a Koran' day. The group intends to put up 750 display tables in front of post offices, libraries, churches, and synagogues to distribute leaflets selectively highlighting verses in the Koran so as to make them appear to advocate violence, slavery, and the domination of women. All told, those developments point to an enduring Western tendency to denounce Islam.

As the authors featured in this volume point out, excluding Muslims is not confined to the America. Across Western societies, Islamophobia manifests in various forms, most notably as resistance to immigration and asylum seeking. In Australia, politicians have issued alarming cries over the 'invasion of boat people' portrayed as criminal – or worse terrorist – threats. Shortly after 9/11, then Defence Minister Peter Reith (2001), announced plans to bolster border security .. 'look you've got to be able to control it otherwise it can be a pipeline for terrorists to come in and use your country as a staging post for terrorist activities.' Increasingly, the 'boat people' are refugees from US-led wars in Afghanistan and Iraq, and it is often their Islamic background that has added tension to the debate over immigration. A recent survey found that Australians out-worry Americans on immigration. The study reports that 69 per cent of Australian respondents agree that their country 'is taking too many immigrants', as compared to 62 per cent of Americans. Overall, '76 per cent of Australians believe that increasing numbers of asylum seekers and illegal immigrants are an important problem for the country' (United States Studies Centre 2010: 1, see Iyengar and Jackman 2010). As Islamophobia crept further into mainstream Australian politics, the government deleted the term 'multiculturalism' from the title of its immigration service: renaming the Department of Immigration, Multiculturalism, and Indigenous Affairs (DIMIA) the Department of Immigration and Citizenship (DIAC). Unsurprisingly, the hard line against refugees amplified under Howard would survive well into the Gillard government, including tactics of deterrence embodied in mandatory detention and offshore processing. With an eye on national – and cultural – identity, Gillard argued that: 'it was wrong to characterize those who were fearful of the return of asylum boats as 'rednecks', or to try to smother legitimate debate under a blanket of 'political correctness' (Manne 2010: 12). Gillard would go on to say that even her own migrant parents (from Wales) were appalled at the idea that refugees were jumping the queue to receive preferential treatment. 'When Gillard travelled to Darwin, she boarded a coastal patrol vessel in the presence of the member for Lindsay, David Bradbury, to reassure the voters [the 'battlers'] from western Sydney that they were now safe' (Manne 2010: 12, see Burke, 2008, Welch 2012).

Politics of fear are a prominent dimension of Islamophobia, whether in America, Australia, or Europe. As we have seen from time to time, violent incidents – even those not involving Muslims – are quickly distorted to portray Islam as dangerous to Western (Christian) society. The reaction by some newspapers to the 2011 massacre in Oslo is instructive. In Britain, Rupert Murdoch's newspaper, *The Sun*, ran a front-page headline that read, "Al-Qaeda' Massacre: Norway's 9/11'. Murdoch's *Wall Street Journal* also initially blamed 'jihadists', reporting that: 'Norway is targeted for being true to Western norms'. Similarly, on the *Washington Post's* website, Jennifer Rubin cautioned, 'This is a sobering reminder for those who think it's too expensive to wage a war against jihadists'. Putting those claims in their proper perspective, constitutional lawyer and political commentator, Glenn Greenwald, weighed into the controversial media coverage of the attacks in Norway.

> When it became apparent that Muslims were not involved and that, in reality, it was a right-wing nationalist with extremely anti-Muslim, strident anti-Muslim bigotry as part of his worldview, the word 'terrorism' almost completely disappeared from establishment media discourse. Instead, he began to be referred to as a 'madman' or an 'extremist'. It really underscores, for me, the fact that this word 'terrorism', that plays such a central role in our political discourse and our law, really has no objective meaning. It's come to mean nothing more than Muslims who engage in violence. (Greenwald 2011)

Once again, we are met with a prevailing calculus: Muslims equal terrorists. Some observers might be quick to dismiss such biased (Murdoch) news coverage, citing Jerry Seinfeld who quipped: 'People who read the tabloids deserve to be lied to.' However, that would be a missed opportunity. As the contributors to this book convincingly argue, the role of the media in demonizing certain Others is central to the analysis of Islamophobia. Of course, the media is just one of several important drivers. While this volume is committed to outlining the many sources of Islamophobia, it also offers a critique of the way we investigate and understand this particular expression of fear. While the chapters deliver precise examples of global Islamophobia, there is a conscious effort to improve sociological interpretation by re-working the theoretical underpinnings of moral panic: a turbulent and exaggerated response to a putative social problem (Cohen 2002).

In this wide-ranging but focused work, moral panic over Muslims is understood as a popular demonology that produces folk devils at the local and national as well as international levels. The theoretical thrust of the chapters derives from radical sociology, a strain of intellectualism that has challenged mainstream social science since the 1960s. The analysis of moral panic via radical sociology, however, does not rely on a static paradigm. As the authors herein demonstrate, the moral panic model continues to benefit from cross-national and comparative case studies that attend closely to the shifting dynamics of fear and anxiety. In the pages to follow, moral panic theory is subject to renovation in ways that facilitate a sharper depiction of social constructionism and its negative consequences. Whereas moral panic – by definition – ebbs and flows, it typically leaves in its wake long-standing institutional changes that continue to affect adversely the marginalized (e.g., ethnic and religious minorities, the poor, the disenfranchized). Indeed, much of the evidence is staring us in the face. Popular politics that permeate local as well as national anxieties increasingly absorb the 'dangerous world' mindset, prompting even progressive Western cultures (for example the Netherlands, Sweden) to adopt right-wing policies. Heavy investments in policing strategies and technologies designed to target and contain those 'who don't belong' are more often the norm instead of the exception. It is through those security manoeuvres that state power makes contact with the Muslim Other. Overall, such mechanisms of social control have proven to be ironic in the sense that they are counter-productive. Especially with respect to the vague 'war on terror', greater reliance on surveillance, policing, and detention rarely make us feel safe; rather, it operates as a treadmill transporting us from one fearful episode to the next. Along the way, political actors routinely justify even greater expenditures on security while scaling back civil liberties (Glassner 1999, Welch 2009).

Moral panic theory is not intended to be grand and all-encompassing. If it were, it would not be a theory but rather an ideology. Still, over the past several decades the moral panic literature has taken up a host of social problems, ranging from youth culture to drug abuse to asylum seekers (Welch 2006b, Welch, Price, and Yankey 2002, Welch and Schuster 2005a, 2005b). Whereas the central topic of this book is Islamophobia in a global context, its contributors select different angles from which to view the phenomenon. Readers will appreciate the breadth and depth to which the chapters explore the demonization of Muslims. Correspondingly, conceptual issues, such as morality, are put to the forefront of analysis, allowing us to see the progression of traditional sociological theory toward its radical offshoot. Similarly, concerns over power exercised at the local, state, and global levels are given proper scrutiny.Altogether, the volume delivers a unifying theme as it sets out to decipher the ways in which Muslims have been framed as threats to Western societies, its presumed values, and way of life. By doing so, we also are shown the corrosive effects of scapegoating. As sociologist W.I. Thomas (1923) observed while studying immigrant neighbourhoods in Chicago in the early 20th century, what people believe to be real will be real in its consequences.

References

Abdel-Fattah, R. 2010. 'Ground Zero Mosque is an Antidote to Extremism. *Sydney Morning Herald*, September 18-19: 9.

Burke, A. 2008. *Fear of Security: Australia's Invasion Anxiety*. Cambridge: Cambridge University Press.

Cohen, S. 2002. *Folk Devils and Moral Panics: The Creation of Mods and Rockers*. 3rd edition. London: Routledge.

Gabriel, B. 2008. *Because They Hate: A Survivor of Islamic Terror Warns America*. New York: St. Martin's Griffin.

Glassner, B. 1999. *The Culture of Fear: Why Americans are Afraid of the Wrong Things*. New York: Basic Books.

Goodstein, L. 2011. 'Drawing U.S. Crowds With Anti-Islam Message.' *New York Times*, March 7: A1, A6.

Greenwald, G. 2011. *Norway Attacks Expose U.S. Media's Double Standard on 'Terrorism.'* *Democracy Now* [Online: 26 July] Available at: http://www.democracynow.org/2011/7/26/glenn_greenwald_norway_attacks_expose_us [accessed: 13 September 2011].

Iyengar, S. and Jackman, S. 2010 *Australian and American Attitudes to Illegal Immigration: Media release (19 August)*. Sydney: The United States Studies Centre, University of Sydney.

Manne, R. 2010. 'The Nation Reviewed: Comment, Asylum Seekers,' *The Monthly: Australian Politics, Society and Culture*, September: 8-14. *New York Times* 2011. Peter King's Obsession. Editorial, 7 March: A21. Reith, P. 2001. Interview with D. Hinch, [Online, 13 September] Available at: www.defence.gov.au/minister/2001/1309013. doc [accessed: 6 February 2007].

Seinfeld, J. 2011. *Brainy Quotes*. [Online] Available at: http://www.brainyquote.com/quotes/authors/j/jerry_seinfeld.html [accessed: 5 August 2011].

Shane, S. 2011. For Lawmaker Examining Terror, a Pro-I.R.A. Past. *New York Times*, 8 March: A1, A8.

Thomas, W.I. 1923. *The Unadjusted Girl*. Boston: Little, Brown.

United States Studies Centre 2010. *Australian Out-worry American on Illegal Immigration: A Comparative Study*. Sydney: The United States Studies Centre, University of Sydney.

Welch, M. 2006a. *Scapegoats of September 11th: Hate Crimes and State Crimes in the War on Terror*. New Brunswick, New Jersey and London: Rutgers University Press. Korean edition, translated by J. Park (2011) Seoul, Korea: Galmuri.

Welch, M. 2006b. *Moral Panic*. In *Encyclopedia of Activism and Social Justice*, edited by G. L. Anderson and K. Herr. Thousand Oaks, California: Sage Publications.

Welch, M. 2009. *Crimes of Power and States of Impunity: The U.S. Response to Terror*. New Brunswick, New Jersey and London: Rutgers University Press.

Welch, M. 2012. The Sonics of Crimmigration in Australia: Wall of Noise and Quiet Maneuvering, *British Journal of Criminology*, in Press.

Welch, M., Price, E. and Yankey, N. 2002. Moral Panic Over Youth Violence: *Wilding* and the Manufacture of Menace in the Media. *Youth and Society*, 34, (1): 3-30.

Welch, M. and Schuster, L. 2005a. Detention of Asylum Seekers in the UK and US: Deciphering Noisy and Quiet Constructions. *Punishment and Society: An International Journal of Penology*, 7(4): 397-417.

Welch, M. and Schuster, L. 2005b. Detention of Asylum Seekers in the US, UK, France, Germany, and Italy: A Critical View of the Globalizing Culture of Control. *Criminal Justice: The International Journal of Policy and Practice*, 5 (4): 331-355.

Introduction: The Transnational Folk Devil

George Morgan and Scott Poynting

'a necessary act .. a war against the rule by Muslims.'

Anders Behring Breivik

We write this introduction in the grim aftermath of the Oslo massacres of 22 July 2011 in which 77 people died. Most of the victims were members of the youth wing of the Norwegian Labour Party, a party with a history of support for multiculturalism and religious tolerance, and early media speculation suggests that Anders Behring Breivik, who has admitted carrying out the bombing and shootings, believed he was part of a violent crusade against Islam, a shock trooper in the clash of civilizations. His lawyer has suggested that he is probably insane, a remark endorsed by some media and political commentators. Whether or not such a diagnosis is confirmed through legal process, it is important to recognize that by constructing the perpetrator as a deranged monster, one who had lost all sense of moral proportion or attachment to reality, we evade some complicated questions. These concern the rise of new racial politics in the contemporary West, specifically Islamophobia, that attacks the liberal democratic state and calls into question its ability to manage globalization, immigration and cultural difference. The contributions to this book address precisely these questions around what we have called Global Islamophobia. The Oslo massacre shows the clear imprint of a revanchist nationalist politics that has gained popularity in many parts of the contemporary West and is expressed with varying degrees of fanaticism. Far from being completely random and aberrant, the slaughter was very much grounded in a particular conjuncture framed by acute social and cultural tensions. While right-wing political organizations have scurried to denounce Breivik and the murders for which he has claimed responsibility, it is clear that he drew on their (tortured) political logic to rationalize his actions.

Various commentators have observed (Poynting et al. 2004, Welch 2004, 2006, Bonn 2010) that, in the global 'West', the racialized 'Muslim Other' has become the pre-eminent 'folk devil' of our time. This process did not begin with 9/11, but since then has expanded rapidly to reshape the politics of multiculturalism in various societies. While nationalism and indeed imperialism retain their ideological salience, the new xenophobic politics has profoundly undermined cultural pluralism that has been so central to liberal democracy. The first key aim of the book is to demonstrate the globalization of this contemporary Islamophobia. The elements of this popular demonology, the processes of assembling the various local and national Muslim folk devils at issue, and the methods of social containment of the communities of deviance associated with this demonization, are startlingly similar internationally, as the cases in this volume demonstrate.

The second aim of this book is to show that the moral panic framework, drawn from mid-twentieth century radical sociology, can and should be suitably developed to recognize the influence of globalization over the social processes which the framework has described and explained. We will argue that in renovating the moral panic model for a global era, questions of geographic scope, of relations between the local/national and the global, and also of duration and fixity of the panics need to be addressed. Thus updated, the model can usefully comprehend how Western societies have increasingly responded since the 1970s and 80s to 'global' Islam and to Muslim minorities amongst their citizens. In the post-9/11 West, some categories of citizen are represented as dangerous to 'our way of life', and their communities are suspected of harbouring enemies of the nation. This demonization conflates particular cultural forms with disregard for the law and enmity towards the nation. In this ideology, Muslim minorities appear as a corrosive influence, refusing to integrate, and undermining national values. Media coverage of 'radical' Islamists along these lines encourages the inference that many from Muslim backgrounds are using the cover of liberal democratic freedoms to subvert liberal democracy. The familiar hysteria is circulated and othering is amplified, stern measures are called for and tough responses are elicited from the state.

Moral Panic Still Goes

We thus take as a starting point that the concept of moral panic (Cohen 1972, Hall et al, 1978, Goode and Ben-Yehuda 1994, Critcher 2003, Garland 2008) is useful for understanding how Islamophobia is manifested in the public sphere and shapes political process. Key moments or elements of the moral panic framework are useful for making sense of the ways Western nations have responded to 'global' Islam and to Muslim minorities amongst their citizens. These include:

i) *Volatility*: The public expression of concern (by media, primary definers, etc) about a condition or set of events is mercurial, often erupting and subsiding very suddenly, and sometimes over longer and recurring cycles. Moral panics can be a long time brewing but they boil over rapidly. Then they subside, but the ingredients may remain simmering for the next cycle of bubbling up. These days, those ingredients are sourced globally.

ii) *Hostility*: In the course of this eruption, folk devils are identified and forced to endure intense scrutiny. They are cast as outsiders, enemies of society, subject to strong measures by the state and identified as deserving of harsh punishment. Sometimes these are 'internal outsiders': enemies within. As Hall et al. (1978) showed in *Policing the Crisis*, this out-casting can be linked very powerfully to racialization.

iii) ***Projection***: It is often the case that underlying social anxieties are 'projected' onto these folk demons, such that they can be scapegoated for all manner of perceived social ills, from indiscipline among young people, to street violence, to cultures of misogyny and outbreaks of sexual violence, to national disunity, to demographic change, to unemployment. In the current conjuncture, many of these anxieties arise structurally from globalization processes. There is an important moral dimension to this blaming process, in which social values and 'goods' that are under tension are ideologically reasserted by 'right-thinking' people, and those who fail to subscribe to them sufficiently in the judgment of moral entrepreneurs, are called to task.

iv) ***Disproportionality***: In the circumstances of moral panic, the state's reaction, the measures instituted to address the problem, are out of proportion to the magnitude of the threat posed. These stern measures are invariably called for by popular media, which exaggerate the perceived problem and predict dire consequences if the state fails to respond dramatically. They are often the subject of an 'auction' by political leaders in populist mode: each side seeking to show action and decisiveness in the face of the 'problem', and to avoid portrayal as 'weak', ineffectual and vacillating. They are also often accompanied by new or extraordinary powers demanded by the repressive arms of the state, which use the popular media to press these demands. In the context of the 'global war on terror', these powers are increasingly mirrored or indeed shared between nation states.

Renovating the Moral Panic Model

From the famous opening paragraph of Stan Cohen's highly influential *Folk Devils and Moral Panics* (2002: 1)[1], we can discern three respects in which the model might well be updated to take account of social changes over the four decades since it was written. Many have suggested revisions to the theory or the concept of moral panic, and many have critiqued the model for other reasons; our point here is that renovating but retaining the model enables us better to grasp contemporary global Islamophobia. Cohen writes of 'periods of moral panic' as emerging 'every now and then'. Such periods end when 'the condition' 'disappears' and 'submerges', and have prolonged effects when it 'deteriorates and becomes more visible' (2002: 1). These aspects of emergence and submergence go to the question of the timing

---

1 'Societies appear to be subject, every now and then, to periods of moral panic. A condition, episode, person or group of persons emerges to become defined as a threat to societal values and interests; its nature is presented in a stylized and stereotypical fashion by the mass media; the moral barricades are manned by editors, bishops, politicians and other right-thinking people; socially accredited experts pronounce their diagnoses and solutions; ways of coping are evolved or (more often) resorted to; the condition then disappears, submerges, or deteriorates and becomes more visible' (Cohen 2002: 1).

of moral panic. Over the last thirty years several influential social theorists (see for example Beck 1992 and Giddens 1990) have argued that precariousness and risk have created a pervasive and ongoing sense of social anxiety. This suggests that something like moral panics may be more or less ongoing and permanent, and not cyclical and sporadic. Yet Cohen (2002) claimed that the notion of enduring moral panic was a contradiction in terms (2002: xxxvii): 'A panic, by definition, is self-limiting, temporary and spasmodic, a splutter of rage which burns itself out'. It is important to distinguish the highly charged conditions of moral panics (such as have followed, for example, from the British riots of August 2011) from the times in which media coverage and public debate can be conducted in a more sober register. However, there is a case for directing more attention to the connection between discrete moral panics, and recognizing that the process of producing folk devils is ongoing and cumulative. In the case of global Islamophobia, it is now clear, however, that the sort of folk demonizing that has constructed little Bin Ladens in localities across the globe is still with us ten years after 9/11, and the Islamophobic raging might be a very long splutter indeed. To put it another way, this is a case where moral panic has long since deteriorated and become more visible, engendering cycle after cycle of panic, of a variety of scope and localities. Can we use the concept of moral panic to denote the global stock upon which each of these 'splutters' draws? Greg Noble, in his chapter of this book, refers to what we are here calling a 'global stock' as 'moral turbulence'. It is clear that this occurs at a different 'level' from the local/national and more temporally bounded moral panic of the 'splutter of rage' type that served well to describe the reaction to the Mods and Rockers.

Beyond the question of timing, we need secondly to consider the scale of what Goode and Ben-Yehuda (2009: 43) call the *locus* of moral panics. How big a constructed collectivity, over what geographic space, has its 'values and interests' (Cohen, 2002: 1) affronted by the folk devil at issue? In Cohen's study of the conflict between the Mods and Rockers, the initial outrage might have been local in each instance, but the media inventory soon ensured that it became aggregated into a *national* panic. It is certainly the state – and that ultimately means the nation-state – that is called upon for the requisite 'show of force' (2002: 98-9). However, the moral panics around Islam are globalized in a way that sets them apart from the twentieth century counterparts. The presentation of the threat to 'our civilization' as transnational provides a pretext for synchronized action amongst nations of the West: from developing common counter-terror measures to remarkably similar national debates about the supposed failure of multiculturalism and the refusal of Muslim immigrants to integrate. Along with this, we would argue, there is a sense of a beleaguered transnational imagined community in the global north.

Contemporary Islamophobia differs from the moral panics of the mid to late twentieth century in being grounded in popular anxieties around transnationalism. If the cultural anxieties and punitive politics of this earlier era were about the failure of immigrants to assimilate, to practice ways of life and embrace the dominant values of the host society, then transnationalism adds an extra dimension.

It suggests not only an enduring allegiance to another place/people/set of values, however romantically constructed, but also the operation of a global cultural space in which this alternative transnational imagined community is nourished. As Basch et al (1992: 2) say, contemporary immigrant communities 'take actions, make decisions, feel concerns, and develop identities within social networks that connect them to two or more societies simultaneously'.

So it is important to recognize the third aspect of Cohen's model that requires renovation. Cohen identified the media as key players in moral panic, but these have passed through epochal changes: they are now global and virtually instantaneous. The growth of new social media alongside the old mass media has profoundly altered both the ways in which the news is covered and public opinion formed. Cohen (2002: 11) recognized in 1972 that 'The gallery of folk types – heroes and saints, as well as fools, villains and devils – is publicized not just in oral tradition but to much larger audiences and with much greater dramatic resources'. How much larger the audience now, and how more instantaneous the publicizing? In the era of the 'war on terror', a folk devil can be a globalized one, and the deviancy amplification spiral subjected to temporal as well as spatial compression. The local coverage of 'citizen journalists' can through new media contribute to the process of producing or challenging contemporary panics and folk devils.

The twentieth century moral panic model tended to towards a 'supply-side' emphasis on the role of old media. Yet, as social scientists such as Goode and Ben-Yehuda (2006: 39) have observed in critiquing what they see as overly structuralist, deterministic or indeed conspiratorial notions of moral panic, notably Hall et al.'s *Policing the Crisis*, moral panics must involve people expressing anxieties actually experienced in their everyday lives. Such panics cannot simply be conjured at will by ruling elites manipulating public opinion. Each of the cycles of moral panic that is instanced in this book melds local grievances and fears, inflected by xenophobia, with a globally constructed 'radical Muslim' folk demon in what is arguably a long-term and large-scale process of Islamophobic moral panic. While recognizing local conjuncture, peculiarities and distinctiveness, and of course conscious agency, if we do not grasp the big structures and processes, the global patterns and the forces that shape them, we have no *context* for understanding the lived and the local and no way of explaining the astonishing similarities between one local Islamophobic panic and another, from one western, first-world nation to the next.

Scapegoating as the Ideological Resolution of Real Contradictions

Moral panics usually involve a supposed identification of a society's ills – fixating on and aggregating a range of symptoms – and prescriptions to remedy these by both accredited experts and ordinary people. What makes the diagnoses 'ring true' is that they resonate with ordinary people's experiences; those suffering from particular anxieties about, say, the direction or extent of social change, can identify elements of their worries as a generalized and shared sense of a social ailment.

'Explanations' offered by the 'experts' take up their inchoate concerns, render them more articulate, plausible, and sometimes even scientific-sounding, and deliver them back to the anxious audiences in a feedback loop which works to the extent that it reverberates with popular anxieties. 'Folk devils' serve as simplified, easily grasped apparent causes of the problem (often obscuring real structural causes). *The problem* is thus invariably presented as straightforward and without complexity. A range of simplistic 'solutions' is accordingly proposed: often hardline state responses. Each instance of local moral panic about the 'Muslim Other' examined in this volume follows this pattern, and each involves the integration of local concern and outrage with a globally circulating construction of an Islamic folk devil.

One final preliminary comment about racialization and folk-devilry. In the preface to his third edition of *Folk Devils and Moral Panics* (2002: viii-xxvi), Cohen identifies seven themes that have been central to moral panics over the thirty years since his first edition, the last of which is 'Refugees and Asylum Seekers: Flooding our Country, Swamping our Services' (Cohen 2002: xxii-xxvi). The construction of folk devils often involves xenophobia or indeed racism and the moral community allegedly under threat is ethnically constructed, with the racialized other as the corresponding folk devil. Pearson (1983) cleverly traces the history of moral panics about gangs of violent working-class young men, narrating backwards to the seventeenth century when the class was first coming into being, and shows the deviant violence is invariably attributed to the pernicious influence of foreignness. Garotting is unBritish, stabbing is unBritish; fighting as a gang rather than one-to-one is unBritish, hooligans are unBritish and are accordingly so named, and are a threat to the Empire. Hall et al's (1978) study of the 'mugging' moral panic is, as remarked above, a classic study of moral panic which grasps the centrality of racialization: the folk-devil figure of the mugger is Black, and the notion is imported from the US in the 1970s, finding its moment in the context of economic crisis and the advent of the New Right. Goode and Ben-Yehuda (2006: 38) note that the increased hostility toward the 'Other', that is a precondition for constructing folk devils, lends itself to racist stereotyping. We suggest the need to go further than they do, beyond conceiving of this process as merely the sort of denigration and dehumanizing associated with cartoon caricatures of phenotype, prolific and potent as these have been in global Islamophobic moral panic. We probably need to look to the construction of imagined moral communities associated with nation and empire – as well as nascent transnational communities – if we are to understand the moral condemnation in global Islamophobia. If orientalism (Said 1995) arose from earlier practices of empire and the ideological standpoints of earlier empires, some of the old coinage still circulates, and still has currency.

Anti-Muslim Moral Panic and the 'Glocal'

Beyond reasserting the relevance of the moral panic model to the contemporary global climate of Islamophobia, in this book we recognize simultaneously the need to renovate the model to take account of the global scale and its interrelationship with local concerns and issues.

Popular politics usually has a local applicabilty. People come to understand wider problems, to articulate their politics, through immediate reference points in their everyday lives. The politics of global fears are to do with a growing sense that the power of the state to deal with global threats (in their many and various forms) and challenges has diminished. So there arises a cultural vigilantism with more people embracing far right politics, as now in many parts of Europe that were erstwhile progressive strongholds – such as the Netherlands and Sweden, that are focused upon in case studies in this book. Clearly, the nation-state is still where 'state' power operates, but it is also increasingly the case that popular fears are encoded in the language of globalization. This can produce a xenophobia and reactionary gestures from politicians (such as deploying surveillance against 'radicalization', or mandating citizenship tests to enforce 'integration') that imply that the power of the nation state is being strengthened. Yet at the same time there is ever more bilateral and multilateral collaboration between 'Western states' involving their police forces and security services, and a standardization, and indeed often 'policy-laundering', of draconian laws to deal with these 'global problems'.

Beyond and behind the repressive apparatuses of the state, the ideological apparatuses that build hegemony and construct consent assemble and maintain a repertoire of Islamophobic ideological elements which circulate globally and are drawn upon in panics at the local and national levels. News Corporation, to name but one global media conglomerate, has all along stridently supported the 'war on terror', whatever that has meant at the time, and has certainly urged and cheered on the US-led interventions in Afghanistan and Iraq, while staunchly defending the Israeli state, whatever state terrorism it may engage in. In an era of globalized media, the spurious claims and specious arguments of a Mark Steyn operating from North America can reinforce and draw upon those of a Melanie Phillips in London, and be lazily if enthusiastically taken up in a local context in moral panics in, say, Australia, drawing upon urban myths and sensationalist reporting from France, as Daglistanli's and Grewal's chapter in this book shows. Thus an imagined dystopia of 'Londonistan' or 'Eurabia' can furnish the 'moral' for a story about Sydney, in a cautionary tale about the amorality and barbarism of Muslim young men half a globe and half a second away. This book is based on the conviction that there is no single political template for dealing with the presence of Islam and Muslim minorities in the West and therefore presents a series of case studies taken from Europe, North America and Australia. The relative pulls of xenophobia, assimilationism and multiculturalism should be understood in terms of the conjunctures/balance of forces prevailing in particular nation states.

Islamophobia and the politics of 'race'/ethnicity are played out through specific national institutions and power blocs.

But for all of this, the book is based on the recognition that the theory of moral panics requires renovation to take account of globalization. In the last three decades of the twentieth century the dynamics of moral panics around immigration and cultural difference were largely tempered by the discourses of 'tolerance' and cultural pluralism. A racialized backlash against Indochinese asylum seekers and immigrants in Australia in the early 1980s, for instance, obtained little political purchase in the context of bipartisan commitment to multiculturalism. Even the moral panic about Muslims in Britain in the wake of the Salman Rushdie affair in 1989 was couched in terms of 'tolerance' and cultural pluralism – these being convenient sticks with which to beat supposed intolerant book-burning fundamentalists – rather than understanding the offence and hurt that the publication of *The Satanic Verses* caused Muslim communities. There were limits to the state's response to those who appeared, in racialized ideology, to pose a moral threat.

In the post-9/11 world, however, the idea of collective insecurity has been used throughout the 'West' to justify the erasure of base-line national civil and cultural liberties, on the presumption that some communities indulge a sort of 'fifth column', a danger to 'our way of life', and that their communities give succour to enemies within the nation and support to enemies outside. This did not begin on 11 September 2001, and forerunners of the contemporary phenomenon can be seen during and after the Gulf War of 1990-1 (Poynting and Mason 2007). It taps into a popular xenophobia which takes certain elements of immigrant cultures for evidence of deprecation of the supposed national culture and rejection of expectations that they integrate with it. From this perspective, Muslim minorities appear as an inscrutable and inherently volatile presence, as a subversive influence, immune to the interpellations of citizenship. Media campaigns against supposedly indulgent and morally relativist multiculturalism combine with sensationalist scapegoating of new 'suspect communities' (Hillyard 1993, Pantazis and Pemberton 2009) to encourage a knee-jerk reactionary communitarianism which stands in stark contrast to liberal and social-democratic universalism.

It is a truism that globalization offers political challenges that are difficult to resolve within the framework of the modern nation state. Some commentators have noted that globalization (in its various forms: economic, cultural, political) ironically often accentuates nationalism and xenophobia. It has produced reactions based on a retreat from cultural pluralism and towards monocultural communal imaginaries. This collection examines the part played in this process by Islamophobic moral panics since the turn of the millennium.

This trend is played out in various ways. Firstly, there are struggles over the symbolic presence of Islam in Western (particularly global) cities. At various times and places governments have responded to Islamophobic populist campaigns to ban the building of mosques, minarets, Muslim schools and prayer rooms. The right of Muslim women to wear the 'veil' (hijab, jilbab, niqab, burqa) in various public places has been challenged in a number of nations, especially in educational settings. More nations are resorting to patriotic testing and scrutiny of applicants for residency and citizenship and demanding (often ridiculously contrived) demonstrations of national allegiance or cultural appropriateness from immigrants. Secondly, global fears have provided the pretext for states to adopt coercive/punitive measures, and regimes of surveillance (Poynting and Mason 2008), the extent of which would have been unthinkable in the West during the latter part of the twentieth century. This has meant a blurring of the boundaries between policing and counter-terrorism so that police in various societies can now undertake activities previously the domain only of espionage or military personnel. Thirdly, there have been challenges to the rights to free expression and association of demonized minorities. While in some places this is given official sanction and informs policing, security services, and prosecutorial practice, in others it takes the form of authorities turning a blind eye to racist vilification and violence, along with their consequences – a form of 'permission to hate' (Perry 2001, Poynting and Perry 2007).

Paradoxically, these foreclosures of cultural pluralism and political liberties, and the rise of xenophobia, have taken place as public discourse assumes a more global character. Today we are seeing greater levels of cooperation between nation states towards standardizing strategies of policing of, and punitive response towards, those deemed to be 'outsiders' and to pose a threat. National debates about cultural symbols are framed in international contexts. Local resistance to the establishment of a mosque in, for example, Western Sydney or London's East End, might well refer to the referendum banning the construction of minarets in Switzerland. Ironically, these global circuits are completely compatible with the emergence of local siege mentality and its official and political consequences.

Cases Considered in this Book

In Chapter 1 dealing with the furore that unfolded in the German press in 2006 around Rütli High School in Berlin, Bruce Cohen and Catharina Muhamad-Brandner trace a moral panic in which this disadvantaged working-class school became infamous nationally and indeed internationally as 'the worst school in Germany'. The media coverage stemmed from a leaked letter from the school's director pleading for help, after acts of violence and threats to fellow teachers in this school, which has a high number of children from migrant backgrounds, notably Turkish and Arab. The moral panic model here explains how the press overwhelmingly presented these children and their families as folk devils. Local and national press coverage – both tabloid and broadsheet across the political spectrum – was surprisingly uniform in the problematization of such migrant groups. This moral panic instances continuing problematization of non-western migrants and their descendents by the dominant order in German society. It is a continuation of the process of 'othering' against such populations that, post-9/11, has intensified into the realms of Islamophobia, and resonates with calls to restrict immigration of those who cannot 'integrate'.

Although the Netherlands is traditionally thought of as one of the most tolerant Western nations, the last decade there has seen the emergence of hostile and excluding social discourses in relation to immigrants, asylum seekers and Muslims, as evidenced in Chapter 2 by Francis Pakes. It is in particular youngsters of Moroccan descent that bear the brunt of this racialization, despite the fact that they are often second-generation immigrants, born and bred in the Netherlands. Their over-involvement in the criminal justice system is well documented, as are under-achievements in education and employment. The chapter examines whether the hostile social discourse is caused by or evidence for a moral panic, in the aftermath of the events of 9/11, and subsequent events that have been said to have caused a cultural trauma. These include the murder of maverick right-wing politician Pim Fortuyn in 2002 and the murder of film-maker, columnist and TV personality Theo van Gogh in 2004. The chapter reflects on the state of Dutch tolerance and the impact upon it of events shaped by globalization.

Bruno Cousin and Tommaso Vitale demonstrate in Chapter 3 how the intellectual field played a determinant role in the development of Islamophobia in Italy during the first decade of the 21st century. Beyond the public declarations of right-wing anti-multiculturalist politicians who regularly denounce the moral inferiority of Islam, and a level of popular and institutional hostility towards Muslims that is the highest in Western Europe, Cousin and Vitale find the mobilization of cultural producers behind an intellectual Islamophobia in Italy. Highly publicized journalists/writers – such as Oriana Fallaci and Magdi Allam – as well as the intellectuals of Berlusconi's party, numerous clerics and academics close to the Catholic Church, and several of their secular conservative colleagues, have contributed to legitimate and reinforce an anti-Islamic *Zeitgeist* that has developed and reinvented the common sense about the 'migration question' and generated a specific xenophobia against Muslims.

In Chapter 4, Diana Mulinari and Anders Neergaard analyze how Sweden, once seen as a pillar of tolerance in Europe, today evinces racism against Muslims of the most central, visible, and normalized variety. They analyze the double-edged relationship between women and migrants and the Swedish xenophobic populist party, Sweden Democrats (SD), and the specific discourse the party embodies emphasizing conservative gender values, anti-Islam, anti-Arab and anti-Muslim racism, while propagating notions of Swedish and European values. The research is theoretically framed within feminist and postcolonial studies; methodologically the study is based on in-depth interviews and life-stories with women and migrants representing SD in municipal councils, and text analysis of policy documents, party-political material and media. Gendered aspects are stressed in the Islamophobia of the SD, often reinforced by the media and some academics. Muslim Others are represented as monolithic and patriarchal in their religiosity, as against a women-friendly, secular welfare state. For the SD, the

Muslim Other is the representation of the general Other, the opposite of all that is Sweden; the party defines Muslim populations as unnatural to the Swedish nation.

Scott Bonn details in Chapter 5 the case of moral panic that he sees as elite-engineered at the level of the nation state, indeed of the world's remaining superpower. Bonn argues that the administration of George W. Bush initiated a propaganda campaign linking Saddam Hussein and Iraq to the events of 9/11 almost immediately after these terrorist attacks. So successful was the 18-month campaign that most of the US public believed that Iraq was directly involved in 9/11 by the time of the US-led invasion of Iraq in March 2003. The Bush administration was able to exploit a legacy of negative media framing of Arabs that predisposed the US public to punitive action toward Iraq even before 9/11. The framing of Saddam Hussein and his followers as folk devils by the administration and the news media after 9/11 interacted with negative stereotypes of all Arabs in the US, so as to prime hostile and retaliatory public attitudes toward Iraq, which led to popular support for the invasion, inscribing it into the ongoing narrative of the 'war on terror'.

In Chapter 6 Ryan Al-Natour and George Morgan examine how a proposal to construct a Muslim school in a small town of Camden on the south-western fringe of Sydney provoked an outpouring of local xenophobia. The development appeared of a modest and innocuous nature but global stereotypes and alarmist narratives about Islam fuelled popular resistance. Much of this resistance was framed around a defence of the space of Australia, as symbolized by Camden's old-fashioned community, against the encroachments of the dysfunctional global-multicultural city. Although the ostensible reasons used by authorities to reject the development application concerned town planning considerations, few were in doubt that the decision was governed primarily by the desire to conserve the local Anglo monoculture.

Selda Dagistanli and Kiran Grewal in Chapter 7 trace the trajectory of local discursive formations around 'Muslim' gang rape and immigration in France and Australia, into a global discourse of contemporary orientalism and Islamophobia. The speed with which local anti-multiculturalism becomes global orientalism and Islamophobia is attributed to three interrelated factors. First, the local anxieties that are caused by the shrinking of borders between East and West as a result of globalization; second, the technologically mediated associations (in racist websites, blogs and other media) that are made between gang rape and Islamophobic anti-multiculturalism; and finally, the wider orientalist connections made between Islam and violence in a post-9/11 context. The central argument here is that these factors are inseparable in the dialectic formed between local and global resurrections of traditional Orientalist discourse.

In Chapter 8 Kevin Dunn and Alanna Kamp provide a case study of an attempt to orchestrate a local Islamophobic reaction for political purposes during the 2007 Australian Federal Election campaign. Members of the conservative Liberal Party of Australia distributed leaflets purporting to be from an Islamist group (which was in fact non-existent) that advocated a vote for the opposition Labor Party.

The political chicanery was uncovered and those responsible were prosecuted. However, the case demonstrated the ways in which elite political representatives have sought to manipulate popular fears about Islam to shore up support for right-wing political parties.

In Chapter 9, Joanne Massey and Rajinder Singh Tatla examine 'riots' in the north-west of England in summer 2001 that were globally reported and worried about nationally for years afterwards, leading to state interventions focusing on non-integration of South Asian Muslim immigrant communities. Islamophobia and moral panic characterized both the reporting and the state response. As the events occurred two months before 9/11, and four years before the 7/7 London transport attacks, this case shows the Islamophobic elements that were already then embedded and circulating in common sense. The authors analyze media representations of the targeted communities in the light of the preconditions and contributory factors to the riot – institutional racism and the related 'segregation', unemployment, the agitation of right-wing organizations such as the British National Party (BNP) and National Front (NF) and the anti-multiculturalism which they espoused.

Anneke Meyer's contribution, Chapter 10, is a UK case study of the role of media representations in the creation of Muslims as folk devils and Islam as a 'major threat to the nation' in the 'war on terror'. It focuses on media coverage of Abu Hamza, a London-based Muslim cleric made infamous in British newspapers, especially tabloids, since 2001. Abu Hamza made several speeches classed as 'extremist' and 'inciting hatred' and he was convicted of several crimes, including soliciting murder, in 2006, in which disproportionate state response followed the media furore. Hamza's hook replacement for his right hand makes him a visually distinct and instantly recognizable folk devil – universally demonized and held up as an object of hatred in the media. Meyer investigates recurrent themes in the media coverage of Islam: fundamentalism, radicalization, terrorism and asylum. These elements and the ways in which they are connected are central to understanding how fear and phobia regarding Islam are manufactured in the British media.

In Chapter 11, Joanna Gilmore details the disproportionate, violent and ethnically targeted state reaction in Britain to mass protests, vigils and occupations following the Israeli incursion into Gaza from late December 2008. Scores of young Muslims who attended the demonstrations were subjected to dawn raids, severe criminal charges, onerous bail conditions and lengthy prison sentences and were vilified in the right-wing press as 'extremists' and 'fanatics'. This chapter discusses the extent to which the discourse of terrorism has served to criminalize Muslim protesters and to intimidate their communities to withdraw from political activism. Based on an ethnographic study of the protests and their aftermath, the chapter demonstrates how politically 'radicalized' Muslims have been labelled as a 'threat', justifying an extreme response from the state with damaging consequences for civil liberties.

To conclude by raising some theoretical questions that elucidate each of the foregoing national and local cases studies, Greg Noble asks in Chapter 12 'Where is the moral in moral panic?' He examines the highly moralized discourse of Islam, evil and moral order that has re-emerged over the last decade, not just as a result of the 'war on terror' but also in the wake of the resurgence of conservatism and its critique of the moral relativism of Western liberalism. Noble argues that it is part of the process of hardening the boundaries between good and bad, between law-abiding citizens and wrongdoers, endemic to the global culture of fear. Moral panic theory is well placed to analyze the appeal of moral enterprise and yet lacks a sustained discussion of the 'moral' dimensions of panic. It is as yet more comfortable describing the construction of folk devils than with deconstructing how 'deviance' articulates moral and social order.

Collectively, the contributions of this volume demonstrate that Islamophobia now permeates the global 'West' with a general repertoire of racialization upon which local moral panics continually draw. The consequences are momentous. As we write, the blogosphere echoes the recognition that 'We are all Norwegian now'. Perhaps it is time to recognize that we are all Afghans and Iraqis too.

References

Basch, L., Glick Schiller, N. and Szanton Blanc, C. 1994. *Nations Unbound: Transnational Projects, Postcolonial Predicaments, and Deterritorialized Nation-states* Langhorne: Gordon and Breach.

Beck, U. 1992. *Risk Society: Towards a New Modernism* London: Sage.

Bonn, S. 2010. *Mass Deception: Moral Panic and the U.S. War on Iraq* New Brunswick, NJ: Rutgers University Press.

Cohen, S. 2002. *Folk Devils and Moral Panics* Third edition. Abingdon: Routledge.

Critcher, C. 2003. *Media and Moral Panics* Buckingham: Open University Press.

Garland, D. 2008. 'On the Concept of Moral Panic', *Crime, Media, Culture*, 4 (1), 9-30.

Giddens, A. 1990. *The Consequences of Modernity* Cambridge: Polity.

Goode, E., and Ben-Yehuda, N. 1994. *Moral Panics: The Social Construction of Deviance.* Cambridge, MA: Blackwell.

Hall, S., Critcher, C., Jefferson, T., Clarke, J. and Roberts, B. 1978. *Policing the Crisis: Mugging, the State and Law and Order* London: Macmillan.

Hillyard, P. 1993. *Suspect Community: People's Experience of the Prevention of Terrorism Acts in Britain* London: Pluto Press in association with the National Council for Civil Liberties.

Pantazis, C. and Pemberton, S. 2009. 'From the 'Old' to the 'New' Suspect Community: Examining the Impact of Recent UK Counter-terrorist Legislation', *British Journal of Criminology* 49, 5, 646-666.

Pearson, G. 1983. *Hooligan: A History of Respectable Fears* London: Macmillan.

Perry, B. 2001. *In the Name of Hate: Understanding Hate Crimes* New York: Routledge.

Poynting, S., Noble, G., Tabar, P. and Collins, J. 2004. *Bin Laden in the Suburbs: Criminalising the Arab Other* Sydney: Institute of Criminology.

Poynting, S. and Mason, V. 2007. 'The Resistible Rise of Islamophobia: Anti-Muslim Racism in the UK and Australia before 11 September 2001', *Journal of Sociology*, 43 (1), March, 61-86.

Poynting, S. and Mason, V. 2008. 'The New Integrationism, the State and Islamophobia: Retreat from Multiculturalism in Australia', *International Journal of Law, Crime and Justice* 36, 4. Special issue on Muslim Communities post 9/11 – citizenship, security and social justice, guest editor B. Spalek, 230-246.

Poynting, S. and Perry, B. 2007. 'Climates of Hate: Media and State Inspired Victimisation of Muslims in Canada and Australia since 9/11', *Current Issues in Criminal Justice* 19, 2, November, 151-171.

Said, E.W. 1995. *Orientalism* London: Penguin.

Welch, M. 2004. 'Trampling Human Rights in the War on Terror: Implications to the Sociology of Denial', *Critical Criminology* 12 (1), 1-20.

Welch, M. 2006. *Scapegoats of September 11th: Hate Crimes and State Crimes in the War on Terror* New Brunswick, NJ: Rutgers University Press.

Chapter 1

A School for Scandal: Rütli High School and the German Press

Bruce M. Z. Cohen and Catharina Muhamad-Brandner

Introduction

With global migration patterns intensifying over the past fifty years, contemporary moral panics have taken on a more overt racialized form which often links 'race' with youth and crime (Cunneen 2007; White 2007). The classic example of this variety of moral panic has been outlined by Hall et al. (1978) in their analysis of the 'mugging crisis' in Britain in 1972 and 1973. Despite there being little evidence to suggest a 'crime wave' of mugging at the time, the ensuing moral panic came to symbolize 'a crisis in law and order' and to portray young black males as the archetypal folk devil, 'dangerously prone to gratuitous violence' (Critcher 2003: 14). It is argued here that the work of Hall et al. and the Centre for Contemporary Cultural Studies (CCCS) Mugging Group remains highly useful in examining post-9/11 media portrayals of young minority groups, including the 'Muslim Other'.

The concept of 'moral panics' has, however, been criticized on a number of accounts. McRobbie and Thornton (1995), for example, argue that, with the development of 'multi-mediated social worlds', connections between 'the media' and 'social control' are no longer so clear-cut; folk devils are not as marginalized as they once were because they also have access to forms of media (e.g. online media) and thus can attempt to resist (or heighten) such moral panics for their own ends. Focusing specifically on Hall et al.'s (1978) research, Waddington (1986) also offers a significant criticism, claiming that the concept represents academic polemic rather than any reality of media reportage. Waddington criticizes Hall et al. (1978) for an inadequate review of the evidence on 'mugging'. He also comments that the issue as to whether the media representations of the crisis really represented a moral panic remains 'essentially a value judgement' (Waddington 1986: 257). On the basis of these criticisms, we believe that it is important to return to testing the validity of the moral panic concept through measuring research results against established criteria. In this chapter, we utilize the criteria from the CCCS Mugging Group's 'signification spiral' (cited in Poynting and Morgan 2007: 3–4) to analyse whether the German press's coverage of Rütli High School represents a moral panic. The criteria are outlined below and will be returned to in our discussion:

a. The intensification of a specific issue;
b. The identification of a 'subversive minority';
c. 'Convergence' or the linking by labelling of the specific issue to other problems;
d. The notion of 'thresholds' which, once crossed, can lead to further escalation of the problem's 'menace' to society;
e. The element of explaining and prophesying, which often involves making analogous references to the United States – the paradigm example;
f. The call for firm steps.

Background

Migrants in Germany

Currently around 19 per cent of the population (15.3 million people) living in Germany has a migration background (Kristen and Granato 2007: 345; Statistisches Bundesamt 2006: 73–9). Based on a *sui generis* notion of bloodlines, Germany's integration and citizenship policies have been highly exclusive and restrictive (Green 2002). Apart from those – such as the *Spätaussiedler* ('late repatriates', mainly from the former Soviet Union) – who can prove German ancestry, migrant populations have been denied the rights that German citizens enjoy, including the right to peaceful assembly, freedom of movement, freedom of association and freedom of occupation. This has included the second- and third-generation children of migrants who have been born and raised in Germany. Such populations are still officially recognized as 'foreigners' (this includes 26 per cent regarded as 'Turkish', eight per cent as 'Italian', seven per cent 'former Yugoslavs', and five per cent 'Polish'). The majority of the 'foreign' population (56 per cent) are the descendants of *Gastarbeiter* (literally, 'guest worker') families who arrived in the 1960s and 1970s (see Bundesamt für Migration und Flüchtlinge 2006: 82).

On this basis it has been argued that Germany's citizenship laws have sought to deny many migrants full political rights and, consequently, have undermined the development of multiculturalism and integrationist policies in the country (Kaya 2001). In contrast, the dominant discourse on immigration in the last decade has focused on the perceived inability of certain migrant populations to 'integrate' *into* German society (Ha 2005). With specific references to problem migrant groups from 'Muslim countries' (Hewitt 2010) and such issues as 'honour killings', attitudes towards homosexuals, and religious intolerance, post-9/11, this discussion has taken on a heightened sense of Islamophobia. An anxiety permeates the dominant (white) German discourse on immigration, integration and multiculturalism in the face of a declining birth rate and ageing population, with occasional calls for the promotion of an alternative *Leitkultur* (a guiding national culture) to challenge what is sometimes perceived as the 'watering-down' of 'German culture' (this, of course, has some dark historical undertones in Germany) (Karnitschnig 2010).

As a country of 70 million Muslims, the possible entry of Turkey to the European Union has only increased this fear of a 'clash of cultures' and religions in Germany (Arnold and Schneider 2007: 116).

Rütli High School

Rütli-Hauptschule (Rütli High School) is located at the northern tip of Neukölln, a large inner-city district in the south of Berlin. The immediate area surrounding the school is known locally as *Reuterkiez* (*Reuterstraße* is a main street running through the area, *Kiez* is a Berlin expression which can be roughly translated as 'local community'). Traditionally working-class, *Reuterkiez* has high levels of social and economic deprivation (Cohen 2008: 103). Neukölln was a cheap area to house *Gastarbeiter* families in the former West Berlin, so it is little surprise that, compared to an average of 13 per cent of 'foreigners' living in the city as a whole, Neukölln has a larger share of minorities living there (22 per cent); 30 per cent of school children are also denoted as 'foreign populations' in Neukölln, compared to a city average of 16 per cent. These figures are further accentuated in *Reuterkiez* (Cohen 2008: 103).

The *Hauptschule* (literally, 'high school') is one of three types of school which form Berlin's tripartite system of secondary education. Steinbach and Nauck (2003: 14) have explained the German system as follows:

> It is easiest to gain entry into the *Hauptschule*, which offers a general education in preparation for a vocational career ... Lesson plans in the *Realschule* are more difficult than in the *Hauptschule*, but a *Realschule*-diploma qualifies graduates also only for vocational training. These diplomas, however, do grant access to career tracks in a wider range of professions ... The *Gymnasium* offers an exclusively college preparatory curriculum ... A diploma from a *Gymnasium* ... grants automatic access to all higher level educational tracks.

On 28 February 2006, Rütli High School's teaching staff sent a two-page letter to the Berlin Senate for Education, Youth and Sports outlining their concerns for the school's current situation; this letter later became known as the *Brandbrief* (Miller 2006b).[1] After one month had passed without any acknowledgement of the school's distress, the letter was leaked to the German media and the first news article on the school was published on 29 March 2006. To be able to determine whether the response of the German press to the problems of the school constitutes a moral panic, we utilize the contents of the *Brandbrief* as our baseline data. That is, our analysis will compare the issues outlined in the letter with the resulting responses in the media. For this reason it is important to briefly outline the contents of the *Brandbrief* itself.

---

1   In Germany, a written appeal for help outlining existing shortcomings is colloquially called a *Brandbrief*.

The Brandbrief

The *Brandbrief* summarized a number of issues which the teaching body of Rütli High School wanted to see addressed by the Berlin Senate for Education, Youth and Sports (Eggebrecht 2006). The letter begins by outlining the school's steadily increasing proportion of pupils with a migration background (then at 83 per cent), noting that those with an Arabic background are most strongly represented amongst the student body (35 per cent) followed by just over 26 per cent of Turkish pupils. The teachers then remark that, 'there are no staff members from other cultures at our school'.

A general atmosphere in the classrooms of 'aggression, lack of respect and ignorance' is described. Few students take interest in the lessons, and violent behaviour in the school – doors being kicked in, paper bins being used as footballs, firecrackers being let off, and picture frames being ripped from the walls – is on the increase. The general culture of the student body is blamed for the current atmosphere: students' misbehaviour and aggressiveness elicits respect amongst other peers. The role of the students' parents is highlighted, remarking that little support is forthcoming in encouraging students to obey school rules, that arranged meetings with the parents are not kept, and that telephoning the parents is difficult because of 'a lack of language skills'. Widely reprinted in the media a month later, the letter states that *Wir sind ratlos* ('we are helpless'). It is explained that the school remains under-staffed due to maternity leave, illness and retirement, and that the residual teaching body is over worked with no time for developmental activities.

The teachers then question the logic of placing all disadvantaged students together in one type of school (i.e. *Hauptschule)*, where the chances of progressing further in education and the labour market are seriously limited. Their students do not see the value of education, rather, they are more interested in their mobile phones and fashion trends. The school has also become a site of power struggle where the troublemakers becoming the role models. They conclude that the *Hauptschule* isolates and separates these students from mainstream society. For these reasons the letter then suggests that *Hauptschule* in general should be phased out and a new type of school developed in its place. While the letter notes that this is a long-term solution, it states that Rütli immediately requires more teaching staff. Likewise, they also state that they require regular financial support to fund other education professionals (e.g. social workers and psychologists) for crisis intervention with students and parents. With the school's centenary approaching (in 2009), the letter finishes with the hope that, by this point in time, both the teachers and students at Rütli will be experiencing education and learning as positive activities.

Methodology and Analysis

The media storm that followed the publication of the *Brandbrief* on 29 March 2006 continued for several months afterwards. However, we wished to gain an overview of the initial period of intensive newspaper coverage in Germany to determine the extent to which this could be considered a moral panic, in and of itself. To do this we chose six news publications over a ten-day timeframe (29 March to 7 April 2006). The publications chosen for this analysis are outlined below:

- *Berliner Zeitung*: a regional centre-left daily broadsheet which sells over 200,000 copies a day, and is published by the Berliner Verlag;
- *Bild*: a national daily tabloid which sells nearly four million copies per day, it is right wing in political orientation and owned by the Axel-Springer corporation;
- *FOCUS*: a popular national weekly newsmagazine which sells close to 800,000 copies a week, it is conservative-leaning, supports economic liberalism, and is published by Helmut Markwort;
- *Der Spiegel*: a weekly national news journal which sells in excess of a million copies a week, it tends to accentuate conservative neo-liberal politics, and is owned by the publishing company Gruner + Jahr (a subsidiary of Bertelsmann);
- *Der Stern*: as with *Der Spiegel*, this is a national weekly news magazine which sells over a million copies per week and is published by Gruner + Jahr, however *Der Stern* is left-liberal in political orientation;
- *Süd-Deutsche Zeitung*: a regional liberal-centralist daily broadsheet which sells over half a million copies per day, and is published by Südwestdeutsche Medien Holding.

These publications were selected to provide a cross-section of tabloid and broadsheet newspapers at both the regional and national levels. Both daily and weekly publications were chosen, and, most importantly, the publications embody a diversity of political orientations. Using the key search word 'Rütli' and time-restricting the search from 29 March 2006 to 7 April 2006, the online news sites of the selected publications were reviewed for potential articles. From the resulting 189 search results, 48 were excluded from the final analysis as they were found to either be unrelated to Rütli High School or were blog commentaries. A total of 141 relevant articles were identified for final analysis; this sample included a variety of article types such as news pieces, brief headline reports, elaborate exposés, interviews, opinion pieces, and fact collections. Table 1.1 (below) provides an overview of the number of articles published by each newspaper/news magazine on each day of the selected time period. Nearly two thirds of the sample stems from two sources only, *Berliner Zeitung* and *Der Spiegel*. A general peak in the number of articles can be noted on the third day of the Rütli High School story.

Table 1.1 Number of newspaper articles analysed between 29 March 2006 and 7 April 2006

Newspaper	Wed 29 Mar	Thu 30 Mar	Fri 31 Mar	Sat 1 Apr	Sun 2 Apr	Mon 3 Apr	Tue 4 Apr	Wed 5 Apr	Thu 6 Apr	Fri 7 Apr	Total
Berliner Zeitung		1	7	8		6	8	7	7	6	**50**
BILD		1	3	3	3	1	1	2	1	1	**16**
FOCUS	1			2		2	1	2	4	1	**13**
Der Spiegel		8	7	5	1	5	5	6	5	1	**43**
Der Stern		1	1	1	1	1		1	1		**7**
Süd-Deutsche Zeitung		2	5		1		1	1	1	1	**12**
Total	**1**	**13**	**23**	**19**	**6**	**15**	**16**	**19**	**19**	**10**	**141**

Results

Day 1

Table 1.1 highlights that only one article was published on Rütli High School on the first day of our time frame. Based on a *Tagesspiegel* article which was published the following day, the online version of *FOCUS* (2006a) led with the headline *Gewalt im Unterricht: Rektorin bittet um Schul-Auflösung* ('Violence in the classroom: Principal asks for school-closure'). The *FOCUS* article provided a basic introduction to the school's problems with violence and claims that the teachers' solution to this was the closure of their school. One sentence notes the low proportion of 'German' pupils amongst the student body, yet no mention is made of the high Arab or Turkish populations.

Day 2

On the second day of our time frame, most media reports draw a picture of Rütli as a 'terror school': violence (especially between Arabs and Turks) and disrespect reigns, weapons set the rules, and instead of school students, *Kriminelle und Terroristen* ('criminals and terrorists') are produced there (Bild 2006b; Bock 2006; Der Spiegel 2006c; Süd-Deutsche Zeitung 2006a). The high proportion of non-Germans and their power over the school are commonly highlighted as a matter of concern. *Der Spiegel* and *Bild* note that the intimidation of 'German' students has reached such an extent that those students have adopted the resistant demeanour of the majority of the student body; Germans could either be a *Schweinefresser* ('pig-eater') or become 'one of them'. The articles also draw a stereotypical picture of the male student at the school: he is macho, disrespectful of girls who do not wear headscarves, and speaks in a Turkish-German accent with frequent swearwords. While almost all articles mentioned that the troublemakers came from Arab or Turkish backgrounds, only one article (Miller 2006b) explicitly stated that one aspect of the problem was rooted in the fact that the *islamisch geprägten Schülerschaft* ('Islamic characterized student body') denies the authority of teachers, especially female staff members.

Many articles also featured observations from outside the front gates of the school where it is reported that young males intimidated journalists with aggressive poses, as well as throwing stones and yelling and spitting. It was commonly noted that the school was due to receive police protection and that students would be searched for weapons. While most articles focused on the apparent chaos at the school, Musharbash's (2006) and Padtberg's (2006) articles in *Der Spiegel* began to investigate the broader issues of youth violence, and the *Hauptschule* as a catchment school for the most marginalized in German society.

Days 3 and 4

The interest in the Rütli controversy peaked on day three of our analysis. Many articles still made mention of the continuing media spectacle outside the school gates, highlighting that the police had moved onto the school grounds while also noting that the promised search for weapons had not in fact taken place. The ethnic mix of the student population at the school remained the centre of attention, as did the issues around *Hauptschule*. Articles mention that this type of school can be considered a *Restschule* where all the leftover students are held until the completion of their compulsory education. The students are said to lack any perspective for the future because of the stigma that surrounds *Rütli* and *Hauptschule* in general.

A small number of articles stress that the students' difficulties at school are not linked to their ethnicity but to their socio-economic background. Nevertheless, the migrant backgrounds of the majority of the students – and the failures of this population to 'integrate' into German society – are frequently explored as a factor of the *Rütli* controversy. The parents of the students are blamed for failing to support their children's integration by removing themselves from German society, for commonly not speaking German themselves, for instilling traditional – sometimes denoted in articles as 'Islamic' – gender roles, and for not valuing education. Conservative politicians such as Friedbert Pflüger (candidate for Berlin mayor) and Bavaria's *Minister-Präsident* (Premier) Edmund Stoiber argue for a need to focus on the political failure to *enforce* integration and assimilation of such migrant populations. Both call for strict sanctions such as cuts in benefits and even for the deportation of delinquent youth or of those who refuse to participate in German society. Other commentaries focused more specifically on the lack of German language skills in hindering the integration and educational success of migrant youth. Here the contributions ranged from offering more targeted support and encouragement for language development to compulsory German language tests as prerequisites for admission to primary school.

Day 5

The increasing and widespread violence at schools was illustrated by some of the articles on Day 5, using examples drawn from other parts of Germany. For example, a *Bild* report (Tackmann et al. 2006) lists five such acts of violence. Strikingly, the article does not mention if the young people involved came from migrant backgrounds. Politicians promise an increase in the number of teachers for problem schools, the extra support of social workers and psychologists for problem students, and measures to compel migrant parents to support the 'proper' raising of their children. Any criminal behaviour at school would be met with expulsion or, in extreme cases, delinquents could be sent to what Jörg Schönbohm (the Interior Minister for Brandenburg) calls a *Schnupperknast* (a trial prison) (*Der Stern* 2006).

Days 6 and 7

Day six includes two magazine articles (Berg et al. 2006; Desselberger et al. 2006) which provide further insights into the situation at the school and some of the social issues raised in the *Brandbrief*. However, Berg et al.'s (2006) cover story for *Der Spiegel* on Rütli High School titled *Die verlorene Welt* (*The Lost World*) begins as follows:

> *Was soll der Scheiss?* [What is this shit?]
> This is how the inhabitants of this world speak. *Ey, man, ey* [hey, man, hey]. *Nutte* [whore]. *Killer*. *Krass* [cool]. There are a lot of 'sch'- and 'ch'-sounds in this language, hardly any complete sentences. They talk in dirty German.
> In this world, in many places in Germany, there is only one value: respect. Respect is who is cool and who is strong, who wears the right clothes, who speaks the right language, listens to the right music, who has the right friends and the right gang. Respect comes to those who protect their own Turkish or Lebanese sister from sex and love in this big glittery West, whilst they themselves fuck German sluts.

Despite the inclusion of such racist stereotyping, Berg et al.'s article (2006) does offer a detailed exposé of the young people in *Reuterkiez* which includes giving voice to the current teachers at *Rütli*. Debates around Germany's school system and the broader social context of many *Hauptschule* students are outlined: the articles note that the students' experiences of long-term unemployment within their own family, their own lack of future perspectives, and the knowledge of racism and discrimination in the employment market, create clear frustrations. It is argued that such students adopt the only identity position that can still bring 'respect' and 'honour': that of being a disruptive and aggressive teenager. Parents are represented as showing no interest in their children's education or upbringing, therefore contributing to their lack of basic social skills. An argument emerges stating that the changing of the school system alone will not solve these wider social problems (Zinser 2006). Overt references to the integration debate also continue in the new week. Concerns regarding the low level of German language skills of students are still strong; especially as readers are reminded of Bavaria's recent policy changes in this area (pre-school language testing was made mandatory in the State earlier in the year).

Days 8 and 9

Details of a planned 'integration summit' emerge, with a general notion of making integration a national issue and getting representatives from various interest groups involved. 'Integration' and 'assimilation' can no longer remain an *option* to migrants but has to be, as Wolfgang Schäuble (Federal Minister of the Interior) puts it, *Pflicht* (obligation) (Averesch 2006). Calls for strict sanctions and deportation continue to be frequent in the media. At the same time, initiatives to support integration – such as integration and language courses – are to be introduced or extended (Bühler 2006; Emmerich 2006).

Der Spiegel (2006b) and the *Berliner Zeitung* (Leo and Majica 2006) report on the Interim Principal's (Helmut Hochschild) first day at Rütli. They both highlight his criticisms of the media's portrayal of the school. The same report also notes a student representative's view on the media's handling of the Rütli situation: she criticizes the exaggerations of the school's problems, and adds her voice to a number of commentators who begin to suggest that some Rütli students were paid by the media to 'act up' for their cameras (Mösken 2006).

Day 10

Süd-Deutsche Zeitung (2006b), *Der Spiegel* (2006a) and *FOCUS* (2006b) all provide space for the views of politicians on Day 10, including Wolfgang Schäuble, Ute Erdsiek-Rave (Minister of Education and the Arts for Schleswig-Holstein) and Claudia Roth (leader of the Bündnis 90/Green Party). These articles underscore the ongoing arguments between German politicians regarding sanctions and migrant responsibilities to integrate. *Bild* (2006a), on the other hand, explores concise 'facts' relating to migration in a collection titled *Ausländer-Politik: So hat der Staat versagt* ('Foreigner-policy: That's how the state failed'). The article focuses on the issues of German language and integration, with 'culture/religion' becoming a central concern. It is argued that only Muslims have difficulties integrating into German society. This difficulty is linked to 'radical Muslim groups', and the increase of 'religious practices' such as forced marriages and 'honour killings'. An expert on Islam (Hans-Peter Raddatz) stresses the limited acceptance of German laws when Muslims only interact with other Muslims. After noting migrants' reliance on social benefits, the article investigates the 'ghettoization' of urban areas by such foreign groups.

In contrast, the *Berliner Zeitung* looks at the current Berlin Senate policies with regards to the education of migrant children (Miller 2006a). With all the political rhetoric over the possible introduction of compulsory pre-school language courses and tests for migrant children, the reporter notes that these are in fact already in existence in Berlin (Miller and Thomsen 2006). The last day of analysis underscores not only the existence of these initiatives, but also that the associated language courses in the previous year were well attended, with no parent having to be sanctioned for neglecting or refusing to send their child to the course.

Discussion

In this discussion the results of our media analysis are reviewed, using the *Brandbrief* as a baseline for comparison of the 'reality' of the events at Rütli High School. With reference the CCCS Mugging Group's 'signification spiral', we will now demonstrate that the coverage of Rütli represents a clear case of a moral panic.

a. The intensification of a specific issue

The *Brandbrief* referred to an aggressive and violent atmosphere at the school, and the problems of addressing a growing ethnic mix of students. A constant under-staffing of the teaching body, as well as a lack of financial support for additional education professionals, meant that these problems could not be effectively addressed. As a type of secondary school which offered a lack of prospects for such students, the *Hauptschule* was also heavily criticized in the letter. The exaggeration and intensification of the school's situation by the media happened from the first day of analysis. *FOCUS*'s article claimed that the teachers were asking for Rütli to be closed, whereas the letter makes no such demand. The article also makes 'violence in the classroom' the main issue in the article, noting the low number of 'German' pupils. By the second day of coverage, a correlation between minority students and violence at the school is omnipresent in the media. Reports claim that the *Brandbrief* gave the high number of students with Arab or Turkish backgrounds as the reason for the violence. In fact, the letter made no reference to such a correlation; rather, references are only ever made to the general body of students.

b. The identification of a 'subversive minority'

On the second day of coverage, the young non-western male is identified by the German press as the root cause of the school's problems. This population becomes the archetypal folk devils in the ensuing moral panic; they are the scapegoats that come to fulfil some of German society's chief anxieties and fears. In contrast with Hall et al's (1978) work, however, our analysis notes a heightened sense of anxiety, post-9/11, encapsulated in these folk devils also as the 'Muslim other'. Thus, groups of young people with Arab or Turkish backgrounds are 'criminals and terrorists', they are the classic 'internal outsiders' or enemies within. Although there were only 57 references to Islam or being Muslim in the 141 articles analysed, there is an implied Islamophobia in the 'clash of cultures' discourse which runs through these reports. Berg et al.'s (2006) cover story for *Der Speigel* offers a typical example here. Their in-depth report covers a wider range of issues around the school and the socio-economic problems of the local area, but returns throughout to problematize young Arabic and Turkish males by accentuating their supposed differences (e.g. in behaviour, attitudes and even their German speech) from wider

German society. The 'lost world' of which Berg et al. writes is a dangerous place, a parallel society of aggressive young ethnic males who believe that they must 'protect their own Turkish or Lebanese sister from sex and love in this big glittery West, whilst they themselves fuck German sluts'. It is a proclamation of essential difference between a German (white) Christian culture and a subversive migrant (or 'foreign') Muslim culture.

   c. 'Convergence' or the linking by labelling of the specific issue to other problems.

The consequences of making young non-western males the folk devils of the Rütli saga are that other social ills are then linked to them. The insinuations of violence, crime and 'terror' from the folk devil are quickly added to with a focus on the wider problems of non-Christian (meaning non-white and Muslim) migrant groups integrating or 'assimilating' into German society (words like 'migration' and 'foreigner' were mentioned a total of 464 times in our 141 articles; integration was found to be a significant topic in 55 of the articles). Thus, there is convergence in the media coverage of Rütli with the national anxieties over integration of these communities (something that, again, was never mentioned in the *Brandbrief*). Moral entrepreneurs are called on to offer 'solutions' to this pressing issue. Rütli becomes a *cause célèbre* in denoting the perceived failure of current German integration policies. It is significant in the response of these 'right-thinking' people that they draw on other moral panics against migrant groups – such as those around forced marriages and 'honour killings' (Korteweg and Yurdakul 2009) – to highlight the need for more aggressive 'integration policies' such as compulsory language courses and testing, deportation of 'foreign' delinquents, stricter German citizenship tests, the control of migrant parents, and the promotion of a German *Leitkultur* to combat the influence of other cultural norms and values.

   d. The notion of 'thresholds' which, once crossed, can lead to further escalation of the problem's 'menace' to society

From the above discussion it can be seen how a significant threat is currently posed to the dominant moral order within German society: to ignore the menace of non-western migrants and their children is to face potential catastrophe in the future. This is most blatant when the *Bild* (2006a) comments on the last day of our analysis period that the state has failed on 'foreigner policy' while talking in the same article of 'radical Muslim groups', and an increase in forced marriages and 'honour killings' in Germany. It is clear that such moral entrepreneurs believe a threshold has been reached, the integration of such groups has failed, what is now needed is policies 'obliging' migrants to either integrate or be punished for not wishing to integrate. If no action is taken to rectify the situation, violations of Germany's laws by such groups will grow and the parallel societies (or 'ghettos') they live in will become breeding grounds for fundamentalists and terrorists.

e. The element of explaining and prophesying, which often involves making analogous references to the United States – the paradigm example.

References made to non-German migrant communities living in a parallel society or 'ghetto' are not only done to emphasize difference, but also to prophesize a potential future in which areas in German cities like *Reuterkiez* become worse than the Bronx in New York (as noted in Berg et al. 2006). The use of 'ghettoization' in many of the reports on *Reuterkiez* stereotypes such 'foreign' populations as much as the German politicians do: to live in 'the ghetto' means to be socially, economically and culturally disadvantaged, to be uneducated, unskilled, working class, and, by default, non-western. It is a narrative device used to negatively compare 'the ghetto' with the rest of German society which is seen as enlightened, educated and sophisticated. It is no coincidence that the press used black neighbourhoods in the United States to emphasize such fears. The media also ultilized photos of metal detectors, commenting that this was the only way to stop 'anarchy' at schools in the United States (Berg et al. 2006). It is worth noting again here that the stated acts of physical violence in the *Brandbrief* were against school property rather than people; no mention was made of students having access to or taking weapons to school.

f. The call for firm steps

The need for firm steps and policy changes has been outlined in the above discussion, but some of these are worth returning to here. The frequent demand by moral entrepreneurs for pre-school German language testing and further language support for students with migrant backgrounds is particularly interesting, firstly because many State governments (including Berlin) already had such an initiative in operation prior to the Rütli incident, and secondly, because the *Brandbrief* only mentioned this issue in relation to the German language skills of *the parents* of the students. More typical to the moral panic discourse is the demand for strict sanctions involving such things as benefit cuts or deportation, the moral entrepreneurs insinuating that migrants are lazy, reliant on the state and potential criminals. In this last phase of the signification spiral, recognition is given that action needs to be taken to curtail the folk devil, thereby reinforcing the dominant moral order while justifying the media's initial reaction to the events at Rütli.

Implications and Conclusion

Through performing a systematic analysis of a selection of German newspapers and newsmagazines we have demonstrated that the coverage of Rütli High School between 29 March and 7 April 2006 represents a moral panic against migrant communities. Specifically, we have identified young males with a Turkish or Arab background as a folk devil for the German press. It is disquieting to note that this particular 'signification spiral' – from the media leaking of the *Brandbrief* to the calls for changes to Germany's integration policies – happened in a matter of days, and could be detected in both tabloid and broadsheet publications (regardless of the newspaper's politics).

What this moral panic suggests is a continuing problematization of non-western migrants and their descendents by the dominant order (that is, white, middle class, German society). It is a continuation of the process of 'othering' against such populations that, post-9/11, has intensified into the realms of Islamophobia. A notable part of this 'othering' process is the way in which the German media often mocks and caricatures migrant populations (for example, see the above Berg et al. (2006) quote from Day 6 of our analysis). As Ha (2005: 186) reminds us, '[t]his mockery of immigrants is basically something that happens without almost any scandalization every day in German society. These devaluing practices are, for the German majority, part of their social construction of normality'. This confirmation and reinforcement of the dominant view of 'reality' – a reality which, for example, confirms a 'the clash of cultures' between Germans and foreigners, and which portrays all groups of foreigner as essentially the same – by the German media represents the subtle transference of a hegemonic discourse based on consensual definitions of social problems by which the media avoids accusations of racism. As Muharrar (1998) stresses,

> ... crime, welfare, drug abuse or what have you – is seen by many as a real issue that is only coincidentally about race. The trait of blackness associated with the problem is viewed as nothing more than an unfortunate reality that is secondary to the public hostility and the punitive measures.

In contemplating our results, we take issue with McRobbie and Thornton's (1995) claims that folk devils are now less marginalized than they once were. The young non-western males in our analysis bear striking similarities to Hall et al. (1978) folk devils in the early 1970s – both populations remain at threat of further scapegoating for supposed social ills of that society. The idea that the 'media capital' of such folk devils can offer an effective resistance to media publications from multinational organizations such as Bertelsmann or Axel-Springer appears highly naïve here.[2] Instead, and as with Cohen's (1987) original research on moral panics, though the issues of Rütli High School was imagined by the German press in 2006, it was real in its consequences for migrant communities. Rütli remains associated in the popular German imagination with problematic migrant youth, and the example is continually referred to in ongoing debates over migrants and immigration policy. The racist and Islamophobic moral panic of Rütli has served to reinforce the morality of 'right thinking' white German society while further

---

2   However, see for example Echchaibi (2007) and Scheibelhofer (2007) for discussions on young migrants' use of media in France and Austria, respectively.

problematizing and stigmatizing young people of non-western origin. The result of such moral panics can be seen in the hardening of public attitudes towards migrants groups as well as in policy initiatives to further restrict the flow to Germany of migrants from Turkey and Arabic countries (Karnitschnig 2010).

Since the events of 9/11, the dominant discourse on Muslims or Islam in the West has been narrowed to a 'clash of civilizations' thesis. Kumar (2010) argues that this hegemonic thesis is primarily articulated by the mass media through particular myths, such as the Islamic religion being inherently violent, sexist, irrational and spawning terrorism. At the same time this discourse reinforces an idea of the West as fundamentally rational and democratic. The 'clash of civilizations' thesis can thus be seen as an excuse for the reproduction of racist and Islamophobic views by the western media; a range of issues from poverty and education to immigration and multiculturalism are increasingly represented as serious threats to society from the Muslim and Islamic 'Other'. We have clearly witnessed this discourse in our analysis of the German media's reporting of Rütli High School, where issues of education are recast as a clash between liberal German society and conservative Islamic groups. As mentioned at the beginning of this chapter, moral panics have often been racialized in the past, but what we are witnessing post-9/11 is an increase in the number of moral panics with a distinct undercurrent of Islamophobia. On this basis we predict that, unfortunately, we are like to witness more frequent occurrences of moral panics aimed at migrant Muslim populations in Germany and other western societies in the future.

References

Arnold, A. and Schneider, B. 2007. Communicating separation? Ethnic media and ethnic journalists as institutions of integration in Germany. *Journalism*. 8 (2): 115–136.

Averesch, S. 2006. Schäuble: Integration ist Pflicht. *Berliner Zeitung*. 6 April. [Accessed 30 September 2010]. Available at: http://www.berlinonline.de/berlinerzeitung/archiv/.bin/dump.fcgi/2006/0406/seite1/0035/index.html.

Berg, S., Brinkbäumer, K., Cziesche, D., Hardinghaus, B., Ludwig, U., Röbel, S., Verbeet, M. and Wensierski, P. 2006, Die verlorene Welt. *Der Spiegel*. 3 April. [Accessed 30 September 2010]. Available at: http://www.spiegel.de/spiegel/print/d-46502879.html

Bild. 2006a. Ausländer-Politik. So hat der Staat versagt. *Bild*. 7 April. [Accessed 23 September 2010]. Available at: http://www.bild.de/BTO/news/aktuell/2006/04/07/auslaender-politik-versagen-staat/auslaender-politik-versagen-staat.html

Bild. 2006b. Nach Hilferuf der Lehrer. Polizeischutz für Berliner Hauptschule! *Bild*. 30 March. [Accessed 30 September 2010]. Available at: http://www.bild.de/BTO/news/aktuell/2006/03/30/schule-polizeischutz/schule-berlin-polizeischutz.html#.

Bock, C. 2006. Eskalation der Gewalt. Eine Hauptschule ruft um Hilfe. *Der Stern*. 30 March. [Accessed 30 September 2010]. Availabel at: http://www.stern.de/panorama/eskalation-der-gewalt-eine-hauptschule-ruft-um-hilfe-558618.html.

Bundesamt für Migration und Flüchtlinge. 2006. *Migration, Asyl und Integration in Zahlen*. Nürnberg: Bundesamt für Migration und Flüchtlinge.

Bühler, K. 2006. Werkstatt für die Zukunft. *Berliner Zeitung*. 5 April. [Accessed 30 September 2010]. Available at: http://www.berlinonline.de/berliner-zeitung/archiv/.bin/dump.fcgi/2006/0405/sport/0033/index.html.

Cohen, B. M. Z. 2008. Ethnic and social differences in music behaviour in a fragmented Berlin. in *Sonic synergies: Music, identity, technology and community*. Edited by Bloustien, G., Peters, M. and Luckman, S. Hampshire: Ashgate.

Cohen, S. 1987. *Folk devils and moral panics. The creation of the Mods and Rockers*. 2nd edition. Oxford: Basil Blackwell.

Critcher, C. 2003. *Moral panics and the media*. Buckingham: Open University Press.

Cunneen, C. 2007. Riot, resistance and moral panic. Demonizing the colonial other. in *Outrageous! Moral panics in Australia*. Edited by Poynting, S. and Morgan, G. Hobart: ACYS Publishing.

Desselberger, A., Jach, M., Fuhrer, A. and Plewnia, U. 2006. Gesellschaft. 'Die verachten unser System'. *FOCUS*. 3 April. [Accessed 23 September 2010]. Available at: http://www.focus.de/panorama/boulevard/gesellschaft-die-verachten-unser-system_aid_214702.html.

Echchaibi, N. 2007. Republican betrayal. Beur FM and the suburban riots in France. *Journal of Intercultural Studies*. 28(3): 301–316.

Eggebrecht, P. 2006. *Brandbrief*. [Accessed 6 December 2010]. Available at: www.ruetli-oberschule.de/downloads/iie3.1schulsituation.pdf .

Emmerich, M. 2006. Frauenverein. Ehrenamtliche Hilfe. *Berliner Zeitung*. 5 April. [Accessed 30 September 2010]. Available at: http://www.berlinonline.de/berliner-zeitung/archiv/.bin/dump.fcgi/2006/0405/berlin/0055/index.html.

FOCUS. 2006a. Gewalt im Unterricht. Rektorin bittet um Schul-Auflösung. *FOCUS*. 29 March. [Accessed 23 September 2010]. Available at: http://www.focus.de/wissen/diverses/gewalt-attacken_aid_106892.html.

FOCUS. 2006b. Schulgewalt. Roth gibt Union die Schuld. *FOCUS*. 7 April. [Accessed 23 September 2010]. Available at: http://www.focus.de/politik/deutschland/schulgewalt_aid_107291.html .

Green, S. 2002. *Understanding citizenship and naturalisation. Evidence from eight countries*. London: Home Office.

Ha, K. N. 2005. Liberal racism? The German construction of race and Turkish ethnicity in a television talk show with Feridun Zaimoglu. in *Insider – Outsider. Bilder, ethnisierte Räume und Partizipation im Migrationsprozess*. Edited by IFADE. Berlin: Transcript.

Hall, S., Critcher, C., Jefferson, T., Clarke, J. and Roberts, B. 1978. *Policing the crisis. Mugging, the state and law and order*. London: Macmillan.

Hewitt, G. 2010. Germans argue over 'failure to integrate'. *BBC*. [Accessed 6 January 2010]. Available at: http://www.bbc.co.uk/blogs/thereporters/gavinhewitt/2010/11/how_sarrazin_s_immigration_vie.html

Karnitschnig, M. 2010. Merkel enters immigration fray. *Wall Street Journal.* 18 October. [Accessed 9 September 2010]. Available at: http://online.wsj.com/article/SB10001424052702304250404575558583224907168.html

Kaya, A. 2001. *'Sicher in Kreuzberg'. Constructing diasporas – Turkish hip-hop youth in Berlin*. London: Transcript.

Korteweg, A. and Yurdakul, G. 2009. Islam, gender, and immigrant integration. Boundary drawing in discourses on honour killing in the Netherlands and Germany. *Ethnic and Racial Studies*. 32(2): 218–238.

Kristen, C. and Granato, N. 2007. The educational attainment of the second generation in Germany. Social origins and ethnic inequality. *Ethnicities*. 7(3): 343–366.

Kumar, D. 2010. Framing Islam: The resurgence of orientalism during the Bush II era. *Journal of Communication Inquiry*. 34(3): 254–277.

Leo, M. and Majica, M. 2006. Der Neuanfang. Rektor Helmut Hochschild will aus der Rütli-Schule eine gute Schule machen. Das wollte auch Brigitte Pick einmal. *Berliner Zeitung*. 5 April. [Accessed 30 September 2010]. Available at: http://www.berlinonline.de/berliner-zeitung/archiv/.bin/dump.fcgi/2006/0405/seite3/0001/index.html

McRobbie, A. and Thornton, S. 1995. Rethinking 'moral panic' for multi-mediated social worlds. *British Journal of Sociology*. 46(4): 559–574.

Miller, T. 2006a. Fast alle Kinder erscheinen zu Deutschkursen. *Berliner Zeitung*. 7 April. [Accessed 30 September 2010]. Available at: http://www.berlinonline.de/berliner-zeitung/archiv/.bin/dump.fcgi/2006/0407/berlin/0038/index.html

Miller, T. 2006b. Zu viel Gewalt. Schule bittet um Hilfe. *Berliner Zeitung*. 30 March. [Accessed 30 September 2010]. Available at: http://www.berlinonline.de/berliner-zeitung/archiv/.bin/dump.fcgi/2006/0330/berlin/0067/index.html.

Miller, T. and Thomsen, J. 2006. Zeit der Geschenke. *Berliner Zeitung*. 6 April. [Accessed 30 September 2010]. Available at: http://www.berlinonline.de/berliner-zeitung/archiv/.bin/dump.fcgi/2006/0406/seite3/0016/index.html.

Mösken, A. L. 2006. Rütli-Schule. 'Denken sie an unsere Zukunft'. *Berliner Zeitung*. 5 April. [Accessed 30 September 2010]. http://www.berlinonline.de/berliner-zeitung/archiv/.bin/dump.fcgi/2006/0405/berlin/0052/index.html

Muharrar, M. 1998. Media blackface. 'Racial profiling' in news reporting. *Fairness & Accuracy in Reporting*. [Accessed 22 October 2010]. Available at: http://www.fair.org

Musharbash, Y. 2006. Berliner Problemschule. Pöbeln aus Angst vor dem miesen Image. *Der Spiegel*. 30 March. [Accessed 30 March 2010]. Available at: http://www.spiegel.de/politik/deutschland/0,1518,408829,00.html.

Padtberg, C. 2006. Problemfall Hauptschule. Sammelbecken der Gewalt. *Der Spiegel*. 30 March. [Accessed 30 September 2010]. Available at: http://www.spiegel.de/schulspiegel/0,1518,408835,00.html

Poynting, S. and Morgan, G. 2007. Introduction. in *Outrageous! Moral panics in Australia*. Edited by Poynting, S. and Morgan, G. Hobart: ACYS Publishing.

Scheibelhofer, P. 2007. His-stories of belonging. Young second-generation Turkish men in Austria. *Journal of Intercultural Studies*. 28(3): 317–330.

Der Spiegel. 2006a. Integrationsdebatte. Kultusministerin rüffelt Rausschmiss-Rhetorik. *Der Spiegel*. 7 April. [Accessed 30 September 2010]. Available at: http://www.spiegel.de/schulspiegel/0,1518,410170,00.html

Der Spiegel. 2006b. Solidarität mit der Rütli-Schule. Danke für diesen Brief. *Der Spiegel*. 5 April. [Accessed 30 September 2010]. Available at: http://www.spiegel.de/schulspiegel/0,1518,410009,00.html

Der Spiegel. 2006c. Streit um Schulauflösung. Gewalt-Notruf entsetzt Berlin. *Der Spiegel*. 30 March. [Accessed 30 September 2010]. Available at: http://www.spiegel.de/schulspiegel/0,1518,408808,00.html

Statistisches Bundesamt. 2006. *Leben in Deutschland: Haushalte, Familien und Gesundheit. Ergebnisse des Mikrozensus 2005*. Wiesbaden: Statistisches Bundesamt.

Steinbach, A. and Nauck, B. 2003. *The structural assimilation of the immigrant second generation in Germany. Educational participation and educational success of children and youths from immigrant families*. Chemnitz: Chemnitz University of Technology.

Der Stern. 2006. Gewalt an Schulen. 'Schnupperknast' für Berliner Schüler. *Der Stern*. 2 April. [Accessed 30 September 2010]. Available at: http://www.stern.de/politik/deutschland/gewalt-an-schulen-schnupperknast-fuer-berliner-schueler-558751.html

Süd-Deutsche Zeitung. 2006a. Gewalt gegen Lehrer und Mitschüler. Berliner Hauptschule bekommt Polizeischutz. *Süd-Deutsche Zeitung*. 30 March. [Accessed 22 September 2010]. Available at: http://www.sueddeutsche.de/politik/gewalt-gegen-lehrer-und-mitschueler-berliner-hauptschule-bekommt-polizeischutz-1.893857.

Süd-Deutsche Zeitung. 2006b. Interview mit Wolfgang Schäuble. 'Ich kann die neuen Gefahren nicht ausblenden'. *Süd-Deutsche Zeitung*. 7 April. [Accessed 22 September 2010]. Available at: http://www.sueddeutsche.de/politik/interview-mit-wolfgang-schaeuble-ich-kann-die-neuen-gefahren-nicht-ausblenden-1.436150

Tackmann, V., Weinl, V.. Remke, M. and Schlichtmann, K. 2006. Tatort Hauptschule. Gewalt steht auf dem Stundenplan. *Bild*. 2 April. [Accessed 23 September 2010]. Available at: http://www.bild.de/BTO/news/aktuell/2006/04/02/hauptschule-gewalt/hauptschule-gewalt.html.

Waddington, P. 1986. Mugging as a moral panic. A question of proportion. *British Journal of Sociology*. 37(2): 245–259

White, R. 2007. Taking it to the streets. The larrikins and the Lebanese. in *Outrageous! Moral panics in Australia*. Edited by Poynting, S. and Morgan, G. Hobart: ACYS Publishing

Zinser, D. 2006. Tagesthema. Sich um die Kinder kümmern. *Berliner Zeitung.* 4 April. [Accessed 22 September 2010]. Available at: http://www.berlinonline. de/berliner-zeitung/archiv/.bin/dump.fcgi/2006/0404/schuleinnot/0048/index. html

Chapter 2

A Panicky Debate: The State of Moroccan Youth in the Netherlands

Francis Pakes

In the morning of November 2004 controversial film maker and TV personality Theo van Gogh (distant relative of the painter Vincent van Gogh) cycled along Linnaeus Street in the Dutch capital, Amsterdam. He then was shot eight times by another cyclist, Mohammed Bouyeri, a 26 year-old Dutch-born male of dual Moroccan and Dutch nationality. The offender subsequently got off his bike, stabbed Van Gogh with a curved knife and pinned a letter on Van Gogh's by now dead body with another knife. Bouyeri, arrested soon after the offence, eventually received a life sentence for the crime.

The letter put into the public domain by the Dutch government, contained a key message directed to Ayaan Hirsi Ali, a former Somali refugee who gained political asylum in the Netherlands in the early 1990s. In a remarkable career she became Member of Parliament of the Liberal Party VVD in the Netherlands but has since moved to the US where she established an organization that campaigns for the rights of women under fundamentalist or militant Islam (AHA Foundation, no date). Just prior to Van Gogh's murder she had made a short film with Van Gogh called *Submission* which dealt with the issue of domestic and sexual abuse within a Muslim family. Much of it is a monologue by a Muslim woman describing the experience of having been raped by a family member and physically abused by her husband. The woman addresses Allah in relaying these events. The film was deemed highly offensive to Muslims as it portrayed Holy Scripture inscribed on a woman's naked flesh. It was shown on Dutch television in August 2004, a few months prior to Van Gogh's assassination. In addition, Bouyeri's letter contained threats to Jews, America, and various others and included many phrases borrowed from religious texts.

Predictably, a furore ensued. One commentator wrote that 'something snapped' in Dutch society after Van Gogh's murder (Kluveld, 2009). In a report the WRR, the Scientific Council for Government Policy, referred to the emergence of 'a different way of speaking' about integration of ethnic minorities. Socio-economic factors drifted into the background of the debate whereas issues of culture and religion came to the fore. Historian Van Rossum referred to a 'panicky debate' (Van Rossum, 2005) about Islam, integration and social cohesion. But what happened was more than talk alone. Several Mosques were vandalized in the days after the murder. Van Gogh's funeral, initially intended to be a private affair, was instead broadcast on national television. There was much public soul-searching on the state of the multicultural society, the essence of Dutch-ness and the way forward for immigration and integration of ethnic minorities, in particular Muslims.

The term 'moral panic' obviously presents itself as suitable to describe these events and through which to understand them. Stan Cohen (1972, 2003) identified concern, hostility, consensus, disproportionality, and volatility as key features of moral panic. Although it already featured in Cohen's framework Garland (2008) recently emphasized a dimension of collective introspection that accompanies episodes of moral panics and the notion that the conduct in question must be seen to be somehow symptomatic of wider social malaise.

However, it is questionable whether what happened in the aftermath of the murder was a moral panic. Dutch criminologist De Haan (2007) has argued that the events can better be understood as a 'cultural trauma' than as a 'moral panic'. He draws parallels with the events of 9/11 in the US. Cultural trauma, as described by Sztompka (2000), is about dramatic social change and the way in which societies seek to come to terms with that. This change needs to be perceived to be sudden, radical and imposed or coming from 'the outside'. Finally, it needs to be encountered with a particular mental frame: it must be perceived as shocking, repulsive and posing a threat to previously held assumptions or a way of life. Sztompka lists a number of social changes that may produce cultural trauma, such as revolutions, ethnic cleansing, acts of terrorism and assassinations of political leaders. Such trauma is likely to occur when there appears to be some kind of cultural disorganization or incoherence. When 'the normative and cognitive context of human life and social actions loses its homogeneity, coherence, and stability and becomes diversified or even polarized into opposite cultural complexes' (Sztompka, 2000: 453), we experience cultural disorientation. Cultural disorientation, Stompka says, 'is apt to occur when some significant, sudden and unexpected episode of social change (…) gives a blow to the very central assumptions of a culture' (Sztompka, 2000: 453). Cultural disorientation can also occur due to a clash of new way of life with an old culture, within cultures or between cultures and events. Although a psychological term, trauma is considered both a 'social fact' and a collective phenomenon.

Moral panic and cultural trauma are similar terms. Both use psychological vocabulary to refer to a societal state; both refer to responses to the unexpected, the disturbing, the unnerving and the sudden. They both acknowledge that certain circumstances can act as a trigger. However, moral panics can often be triggered by relatively minor and local situations and events that come to stand for something much larger. Goode and Ben-Yehuda (2009), for example, identified the 'the risk of Horror Comics' in the 1930 that were feared to produce a generation of feral youths, and the panic that emerged in the 1950s when it was reported that scores of young boys had been ensnared in homosexual networks in Boise, Idaho, and argue, that this was nothing more than a 'tempest in a teapot' (2009: 13). What these cases share is that they involve an overreaction by a narrow-minded and too easily scared majority to something that in all likelihood is a relatively trivial matter.

Although not exclusively, moral panics frequently refer to small scale, perhaps isolated events. Van Swaaningen even refers to an 'avalanche of moral panics' (Van Swaaningen, 2005: 298) in the Dutch media when he discusses 'all the drama stories about "robbing Moroccans", "stabbing Antilleans" and "shooting Turks and Yugoslavs"' (Van Swaaningen, 2005: 297). It is criminology challenging and frequently dismissing the preoccupations of dominant discourses in society.

Are the terms 'moral panic' or 'cultural trauma' useful for considering the position of Muslims and particularly of Moroccan youngsters in the Netherlands, or is a wider frame of reference required? The murder of Van Gogh no doubt was a watershed event, a murder so expressive, so public and so gruesome that a notion of collective trauma suffered by a population is probably fairly applied. What made matters worse is that it came only two years after another assassination, that of maverick politician Pim Fortuyn, who was set to make his mark in the national elections of May 2002 on an anti-Islam ticket. He was killed after a media appearance in the town of Hilversum by a native Dutch environmental activist. The mood in the aftermath of that event was arguably even more surreal because it was the first political assassination in the Netherlands for centuries and because of the circumstance that general elections were only nine days away. Pim Fortuyn's party, bereft of its leader, came second out of nowhere. Whereas Fortuyn's murder was a shock, the Van Gogh murder added a layer of abhorrence and anxiety to what was already a state of cultural disorientation. Despite their differences both acts compounded the cultural disorientation. On both occasions the 'blame', was directed away from those who actually committed the acts and towards the 'left'. Leftwing politics was portrayed as an Islam appeasing bogeyman to be blamed for mass immigration, multiculturalism and a softness of issues of crime, culture and integration.

The case that there has been cultural disorientation in the Netherlands is probably quite easily made. It probably took place since 1990 although I have argued elsewhere that its effects in criminal justice mainly came to the fore in the new millennium (Pakes, 2004). As is the case in other European countries, a fear of the 'Islamization' of societies has certainly become part of popular, media and political discourse. Already in 1997 Pim Fortuyn had written a book titled *Against the Islamization of our culture: Dutch identity as foundation* (Fortuyn, 1997), arguing that the Dutch should reflect more on what is essentially Dutch and for Dutch culture to resist soaking up Islamic culture. At that time Fortuyn was a minor public figure and although the book did make some waves, it did not capture the popular imagination to a great extent. Around 2000, Labour man and journalist Paul Scheffer famously referred to the Dutch 'multicultural disaster'; lamenting both the lack of integration of ethnic minorities and their poor socio-economic position. In his piece for national newspaper *NRC Handelsblad* he argued that rapid demographic changes together with present inequalities would lead to the establishment of a sizeable ethnic minority underclass. He referred to the multicultural society as a house of cards and in the process essentialized Islam and argued it is a fallacy to think that the distant outposts of Islam would become moderate blends of Islam, influenced by the liberal and secular home country. Instead, he warned, that diasporas from Turkey and Morocco in the Netherlands are locked into conservative and isolationist modes of religious practice and belief.

Such public expressions indicate that there was unease before 9/11· and the assassinations, but is difficult to gauge how widespread that was. Prior to Fortuyn's rise (which commenced after 9/11), there were no public mouthpieces for discontent, although there were lively debates on integration and ethnic minorities, in newspapers and current affairs magazines, prior to then. That said, although 9/11 occurred over 3,500 miles away, it may well have been the third traumatic event that shaped the national mood in the new millennium.

Van Swaaningen (2005) has argued that it was experienced almost as if it were an attack on the Netherlands. The attacks certainly legitimized a discourse on ethnicity, religion, and integration in which the otherness of immigrants and asylum seekers could be amplified. Islam played a crucial role in that. Fortuyn and others argued that the newcomers failed to integrate. They watched Moroccan or Turkish TV, failed to learn Dutch, continued to yield to militant or extremist imams and stubbornly hung on to anachronistic lifestyles associated with their home countries. In short they were accused of opting out of Dutch values or traditions. A growth of the Islamic population over time through immigration, high birth rates and a tradition of seeking spouses in the 'motherland' of Morocco and Turkey could over time lead to a challenge to the Dutch way of life, the separation of state and religion, the freedom of expression and other freedoms often celebrated as typically Dutch achievements such as in the spheres of euthanasia, soft drugs and sexuality (Pakes, 2006). This is an oft-repeated argument, warning of a putative 'Islamization' of society.

In the meantime there is a steady diet of stories in the media, mainly about misbehaving Moroccan youngsters or other negative stories about ethnic minorities. In last few years they have included stories such as the following

- Extra police in Zandvoort: tough response to beach terrorists. Sea resort tired of groups of Moroccans (*De Telegraaf*, 10 May 2010)
- A call for research into inbreeding among Turks and Moroccans in the Netherlands and possible links to birth defects (*De Telegraaf*, 17 March 2010)
- 'Moroccan tentacles a burden for migrant', a story on how Moroccan authorities ostensibly recall imams preaching in the Netherlands for training but mainly to use them in order to gain control over Moroccan émigrés (Bouddouft and Abdelghafour, 2008).
- Zaltbommel's Burgomaster under protection as threats have been received from Moroccan youngsters *Algemeen Dagblad*, 23 January 2010.
- Communities at war: will there ever be peace between Moroccans and Malaccans in Culemborg? *De Telegraaf*, 5 January 2010.

Stories of the variety 'Moroccan youths make my life a misery' have appeared in relation to Zaltbommel, Ede, Culemborg, Veenendaal and other small or mid-sized towns, most notably Gouda. Although the stories are typically overblown, the trouble of Moroccan youth is now accepted as social fact. Terms that refer to it such as street terrorism, beach terrorism and street terror have become commonplace, invariably in relation to Moroccan youngsters. Twenty-two towns have been designated 'Moroccan municipalities' and receive specific state funding to tackle the problems caused by Moroccan youngsters. The essentialist term '*Marokkanengemeenten*' (Moroccan municipalities) highlights the lack of official restraint in denoting a particular subgroup as worthy of intense scrutiny and intervention. Stol and Bervoets (2002) argue that police officers find dealing with (groups of) Moroccan youngsters particularly problematic.

> According to the police, the teens usually deny what they have done, even if they are caught in the act, witnesses do not tell the police what they have seen because they fear the boys will take revenge. The police also see that the boys cause disturbances through loitering and harassing people. Furthermore, police officers feel they are not respected by the boys. In situations where the police seek to restore public order, the boys often turn against them, warning their friends via mobile telephone and in an instant the police find they are confronted with a large group of aggressive boys. Not surprisingly, many officers are fed up with these boys and their behavior (Stol and Bervoets, 2002: 192).

Thus, in analysing the state of Moroccans in the Netherlands, we need on the one hand to appreciate the potency of traumatic events such as the murders of Van Gogh and Fortuyn, but at the same time the continuous focus on 'minor events' and antisocial behaviours that reach public consciousness to portray Moroccan youngsters as aggressive, misogynist, and engaged in terrorizing public spaces. A more or less distant and abstract cultural threat is mixed in with a more immediate crime and public order concern, where one group comes to symbolize problems of youth, gender, immigration and culture.

Ethnic Minorities in the Criminal Justice System

Discourse on race and ethnicity in the Netherlands is dominated by the distinction between those that are regarded as 'allochtone', i.e., 'not from here' or 'autochtone', those that are 'from here', and it is used as a quick shorthand description to separate 'natives' from 'immigrants' but in a loose sense. 'Recognition of, and claims to, ethnic background is a central feature of Dutch society. Whereas, for example, an American of Afghan descent is first of all addressed as an American, even a third generation immigrant in the Netherlands will still be referred to as a Turk, Surinamese, and so on', explain Uit Beijerse and Van Swaaningen (2006:71).[1]

In the Netherlands, ethnic minorities comprise about ten percent of the population. The largest groups are from Turkey and Morocco on the one hand, and from former colonies Surinam in South America and the Dutch Antilles islands in the Caribbean on the other. Citizens from the former two countries were recruited as so-called guest workers from the 1950s onwards and stayed. Ethnic minority groups are mainly concentrated in the four major cities of Amsterdam, Rotterdam, the Hague and Utrecht where about a third of the population is of ethnic minority background. Nearly fifty percent of those under eighteen are of ethnic minority background, although the great majority are born and bred in the Netherlands. Over eighty percent of Moroccan and Turkish youngsters have dual nationality. There is an increased level of segregation within these cities in certain areas. This is particularly the case for Turks and Moroccans in Rotterdam and the Hague.

Distinctions are important in debates around ethnic minorities. Firstly, public unease is mainly directed towards those of the Islamic faith and within that, Moroccan youngsters in particular. It is particularly here that cultural threats and daily nuisance are seen to be coming together to produce a 'dangerous population' (see Aas, 2007). The average age of ethnic minorities is substantially lower than that of the native population, 28.9 versus 40.6 years of age. In 2008, sixteen percent of births in the Netherlands were of second-generation ethnic minority background. Many of these children start their school career with a language disadvantage. In particular Turkish and Moroccan children have a lesser command of Dutch when they enter primary school and this differential persists through primary school with obvious implication for secondary and higher education. Unemployment figures are commensurate with this. Overall unemployment is 3.8 percent for the Dutch population but 11.2 percent for ethnic minorities. For youngsters, this is ten percent as compared with 21 percent figures that are strongly linked to levels of education (Integratiemonitor, 2009). However, there is also evidence that discrimination operates at the stage of application and interview more than at the point where an ethnic minority member has actually established themselves in the workplace (SCP, 2010).

Overrepresentation of ethnic minorities is also strongly apparent in criminal statistics. According to police data 4.8 percent of ethnic minorities versus 1.3 percent of the 'autochtone' (native) population have been suspected of a crime, in 2007 (Gijsberts and Dagevos, 2009). Overrepresentation in the suspect population particularly involves Antillians (7.9 percent), Moroccans (6.4 percent) and Turks (5.3 percent) (Gijsberts and Dagevos, 2009). The prison population is predominantly non-White. Cavadino and Dignan (2006, p.127) refer to this as a 'wildly disproportionate number foreigners and members of ethnic minorities in Dutch prisons'.

---

1   Where I refer to 'Moroccans' etcetera in this chapter, it is with that meaning.

Ethnic youth have particular problems. For 12 to 17 year olds, 8.4 per 100,000 Moroccans have been arrested. This ratio is 8.3 for Antilleans and 5.9 for those of Surinamese descent whereas this figure for the native population is 1.8 per 100,000 (Van der Laan, Blom, Tollenaar and Kea, 2009). However, there are signs that Moroccan youngsters do suffer a degree of unfair treatment in the juvenile justice system (Komen and Van Schooten, 2005). Komen and Van Schooten analyzed 241 youth justice case files and found that ethnic minority youngsters on average were kept in custody for 53 days longer than native youngsters even after controlling for various factors such as the seriousness of the offence. The reasons given included that attitudes and opinions of ethnic minority youths are frequently interpreted more negatively than those of native youngsters which leads to more negative reporting which in turn tends to lead to harsher sentencing.

Weenink looked at 409 juvenile case files and found that ethnic minority youths were 2.5 times more likely to be taken into custody and 2.3 times more likely to be formally charged than their native Dutch counterparts. His analysis also revealed similar patterns of negative interactions between ethnic minority youngsters and professionals in the system. This influences the judges who do the sentencing and heavily rely on the paperwork produced for them by these professionals (Weenink, 2007, 2009). The further one traverses the criminal justice system, the more striking becomes the over-representation of ethnic minority youngsters. Ethnic minority youngsters are over-represented by a factor of four in charge data, but no less than sevenfold in custody rates (Komen and Van Schooten, 2005).

A Decade of Anti-Islam Populism

Since 2001 there is no shortage of political mouthpieces for voices of discontent. Pim Fortuyn was the trailblazer of this movement, strongly arguing against immigration from Muslim countries, for a change to the constitution in order to secure a Christian tradition as the foundation of Dutch society, unilateral withdrawal of UN Charters, abandonment of the Schengen Treaty to reinstate border controls and so on. Even after his death his party, the List Pim Fortuyn acquired 26 seats in parliament (of 150 seats) and entered a coalition government that was rather short-lived as infighting and incompetence characterized the new party, bereft of its figurehead .

Others sought to emulate Fortuyn's approach and success. Liberal Party VVD MP Rita Verdonk broke away from her party to go it alone with newly formed party TON (*Trots op Nederland*, Proud of the Netherlands), established in 2007. Political polling is a weekly pursuit in the Netherlands and at its height Verdonk's Party seemed close to matching Fortuyn's electoral prowess. However, the electorate proved fickle and, having polled a gain of over two dozen seats, TON actually lost Verdonk's own seat in Parliament in the June 2010 elections gaining less than one percent of the national vote. The mantle however, has been taken up by Geert Wilders, also a Former VVD MP. He has already done well in European and local elections although the party only stood in two carefully chosen municipalities. Wilders's stance is violently anti-Islam. He has compared the Koran with Hitler's *Mein Kampf*, and has argued that Muslims who want to feel at home in secular Netherlands need to rip out most of its pages. He has also referred to the prophet Mohamed as a paedophile. He is arguing for stopping immigration from Muslim countries, banning foreign funding of Mosques and limiting the transfer of benefits abroad.

In the June 2010 general elections, Wilders' Freedom Party emerged as the clear winner, increasing its presence in Parliament from nine to twenty-four seats, having acquired 15.5 percent of the votes and achieving third place in parliament after the Liberals, VVD, and the Labour Party, PvdA. The Christian Democrats, traditional centrist stronghold in Dutch politics, imploded, lost twenty seats and came fourth. Coalition formation, never an easy thing in such a fragmented political landscape, took well over 100 days. With high levels of controversy and mistrust between the tradition main parties, Wilders smartly assumed the role of kingmaker. The coalition government that was eventually formed consisted of Liberal Party VVD, the largest party after the elections with the Christian Democrats despite their substantial losses. The coalition secured a majority via the support of Wilders' Party for Freedom although the party is not formally a part of government. Clearly, the corridors of power loom ever closer for Wilders.

Moving beyond the backroom political manoeuvring of the day, it is clear that a strong anti-Islamic stance now has had a decade of political currency in the Netherlands. In Western Europe, that is arguably nothing new as in many countries it was already well established that somewhere between ten and twenty percent of voters are drawn to right wing, populist, anti-immigration and anti-Islam messages (Albertazzi and McDonnell, 2007). In his speech on election night, Wilders said; 'more security less crime, less immigration and less Islam is what the Netherlands has chosen for'. Indeed it seems as if Wilders has become the mouthpiece for a disaffected and politics-mistrusting part of the voting population. In 2009 Freedom Party voters were more likely to be male and less well educated and more likely to be between 35 and 64 years of age than the average voting population. Unsurprisingly, they felt more negatively about immigrants and also about politics and politicians. They were also more likely to report having had negative encounters with members of ethnic minorities, such as threats and name calling and were also more likely to report to have been victimized by an ethnic minority member (Hooghuis and Bank, 2009).

However, the 2010 elections saw a degree of normalization of the PVV voting population. In particular in relation to education their profile increasingly resembles that of the general voting population. It is also important to note that Wilders' stance is a peculiarly Dutch mixture of xenophobia and libertarianism. The Party holds liberal views on women and homosexuality for instance and places a lot of emphasis on that. Rather the discourse is one of ostensive Freedom (allegedly in jeopardy due to immigration and Islam) as well as a conservative nationalism, holding the view that much of what is typically Dutch is under threat due to immigration and Islam.

It is important to note that whilst the Wilders movement is in essence conservative and neo-nationalist, there is a strong international edge to it. On the one hand this may be a matter of fundraising. As the Freedom Party is not a political party in the traditional sense, as it operates without a membership and without Government subsidy, Wilders needs to be innovative and pro-active in raising funds. Although there is a lack of transparency around this, Wilders frequent media appearances at home and abroad may well reflect such efforts. Recently he spoke at the ninth anniversary of September 11th 2001 in New York, for instance. On the other hand, similar movements abroad may offer both lessons and, as it were, encouragement. An example of the latter was the global furore that occurred further to the publication of cartoons depicting the prophet Mohamed in Danish outlet *Jyllands-Posten* in 2005. The outrage probably served to bolster Wilders's anti-Islam case at home and Wilders indeed spoke out in favour of cartoonist Westergaard. Without needing to assume any grand international network or overarching structure, there is an argument to say that neo-nationalism of the Wilders variety is carried along in a global undercurrent. Tellingly, his website www.wilders.nl is mainly in English, embodying the paradox of the neo-nationalist.

Moral Panics, Cultural Traumas and Social Change

Garland (2008) highlights the productive effect of moral panics: they segregate and polarise, and allow for harsher and harsher treatment of those denoted as folk devils or scapegoats. Indeed, the key issue is not so much what moral panics are; the disturbing stuff is what moral panics do. To balance that picture, however, Goode and Ben-Yehuda noted already in 1994 that many moral panics simply fade without leaving a legacy. They even refer to the demise of the moral panic, whereas Garland (2009) recently conceded that perhaps some of the potency of moral panics has been reduced. That said, where the term moral panic does have purchase in the Dutch context is the designating of Moroccan youngsters as cultural scapegoats, or folk devils. They have come to symbolise societal unease with immigration and multiculturalism so that their very depiction serves to amplify those feelings and also to generate a sense of justification for it. The labelling, and the manifestations of rebellion against it are certainly significant processes occurring in the Netherlands at present.

Still, the term moral panics has suffered more recent criticism. Aas (2007) argues that while the concept moral panics may be useful for unveiling certain social constructions, it also fails to provide insight into what she calls structural transformations of modern penality. After all, the case of increased punitiveness against ethnic minority youngsters has indeed been made here, there are much wider processes of exclusion and othering at work, which involve surveillance, identity and mobility. Aas's point seems to be that moral panics suggest a narrow, perhaps even a static perspective on outsiders within established communities and that we should be looking at broader social and cultural transformations, rather than focus on panic, trauma and legacy.

Looking at the boys of Boise, for instance in the early 20th century but also looking at moral panics involving homosexuality or vagabonds in the Netherlands in the 17th century (Schama, 1986), the quintessential moral panics perhaps are local panics although obviously, the 'power' of local panics is frequently that they tap into or make visible an assumed threat that is much more widespread. Their local nature, you might even argue, adds credence to the postulate that they are over-reactions: if we are terribly upset about a certain development in one locality, why do people elsewhere remain unaffected? This, however, is clearly not the case when discussing unease with Islam, immigrants and globalization: these sentiments are widespread around Western Europe and beyond and could even be regarded as globalizing factors in themselves. The transnational and global aspects of immigration and Islam and responses to it may not prohibit the term moral panic to be used, but it does seem that what we are dealing with are not textbook cases. Some moral panics are now global panics and the question is not whether they will subside or not, but rather how the interactions between outsider groups and the process of exclusion, surveillance and control will shape their identity and the way in which they impose themselves on the dominant culture, both locally and globally (see Pakes, 2010). Perhaps the term moral panic in that regard is both too static and too negative.

This point is developed by Obdeijn and De Mas who describe Moroccans in the Netherlands as on the move, knocking on the door, fighting for their place in society (Obdeijn and De Mas, 2003, Crul and Doomernik, 2003). They use cultural and media analysis to show that Moroccans are taking great strides towards establishing themselves. Indeed, the public face of Dutch Moroccans is highly diverse and as a consequence, it is not difficult to find a wide variety of Moroccan role models that exemplify integration and success. Examples include Ahmed Aboutaleb, Moroccan-born Labour rising star and currently Mayor of the port city of Rotterdam, as well as several Members of Parliament across the political spectrum. Moroccan footballers are making their mark on *Oranje*, the Dutch national football team that enjoys enormous popularity. They include Dutch-born players Khalid Boulahrouz and Ibrahim Afellay who were both part of the World Cup Squad in South Africa in 2010. Female public figures include singer Hind, and popular newsreader and presenter Laïla Abid. It is perhaps Najib Amhali who best encapsulates the transcultural existence of Dutch Moroccans. He is a stand-up comedian and actor whose tremendously successful material often involves everyday situations in which Moroccans face situations in Dutch society. Obdeijn and De Mas (2003) indeed predicted that after a few decades in the margins of society Moroccans would make their mark. For better and for worse, there is no doubt that they are doing so.

Thus, the stereotyping of Moroccan youngsters shares features with many moral panics. At the same time, however, we are looking at a situation in which the Netherlands, along with other Western countries, is seeking to come to terms with profound social change due to immigration and globalization. The murders of Fortuyn and Van Gogh probably qualify as cultural traumas that have enhanced and legitimized both feelings of hostility and processes of exclusion. Moral panic theory is perhaps in danger of under-valuing or ignoring transnational and global communications and interactions. But that is not to say that the term is worn out as it continues to represent one of criminology's most celebrated concepts. However, the lens through which to view Moroccan youngsters in the Netherlands needs to be multifaceted. It needs to zoom in on the lived experience, and on the transnational identity that Moroccans carve out (see Pakes, 2010). In addition, it is required to zoom out, to understand the context of Dutch society and then zoom out further in order to come to terms with patterns of migration and the global travel of discourses, fears and ideology. Only then can we fully come to terms with complex patterns of social change in the Netherlands and, for that matter, elsewhere.

References

Aas, K.F. 2007 *Globalisation and crime*. London: Sage.

Albertazzi, D., and McDonnell, D. (Eds) 2007. *Twenty-first century populism the spectre of western European democracy*. London: Palgrave Macmillan.

Bouddouft, S. and Abdelghafour, A. 2008. Tentakels Marokko beschadigen migrant. Trouw, 15 November 2008.

Cavadino, M. and Dignan, J. 2006 *Penal systems: A comparative approach*. London: Routledge.

Cohen, S. 1973/2003. *Folk devils and moral panics*. London: Routledge

Crul, M., and Doomernik, J. 2003. The Turkish and Moroccan second generation in the Netherlands: Divergent trends between and polarization within the two groups. *International Migration Review*, 37, 1039-64.

De Haan, W. 2007. Morele paniek of cultureel trauma? Over de betekenis en gevolgen van de moord of Theo van Gogh. *Tijdschrift Voor Criminology*, 49, 252-264.

Fortuyn, P. 1997. *De puinhopen van acht jaar Paars*. Rotterdam: Karakter.

Garland, D. 2001. *The culture of control*. Chicago: University of Chicago Press.

Garland, D. 2008. On the concept of moral panic. *Crime, media and culture*, 4, 9-30.

Gijsberts, M. and Dagevos, J., 2009. Jaarrapport integratie 2009. The Hague: Sociaal en Cultureel Planbureau.

Goode, E. and Ben-Yehuda, N. 1994 *Moral panics: Culture, politics and social construction*. Annual Review of Sociology, 20, 149-171.

Goode, E. and Ben-Yehuda, N. 2009 *Moral panics: The social construction of deviance*. Chichester: Wiley.

Hooghuis, M. and Bank, M. 2009. *De PVV stemmer: Profiel, achtergrond en motieven*. Report for: NRC Handelsblad, 25 September 2009. Available at: http://www.nrc.nl/multimedia/archive/00251/91221_rap_v_1_01_251044a.pdf

Komen, M. and Van Schooten. E., 2005. Allochtone jongeren gemiddeld langer vast. In: M. Komen (Ed.) Straatkwaad en jeugdcriminaliteit: Naar een algemene of een etnisch-specifieke aanpak? Het Spinhuis, Apeldoorn.

Kluveld, A. 2009. Praat moord Van Gogh niet goed. *Volkskrant,* 2 November 2009.

Nievers, E., and Andriessen, I. 2010. *Discriminatiemonitor niet-westerse migranten op de arbeidsmarkt 2010.* The Hague: SCP.

Pakes, F.J. 2004. The politics of discontent: The emergence of a new criminal justice discourse in the Netherlands. *Howard Journal of Criminal Justice*, 43(3), 284-298.

Pakes, F.J. 2005. Penalisation and retreat: The changing face of Dutch criminal justice. *Criminal Justice*, 5(2), 145-161.

Pakes, F. 2010. Global forces and local effects in youth justice: The case of Moroccan youngsters in Netherlands. *International Journal of Law, Crime and Justice, 38,* 109-119.

Schama, S. 1987. *The Embarrassment of Riches: An Interpretation of Dutch Culture in the Golden Age.* New York: Vintage.

Scheffer, P. 2000. Het multiculturele drama. *NRC Handelsblad*, 29 January 2000.

Stol, W.P. and Bervoets, E.J. A., 2002. Policing Dutch-Moroccan youth. *Policing and Society*, 12, 191-200.

Sztompka, P. 2000. Cultural trauma: The other face of social change. *European Journal of Social Theory* 3, 449-466.

Uit Beijerse, J. and Van Swaaningen, R., 2007. The Netherlands: Penal welfarism and risk management. In: Muncie, J. and Goldson, B. (Eds). *Comparative Youth Justice*, 65-78. Sage, London.

Van der Laan, A., Blom, M., Tollenaar, N., and Kea, R., 2010. *Trends in the geregistreerde jeugdcriminaliteit onder 12- tot en met 24-jarigen in de periode 1996-2007.* Ministry of Justice, The Hague.

Van Rossum, M. 2005. Nederland in crisis? In: *Hoe nu verder? 42 visies op de toekomst van Nederland na de moord op Theo van Gogh.* Utrecht: Spectrum.

Van Swaaningen, R. 2005. Public Safety and the Management of fear. *Theoretical Criminology,* 9, 289-305.

Weenink, D. 2007. De invloed van de etniciteit van jonge verdachten op beslissingen van het Openbaar Ministerie, *Sociologie,* 3, 291-322.

Weenink, D. 2009. Explaining Ethnic Inequality in the Juvenile Justice System An Analysis of the Outcomes of Dutch Prosecutorial Decision Making, *British Journal of Criminology, 49*, 220-242.

Chapter 3

Italian Intellectuals and the Promotion of Islamophobia after 9/11

Bruno Cousin and Tommaso Vitale

During the 2000s, the intellectual field played a determinant role in the development of Islamophobia in Italy[1]. Beyond the public declarations of numerous right-wing political leaders opposed to multiculturalism regularly proclaiming the moral inferiority of Islam, and a level of popular and institutional hostility towards Muslims that constitutes a record for Western Europe (EUAFR 2009), we find in Italy the mobilization of cultural producers behind an intellectual Islamophobia. Highly publicized journalists/writers – such as Oriana Fallaci and Magdi Allam – as well as the intellectuals of Berlusconi's party, numerous prelates and academics close to the Catholic Church, and several of their secular conservative colleagues, have contributed to legitimate and reinforce an anti-Islamic *Zeitgeist* that has developed and reinvented the assortment of stereotypes (Bourdieu 1991, Bourdieu and Boltanski 1976: 61) about the 'migration question' and generated a specific xenophobia against Muslims.

This chapter proposes a review of these different Italian thinkers and promoters of Islamophobia in order to both clarify their respective ideas and describe the relations and links that join them to one another in a cartel branching out through all the arenas of power. It thus presents both a preliminary network analysis and a prosopography (detailing the social properties and the trajectories of the authors and their works) that provide a collective portrait previously undrawn: an indispensible precondition for any approach seeking to identify the processes of reconfiguration in the Italian intellectual field since 9/11, to measure its influence on the public debate about Islam, or to analyze further the role and strategies of a particular group or author without being restricted to the scholastic illusion that often characterizes history of ideas.

The Media Champions: Saga and Prophecies of Oriana Fallaci...

The most well-known figure in Italian Islamophobia is undoubtedly Oriana Fallaci (1929-2006), whose essays (*The Rage and the Pride*, 2001; *The Force of*

1   We would like to thank Alfredo Alietti, Daniel Cefaï, Giacomo Costa and Simone Tosi for their comments on an earlier version of this text.

Reason, 2004; *Oriana Fallaci Interviews Herself – The Apocalypse*, 2004) have been translated and commented on throughout the world[2]. Islam is described in these volumes as a monolithic enemy at war with the West: an ahistorical and undifferentiated monad, without distinctions or internal tensions worthy of analysis. No substantial difference is seen to exist between fundamentalism and moderate or secularized Islam: all Muslims are potential terrorists, and immigrants the vanguard of an 'invasion' that it would be deceptive to believe could be integrated through citizenship or acculturation. Therefore, war and the closing of borders are described as the only solutions to this centuries-long conflict between civilization and barbarism. Fallaci thus denounces the lax attitude of civil societies and European governments, which have done nothing to counter the scourge of migrants and on-going Islamicization, the symptoms of which she sees in any form of tolerance towards the cultural specificities of Muslims. According to her, a grand conspiracy and planned manoeuvres to transform Europe, and particularly Italy, into a province of the Ummah are underway: an entirely Islamicized Europe ('Eurabia') is on the doorstep, so advanced is the insidious action of the allies of Muslim fundamentalism, which are – all together – the social sciences, the anti-globalization movement, the Western governments who have yielded to the sirens of a multicultural society, and the Vatican of John Paul II (accused of preaching benevolence towards foreign immigrants instead of leading the fight against Islam).

Despite their systematic falsification of facts (or multiple glaring errors), their massive resort to conspiracy theories, to describing their opponents as animals, sexual perverts or health hazards, their gutter racism, their homophobic insults and their calls for state violence, all in a form closer to muddled invective than to reasoning, these works have dominated book sales (all genres included) in Italy during the first half of the 2000s and, shortly before her death, their author was awarded the highest civil honours (by several political representatives from both the right and the left). During the past decade Fallaci was an unavoidable reference in the public debate on intercultural relations and the possibility of Muslim integration. How has this exceptional success been possible?

Firstly, the success arose from the sweep and culmination of her career. Her unique path – from 14-year-old courier of the anti-fascist Resistance during World War II, to respected field reporter (notably from the Muslim world) who risked her life many a time, popular novelist, and charismatic feminist icon – is constantly referred to in her works and allowed her to adopt, at the end of her life, a multifaceted dominant posture at the heart of the national intellectual field; a posture made possible from autumn 2001, also because she took on the role of national critical conscience, conservative but non-partisan and supposedly

---

2   For a detailed study on the origins, modalities and effects of Fallaci's intellectual leadership on Islamophobia in the Italian public sphere between 2001 and 2006, we take the liberty of directing the reader to a forthcoming article by the present authors. Elements of analysis have also been presented in previous papers (Cousin and Vitale 2002, 2005, 2007, 2008).

non-conformist, left vacant a few months earlier following the death of Indro Montanelli (1909-2001).

In addition, Fallaci's essays enjoyed huge media launches resulting from an advertising synergy between the two largest national press groups – her publisher RCS and Mondadori, owned by Berlusconi – the three television channels belonging to the latter, and the three public ones he controlled directly as prime minister. The author was also able to draw on her influence among journalists and intellectuals. Last but not least, she enjoyed a singular artistic licence as a consequence of her *multipositionality* (Boltanski 1973): between journalism, literature, the intellectual field and the media; and between Italy and the United States (where Fallaci mostly lived during the last two decades of her life, often claiming she was better known there than in Italy). Her prestige is not the product of a reputation established in a specific national field, progressively expanded to a neighbouring one sharing some institutions or modes of legitimation with the first, and so on. It results instead from crossed and simultaneous guarantees, whose iteration masks the fact that the public image of brilliance Fallaci enjoys is not solidly based in any specific domain.

…Testimony and Hagiography of Magdi Allam

Magdi Allam (born in 1952) was the other main intellectual herald of the anti-Islamic mobilization of the 2000s, in a way that both reinforced and complemented the stands taken by Oriana Fallaci (whose praises he often sang). Allam is a journalist and essayist of Egyptian origin, who was schooled in Italian by the Combonian nuns and the Salesians of his hometown of Cairo, before emigrating at the age of twenty to Italy. Here he studied sociology and started a career in journalism that led him – drifting progressively to the right – to work for *Il Manifesto, La Repubblica,* then *Il Corriere della Sera,* of which he was a deputy editor and a columnist from 2003 to 2008. A fluent speaker and writer of Arabic (in a country where oriental studies, anthropology[3], and critical sociology of migrations are little developed[4]), he moved at the end of the 1990s from the status of chronicler

---

3   Notably because academic themselves often turn to opinion writing. For instance, Ida Magli (born in 1925), once a recognised specialist in cultural and religious anthropology at the Sapienza University of Rome, has now adopted an exclusively critical approach which has set her up as an additional rhetorical force defending Italian cultural heritage by denouncing the 'peril' supposedly represented by immigration in general and Muslim immigrants in particular (see her virulent column published by *Il Giornale*, one of the most aggressive newspapers belonging to the Berlusconi family).

4   Even if Italian journalists/writers and essayists, from the right and the left, sometimes refer to the main international specialists in Islamic studies (rather than to those teaching in Italian universities) to prop up their thesis. This is the case for Fiamma Nirenstein (born in 1945): a journalist who covered the Middle East during two decades, author of several books on Israel and anti-Semitism, lecturer at the LUISS, deputy for Berlusconi's party and

and reporter specialized in the Muslim worlds to that of expert and media-hyped critic, first of the effects of fundamentalist Islam and later of Muslims as a whole.

Although he has less symbolic capital than Fallaci, he has since 2002 written several alarmist books (often autobiographical and all published by Mondadori – Allam 2002a, 2002b, 2003, 2004, 2005, 2006, 2007, 2008, 2009) through which he consolidated a posture of multifaceted legitimacy similar to hers. He presents himself, at the same time: as a heretic breaking with a predominantly violent Islam (which went so far as to sentence him to death and forced him to live under police protection) and with an Italian intelligentsia who underestimates its dangers; as a moralist with anti-intellectual hints invoking the primacy of a clear and normative stance over explanatory quibbles; as a true specialist in the topics he deals with and a 'sociologist' giving in to simplification only for a pedagogical purpose; and as an expert whose advice is appreciated by those few truly enlightened leaders fighting against Islamic violence (be they politicians, magistrates, or the Italian intelligence agencies). However, where Fallaci poses as a martial adversary of Islam, Allam prefers to present himself throughout his books as a still-defiant victim of persecution and tells his life story in the form of a hagiography rather than a saga. At a young age he was deprived of his father whose polygamist attempts led him to abandon his mother, who herself eventually left to work in Saudi Arabia and embraced Wahhabism. He also witnessed the end of the Cairo cosmopolitanism of his youth, dismissed by the rise of Egyptian nationalism after the Six-Day War. Then he experienced repeated humiliations within the Italian journalistic milieu which – he complains – was slow to recognize his value, before scaling its heights through implacably denouncing those he saw as responsible for such misfortunes (and many others to boot).

His successive books thus go back on many of his previous analyses: while in the past he had stated the compatibility of Islam with democracy, praised immigration as salutary for Italy, advocated a balanced Israeli-Palestinian peace process and denounced the Clash of Civilizations thesis, he later adopted the opposite positions. Finally, carried away by the conviction of the moral and spiritual superiority of Christianity, he veered from an attitude of pluralistic critique – engaging in controversies with reformist Islamic thinkers such as Tariq Ramadan and Rached Ghannouchi – to the condemnation of multiculturalism itself and of what he describes since as the death-dealing essence of Islam. This conviction led in 2008 to his apostasy and sensational conversion to Catholicism (he was baptised by the Pope in St. Peter's Basilica during the Easter Vigil), and then to the formation of his party *Protagonists for Christian Europe / I Love Italy*, which enabled him the following year to be elected to the European Parliament on the UDC list (Christian democrat right). It was a turnaround which, like Fallaci's

---

vice-chairman of the Committee on Foreign Affairs of the Chamber, she considers herself a student of historian Bernard Lewis, whose recent analyses of current affairs she helped popularize in Italy (Nirenstein 1999, 2003).

last successes, must be situated in a context of relations structuring the Italian public debate about Islam during the last decade, as we will now see.

The Occidentalist Ideologists of Berlusconism

The success and the vast audiences of Fallaci and Allam cannot be explained without considering the support they received from (Catholic) institutional intellectuals and/or from (Berlusconian) organizational ones (Sapiro 2009) holding key positions both in the political field, and within scholarly and public debates. Indeed, in comparison to the other European countries, the low level of differentiation between these fields is an Italian peculiarity – already pointed out for the nineteenth century (Charle 1996) – that persisted until today. As the careers of these key intellectuals show:

- Marcello Pera (born in 1943), professor of philosophy at the University of Pisa and heir until the mid-1990s to a Popperian tradition that brought him close to the liberal-libertarian claims of the Radical Party, is today the leader of the Italian theoconservative movement: a Berlusconian senator since 1996, he was president of the Senate from 2001 to 2006, and co-wrote or prefaced several books with Joseph Ratzinger (Pope Benedict XVI), notably *Without Roots* (2004) and *Why We Must Call Ourselves Christians* (2008).

- Gaetano Quagliariello (born in 1960) was his adviser for cultural affairs to the Presidency of the Senate. Once one of the national leaders of the Radical Party, he defected to the right, and also pursued a double career in academia and politics: a professor of contemporary political history at the LUISS in Rome, a Berlusconian senator since 2006 and in charge of the Culture department of Forza Italia[5] in 2007-2008, he is notably the author of *Catholics, Pacifists, Theocons* (2006)[6].

- The essayist and journalist Ferdinando Adornato (born in 1945), a former top official of the Italian Communist Party's youth wing, was for his part one of the co-authors of the 2004 'Charter of Values' of FI. He sat as a Berlusconian deputy from 2001 to 2008 (before joining the UDC), and chaired until 2006 the Culture, Science and Education Committee of the Chamber. He recently published *The New Way: West and Freedom after the Twentieth Century* (2003), and *Faith and Freedom* (2007) with future archbishop Rino Fisichella.

- Father Gianni Baget Bozzo (1925-2009) was active in the Christian Democracy and then in the Italian Socialist Party (for which he was twice an MEP) before

---

5   FI was created by Silvio Berlusconi in January 1994, and immediately established itself as the first political party of the country and the kingpin of the right-wing coalitions led by Berlusconi during the following 15 years. In March 2009, it merged with the post-fascist Alleanza Nazionale, as well as with several smaller parties, to form Il Popolo della Libertà (PdL).

6   On his standpoints towards Islam and immigration, see also his website www.gaetanoquagliariello.it.

joining FI in 1994. He also contributed to write the 'Charter of Values' and was the special adviser to Silvio Berlusconi on issues related to Islam (Guolo 2003). A columnist and commentator for several media, and a prolific essayist, he is the author of, among other works, *Facing Islam* (2001), *The Western Empire* (2004) and *Between Nihilism and Islam* (2006).

Pera, Quagliariello, Adornato and Baget Bozzo – like Giuliano Urbani (born in 1937), professor of political science at Bocconi University in Milan, columnist, Berlusconian deputy in 1994-2005 and Minister of Culture from 2001 to 2005 – all warmly praised Oriana Fallaci's 'Trilogy'. In addition to having more or less left-wing past, having played key roles in the FI party machine and at the head of its think tanks (Cousin and Vitale 2006), these people had a proximity to the Roman Curia (and especially to his Congregation for the doctrine of the faith), a status of intellectuals recognized as such both by their peers and by the wider public, and the same publisher (Mondadori). They share a conception of democracy as incompatible with multiculturalism and French-style secularism. Democracy is seen as inseparable from Christian origins, to which it supposedly owes its moral superiority, and which should be constantly recognised and valorized to avoid Western civilization and social order being washed away by migration flows. Moreover, just as they often reduce Christianity to Catholicism, the organic intellectuals of FI regard Islam as a unitary religious and cultural entity, intrinsically violent, particularly threatening for the survival of European 'values' and individual freedoms, and overdetermining the actions of all Muslims, who are therefore by definition unable to integrate, even after a long acculturation process[7].

They bestowed on Silvio Berlusconi's party conservative cultural references and an intellectual critique that part of its electorate had complained to be lacking during the first years of Forza Italia, characterized by more neoliberal leanings (Poli 2001). These ideologists have contributed to setting up one of the convergences that have held the right-wing coalition in place throughout the last decade. Islamophobia and Christian Occidentalism have indeed allowed FI to pledge its xenophobia to its allies of the Lega Nord, which for its part has never really sought to base its essentialist racism on any complex justification (Cento Bull 2009, Biorcio 2010). But they have also simultaneously strengthened its links

---

7   These preconceptions are also fully shared by Roberto de Mattei (born in 1948), professor of history at the University of Cassino then since 2009 at the European University of Rome (created in 2005 by the Legionaries of Christ), and adviser for international affairs to the Italian Government in 2002-2006. His books on Western-Islamic relations (de Mattei 2002, 2009), as well as his many dogmatic, homophobic, anti-feminist and anti-evolutionist thesis, caused a surge of indignation in April 2011 when they were topped with a series of statements arguing that the Eastern Japan great earthquake and tsunami – like the destruction of Warsaw by the Nazis during World War II – were a punishment sent by God. The protest caught on among academics, mainly because the Catholic fundamentalist professor was in 2004-2007 and again since 2008 the vice-president of the National Research Council (the Italian NSF).

with the Christian democrat right and the Roman Church: Forza Italia's defence of Catholicism as a central component of Italian (and European) identity, as well as its positions on bioethical issues and in favour of private Catholic schools, has led them in exchange to tolerate the strong personalization of power to the advantage of Silvio Berlusconi, and the pornocratic dimension of the regime made public over the last three years.

The Catholic Voices: From the Magisterium of the Holy See to the Influence of *Comunione e Liberazione*

The ideological junction of these intellectuals with the Holy See and part of the Catholic hierarchy can only be understood in the light of the evolution of the Church's positions at the end of John Paul II's pontificate, then – in a more distinct manner – when Benedict XVI succeeded him in 2005. Unlike Karol Wojtyła, who was a professor of ethics deeply committed to his pastoral activity and whose pontificate was marked by interfaith dialogue, Joseph Ratzinger (born in 1927) had an exclusively academic career as a professor of dogmatic theology before becoming a cardinal, throughout which he contributed notably to transform the Holy Office (the ex-Roman Inquisition) into the Congregation for the doctrine of the faith, which he then headed from 1981. As the prefect of the congregation, he strongly limited pluralism within the Catholic Church, becoming known for his authoritarianism, his intransigence concerning orthodoxy, and his reservations about ecumenism and the possibility of shared ethics among the major religions. In 2000, his *Dominus Iesus* declaration recalled the primacy of Catholicism in terms of salvation over other Christian and non-Christian denominations. In May 2004, in the thick of the debate on the opportunity to mention European 'Christian heritage' in the preamble to the Treaty establishing a Constitution for Europe, he participated in two conferences with Marcello Pera, extended by an exchange of letters, from which comes the book they published together that same year. In it, Ratzinger denounces multiculturalism as the symptom of Western self-loathing that he defines as pathological. Finally, in 2006, especially since he had become Pope the previous year, Benedict XVI created a worldwide turmoil and built himself a public image tinged with Islamophobia during his now (in)famous Regensburg lecture, when he reflected on a quote from the Byzantine emperor Manuel II Palaiologos[8] reducing the essence of Islam to violence[9].

---

8   It is unclear if the grounding of the speech in such a reference was the result of clumsiness or a tactical choice. The ambiguity often characteristic of the papal word is based – for Benedict XVI – less on the search for consensual wordings simultaneously congenial to the different sections of the Catholic world, than on the succession of statements and subsequent corrections (or even denials) establishing a segmented communication strategy.

9   'Show me just what Mohammed brought that was new, and there you will find things only evil and inhuman, such as his command to spread by the sword the faith he

These positions of the new Pope, supported with scholarly references, were even more willingly welcomed by the Italian right as they concurred with those of the top of the Italian episcopacy – dominated at the time by its most conservative fringe – whose opposition to a national multiculturalism including Islam had been declared many years earlier (Garau, 2010). Since the end of the 1990s, the thesis of the impossibility of integrating Muslim immigrants has been debated at the highest levels of the Italian Catholic hierarchy, where it was vehemently supported by Cardinal Giacomo Biffi (2000a, 2000b) – close to Benedict XVI – and Cardinal Camillo Ruini, who was the president of the Italian Episcopal Conference from 1991 to 2007. The latter declared as early as 1997 that immigrants were not welcome into the country unless their cultural and religious origins were 'compatible with the Italian ones', that is unless they were Christians.

Moreover, the convergence of the ecclesiastical hierarchies and the ideologists of Forza Italia on Islamophobic stances was also the fruit of intense bridge-building carried out by actors firmly and simultaneously installed not only in the political and the intellectual fields, but also in the ecclesial one[10] (whose influence in Italy reduces even more the autonomy of each of the other two), such as Rino Fisichella and the *Comunione e Liberazione* movement (CL).

Archbishop Salvatore 'Rino' Fisichella (born in 1951) was professor of fundamental theology at the Pontifical Gregorian University in Rome until 1998, rector of the Pontifical Lateran University from 2002 to 2010, and president of the Pontifical Academy for Life from 2008 to 2010. A member of the Congregation for the doctrine of the faith, he was handed the presidency of a new Church department in June 2010: the Pontifical Council for promoting the new evangelisation, charged with fighting against the decline of Christianity and the secularisation process in Western countries. His main positions in the public debate, in defence of the 'Christian roots' of Europe and against its 'Islamization', appear in the volume co-authored with Adornato as well as in two other books recently published by Mondadori (Fisichella 2007, 2009a). But Fisichella also organized (Quagliariello 2006: 120) the conferences with Pera and Ratzinger that led to their joint volume; and was Oriana Fallaci's principal confidant throughout her last two years of worsening illness (Fisichella 2009b), the architect of her rapprochement with Benedict XVI (who granted her a private audience in August 2005) and the attentive reviewer of her third Islamophobic essay. Moreover, according to Magdi Allam – whose conversion he encouraged and supported – he is his 'spiritual guide'. Finally, Fisichella is used to getting involved both directly and indirectly in politics: not only because from 1994 to 2010 he was the chaplain of the Chamber of Deputies, but also by regularly defending in the media Silvio Berlusconi's morality. During the second half of the 2000s, he also got closer to

---

preached.' (Palaiologos 1966 – The original text is in Greek and the accuracy of the English translation by the Vatican has been debated).

10   On the pertinence of studying the Catholic Church as a field, see Bourdieu and Saint-Martin 1982.

CL and was, for instance, invited in 2007 and 2008 to speak at the international summer meeting gathering hundreds of thousands of its members in Rimini.

CL began in Milan in the 1950s and grew in importance after 1968, imposing itself as the organizer of a revival of the forms of mobilization among the Catholic youth: more spontaneist than its predecessors – in particular than Azione Cattolica – and nevertheless advocating entryism and cultural confrontation, aestheticism and anti-Marxism (Zadra 1994, Abbruzzese 2001)[11]. Recognized by the Church since 1982 as an association of pontifical right, the 'movement' is today one of the organizations that dominate the field of power in Northern Italy (the economic heartland of the country), where it has several thousand members and tens of thousands of followers. It has controlled the Lombardy Region since 1995, when one of its historic officials – Roberto Formigoni (now Berlusconian) – was elected governor. His clientelist machine and his hold over the several institutional sectors rely widely on the *Compagnia delle Opere*, the operational arm of CL which functions at the same time as an employers' union, a services provider, a welfare and philanthropy consortium, and as an educational and cultural federation (Pinotti 2010). Among the principal Italian politicians belonging to CL, many have encouraged over the last decade the defence of 'Europe's Christian roots' against multiculturalism and Islam. For instance, although usually temperate in his positions, Mario Mauro (born in 1961), vice-president of the European Parliament in 2004-2009, current chief whip of the Berlusconian MEPs, adjunct professor at the European University of Rome, and in charge of the Higher Education department of Forza Italia in 2002-2009, has written several essays on these questions, including: *Europe will be Christian or it will not be at all* (2004), *The God of Europe* (2007) and *Little dictionary of the Christian roots of Europe* (Chiappa and Mauro 2007)[12]. Maurizio Lupi (born in 1959), a Berlusconian deputy and vice-president of the Chamber, was another strong supporter of Magdi Allam's conversion and his godfather at his baptism in 2008[13].

The intellectual influence of CL is also due to the fact that the largest Italian student union is a direct outgrowth of the movement and that the main secular leader of the latter is currently Giancarlo Cesana. Cesana (born in 1948) is a professor of medicine and hygiene at the University of Milan-Bicocca and a

---

11   Concerning the history of CL since 1954, see also the three volumes written by one of its leaders: Massimo Camisasca (2001, 2003, 2006).

12   The last title is a children's book.

13   By contrast, some other political or religious leaders originally from CL – conservative Catholics that did not join Berlusconi or toe the Ratzinger line against multiculturalism – reject the essentialist approach to Islam in favour of interreligious dialogue carried out on a more pragmatic basis. This is the case notably for Cardinal Angelo Scola (born in 1941), the highly influential archbishop of Milan and former patriarch of Venice, but also for Rocco Buttiglione (born in 1948), president of the UDC, professor of political philosophy at the LUSPIO in Rome, exegete of John Paul II, former MEP, former senator, minister of Culture in the third Berlusconi government (2005-2006), and currently vice-president of the Chamber.

high-level manager in the Lombardy health system, whose scientific authority is particularly instrumental in supporting CL's 'pro-life' stances. But, at the 2010 annual meeting of the movement he also proclaimed his indignation against Umberto Eco: explicitly denounced as a eulogist of tolerance and ideological pluralism, as well as for his criticism of religious fanaticism contained in *The Name of the Rose...*

The Secular Conservative Experts and the Figure of the Incompatible Alien

In addition to these Berlusconian and Catholic intellectuals[14], a third group of men – sharing common social properties and similar modalities of taking stances – has contributed to the rise of Islamophobia in Italy; notably by unanimously acclaiming the essays of Fallaci, by criticizing their extreme tone to better celebrate their alleged truthfulness and analytical accuracy. This group is made of liberal-conservative political scientists attached to secularism. Critical supporters of the Italian right, they are careful never to lapse into forms of partisan activism that could undermine the claimed neutrality of their expertise, and they all combine a prestigious academic or professional career with writing op-ed columns.

Sergio Romano (born in 1929), was general director of cultural relations at the Italian Ministry of Foreign Affairs, ambassador to NATO and to the Soviet Union, then professor of history of international affairs at Bocconi University. He is today a prolific essayist often writing on the relations of Italy with Islam and the Muslim world. Ernesto Galli della Loggia (born in 1942) was professor of contemporary political history at the University of Perugia, at San Raffaele University in Milan, and has been since 2009 at the prestigious *Istituto Italiano di Scienze Umane*. He is also the co-author with Cardinal Camillo Ruini (2009) of a book on the social role of Christianity. Finally, Angelo Panebianco (born in 1948) is professor of political science at the University of Bologna. All three have long been columnists for the *Ill Corriere della Sera*, the largest Italian daily newspaper[15] (in which Fallaci published – as first drafts or previews – long extracts of her three books against Islam, and of which Allam was a deputy editor). They don't adopt any Occidentalist perspective neither claim the moral supremacy of Christianity, but in the name of political realism they resort to a culturalist analysis of Muslim countries and their citizens, in order to maintain the difficulties of the latter in accepting a democratic, secular and tolerant society.

Without denying the possibility or even the possibility of a more multicultural Italy these authors make various diagnoses about how Islam hinders it. For Romano (2007), the problem is due essentially to the fact that the Arab countries

---

14   Which of course are not representative of all the diverse positions towards Islam existing within the Catholic Church.

15   Romano also for *Panorama*, the second largest weekly news magazine in the country, owned by Berlusconi.

have not yet met a historical and geopolitical conjuncture favourable to their democratization and to the emergence of a 'modern state', and therefore do not socialize their inhabitants to lead respectful and pluralistic civic lives. According to him, Islam is thus only one causal dimension of this situation (among others). For Galli della Loggia, analyst and promoter since the 1990s of an 'Italian national identity' inevitably filled with Catholicism, Islam poses a specific problem in that it too often denies individual rights and freedoms (notably those of women and sexual minorities) and because it is a religion exclusively based on submission to authority, to texts and to divine law, while Christianity is seen to give more space to *logos* and reason[16]. Finally, for Panebianco, it is the quest for cultural hegemony inherent to Islam (and exacerbated by the Islamist awakening) that renders Muslim immigrants and their children particularly difficult to integrate peacefully into European societies. Thus, for the three authors, the integration problems that Muslims have faced in Italy can only be caused by their lack of conformity and adaptability – contingent for Romano, doctrinal for Galli, and relational for Panebianco – to their new country, while the possibility that the latter could try to reach a compromise over certain specificities of this fraction of its population (which now totals around a million and a half people) is never mentioned.

Actually, this line of analysis, with its culturalist and assimilationist overtones, has also been adopted and legitimated for a decade by the most famous Italian political scientist: Giovanni Sartori (born in 1924), emeritus professor at Columbia University in New York and at the University of Florence, who is also an op-ed columnist for *Il Corriere della Sera*. Since the appendix to the 2002 edition of his book *Pluralism, Multiculturalism and Foreigners* – where he affirms that 'we can only integrate what is integrable'[17] – until the debate that pitted him against Bocconi economist Tito Boeri (Sartori 2009, 2010), he has maintained that all former and recent historical experiences show without exception that Muslim minorities are impossible to integrate, little inclined to tolerance and to the recognition of other religions, often violent, and would therefore be disruptive of order and social peace in any country welcoming them, especially secular democracies. The problem, according to Sartori, is that Islam is a totalizing religion incompatible with secularization. Therefore, in the name of realism, Italy should both seek to attract the 'good' migrants essential to its economy, and do all it can to avoid accepting Muslims and making them citizens. Sartori defends the right of the native majority to xenophobia, that is to the refusal of a cultural otherness that frightens them.

Islamophobic Intellectuals as Moral Panic Entrepreneurs

If the stances taken by these different intellectuals share the common aim of fighting 'cultural relativism' – a claimed aim which is also the feature of a wider

---

16   See, for instance, Galli della Loggia 2006.
17   See also Sartori 2008.

public discourse that has developed in Italy over the last decade (Rivera 2010)[18] – it is the 'values' they declare to defend that distinguish them from each other. Some are more secular and pluralistic (but opposed to political multiculturalism), others essentially based on interpretations of Christianity and more specifically of Catholicism, and most are a combination of the two: seeking to establish in one way or another the necessity of the link between Christianity and democracy. Cultural pluralism is seen as often too permissive towards Muslims, therefore as fostering (moral) disorder and (tolerance towards) barbarism.

The 2000s have indeed been marked by a hardening of these two lines of criticism of Islam, but also by a gradual shift of several intellectuals from a secular position to an alignment with the Vatican, often accompanied by an act of faith. In addition to the already mentioned cases of Oriana Fallaci, Magdi Allam and Marcello Pera, we can also cite, in this regard, the case of Giuliano Ferrara, founding editor of *Il Foglio*, a daily opinion paper controlled by Berlusconi[19]. Moreover, the numerous books of dialogues with high-level Catholic prelates (Pera with Ratzinger, Adornato with Fisichella, Galli della Loggia with Ruini) have further contributed to reconfigure the debate about the place of African immigrants in Italian society in religious terms (Allievi 2005): the 'Moroccans' of the 1990s have been transformed into 'Muslims' 'Islamics' or even 'Mohammedans'[20] in the 2000s. But this renewed influence of the Church hierarchy on several conservative intellectuals is also explained by the historical weakness of the Italian liberal tradition.

The versions and skilful elaborations of Islamophobia presented in this chapter do not however fully make sense outside the comparison with other waves of intolerance – towards, for example, Albanians (Dal Lago 1999) or Roma groups (Vitale and Claps 2010) – that have affected Italy over the last twenty years. In the case of Roma and Sinti, xenophobia doesn't need any intellectual elaboration. It is based on longstanding popular depictions, on the performativity of recurrent public accusations, and on the institutional – and thus instituting – routines that have long stabilized the *reality* of Roma groups, that is the stereotype used against them (Boltanski 2011). They are almost unanimously perceived as a socially homogenous, fundamentally deviant population – whose appearance

---

18   See also the groundbreaking research of Alfredo Alietti and Dario Padovan (2010, 2011) that analyzes how Islamophobic prejudices and attitudes among the Italian population are connected to authoritarian, ethnocentric and anomic systems of representations.

19   A formidable neoconservative polemicist, Giuliano Ferrara (born in 1952 into a communist family) spent part of his childhood in Moscow, was a PCI activist during the 1970s, moved during the 1980s to the Italian Socialist Party of Bettino Craxi (as an MEP) and to the CIA (as an informer), then to Forza Italia as minister in charge of the Relations with the Parliament and chief spokesperson for the first Berlusconi government (in 1994). An ardent promoter of the recognition of Europe's Christian roots and of a moratorium on abortion, during the meeting of CL in August 2005 he publicly announced his embrace of Catholicism.

20   These appellations now have a neo-ethnic acceptation, as shown by Olivier Roy (2004).

provokes repulsion and even physical disgust – constituting above all a social problem[21]. Stories continue to circulate representing them summarily as predatory vagrants, and sometimes as child-snatcher. Similarly, in the case of Albanian and Kosovan migrants, whose religion is only rarely highlighted, the figure of the brutal Balkan bandit predominates, reactivated by the media coverage of the Yugoslav wars during the 1990s. In contrast, until the 2000s there were in Italy no negative narratives or frames peculiar to Islam; hence the recent insistence of Fallaci and her epigones and supporters to innovate by pointing at the alleged dirtiness, violence and/or perversion of Muslims, and to resurrect the 'memory' of the medieval Arab invasions, the Crusades, the wars against the Ottoman Empire, and the rivalry between the seafaring Italian cities and the Barbary pirates[22]; and hence, especially, the necessity of an ideological construct articulated and displayed in various formats (from the populist booklet to the highbrow essay) in order to build the cultural foundations of a well-spread Islamophobic view.

Avoiding any normative perspective (Garland 2008, Rohloff and Wright 2010), it is then as entrepreneurs and promoters of moral panic (Cohen 2004) that the intellectuals presented here must be analyzed. As a result of (notably) the diversity of their respective trajectories, their criticisms after 9/11 denouncing the dangers of Islam and multiculturalism were received in a highly consensual and trans-partisan manner. The Oriana Fallaci of the 2000s – who was eulogized by prominent left-wing political leaders such as Francesco Rutelli[23] and Riccardo Nencini[24] – enjoyed a more widespread favourable reception in Italy than Éric Zemmour in France, Ayaan Hirsi Ali in the Netherlands, Thilo Sarrazin in Germany, Bruce Bawer in Norway, Melanie Phillips in the United Kingdom, Mark Steyn in Canada, or Glenn Beck in the United States[25]. This Italian achievement in terms of Islamophobia is of course due in large measure to the emotions provoked by the Islamist terror attacks in New York, Madrid and London (which in Italy

---

21   In a similar way that – during the heroin epidemic of the 1980s – all drug users were associated with the figure of the 'junkie'.

22   This memory dramatization also took place on screen with the work of Renzo Martinelli (born in 1948), a committed right-wing filmmaker – close to the Lega Nord and to Berlusconi – who describes himself as an 'intellectual'. Generously funded by RAI (the Italian state broadcaster), he made a series of movies on: Al Qaeda in Europe (*The Stone Merchant*, 2006), Alberto da Giussano, the legendary hero of the medieval Lombard League (*Sword of War*, 2009), and the role of Marco d'Aviano during the Battle of Vienna (*September 11, 1683*, to be released in 2012). Besides, in the cinema world, the last books of Oriana Fallaci were acclaimed by director Franco Zeffirelli (born in 1923), well-known for his television mini-series *Jesus of Nazareth* (1977), and who was a Berlusconian senator from 1994 to 2001.

23   Francesco Rutelli (born in 1954) was mayor of Rome from 1993 to 2001, then minister of Culture and vice-prime minister in the second Prodi government (2006-2008).

24   Riccardo Nencini (born in 1959), author of historical essays and novels, was governor of the Tuscany Region from 2000 to 2010.

25   About the 'Eurabia' literature in North America, see Vaïsse 2010.

awoke the fear of terrorism experimented on during the Years of Lead[26]), to the sensationalism of national media and the direct control exercised over many of them by Silvio Berlusconi's entourage, as well as to the regularity with which the most recent waves of immigrants are depicted as 'folk devils' (notably by the right-wing political parties, especially the Lega Nord).

However, one of the deeper causes of this moral panic is probably linked to the unease generated by the quadrupling of immigrants during the last twenty years (from one to more than four million) in an economically stagnant society with very few opportunities for social mobility (Cousin 2009), and lacking any model of integration. The Islamophobic arguments exclude Muslims from a common humanity all the more easily because in Italy local realities are largely stabilized by relations of domestic worth (Boltanski and Thévenot 2006) – which tend to be exclusive towards those who 'aren't from around here' – and don't rely on a meritocracy immediately open to all[27]. Therefore Italians are particularly impervious to antiracist critiques and references to a procedural justice independent of the length of everyone's local involvement.

Finally, we must underline that the contribution to the progression of Islamophobia by the numerous Italian intellectuals we have examined here is not limited to their spoken and written words. It lies also in the laissez-faire attitude, the silence – sometimes embarrassed but often benevolent – with which the majority of them welcome the most obvious populist and instrumental political uses of their ideological constructs and the Islamophobic vulgate following from them. Thus, the crude counter-narrative with which in February 2011 Silvio Berlusconi attempted to publicly clear himself of having hired a 17-year old Moroccan prostitute – spreading in the media that he had 'helped her' to escape a family life of rapes, constant fear, and physical abuse inflicted in the name of Islam and of an archaic culture of honour – didn't provoke any comment despite its many incongruities (or perhaps because of them). This too, then, was supposed to be the fault of Muslim immigrants… and during the following months, commenting on the on-going Arab Spring, many Italian intellectuals worried first and foremost that more will arrive[28].

It is still too early to know if, in the long run, the 2011 geopolitical turn in the Muslim world (impulsed by the Arab revolutions and the killing of Osama bin Laden) and the aftermath of the Oslo-Utøya massacre (whose author was

---

26   The protest cycle of the period 1969-1982, characterized in Italy by the spread of political violence. See for instance Della Porta 1995.

27   We are not referring here to the amoral *familism* (Banfield 1958), the *parochialism* (Almond and Verba 1963), or the lack of a culture of civic engagement (Putnam 1993) supposedly peculiar to Italy or some of its regions (causal analyses that are all highly contested within Italian sociology), but rather pointing the fit of representations and expectations with the local opportunity structure and with the tests that govern it.

28   See for instance the alarmist position taken by Piero Ostellino (2011), former editor of *Il Corriere della Sera*, where he is currently a columnist.

an avid reader of Islamophobic intellectuals) will delegitimize and attenuate the anti-Muslim racism that grew in Europe during the past decade. In Italy, after ten years of Islamophobic advocacy carried by many of the most influential public figures, prejudices and aversion towards Muslims are now widely disseminated in common sense. The variety of the Italian Islamophobic repertoire – both in styles and in axiological traditions, as this chapter shows – contributes to this pervasiveness. Because it is based on a plurality of rationales and narratives, it also makes any attempt of refutation more difficult and complex.

List of Analytical References

Abbruzzese, S. 2001. *Comunione e liberazione. Dalle aule del liceo Berchet al meeting di Rimini: storia e identità di un movimento*. Bologna: Il Mulino.

Alietti, A. and Padovan, D. 2010. Racism as Social Bond: Some Notes on Anti-Semitism and Islamophobia in Italy. *European Journal on Child and Youth Research*, 5, 42-49.

Alietti, A. and Padovan, D. 2012. Racism as Social Bonding. Anti-Semitism and Anti-Islamism in Italy, in *Islamophobia in Western Europe and North America*, edited by M. Helbling. London: Routledge.

Allievi, S. 2005. How the Immigrant has Become Muslim. Public Debates on Islam in Europe. *Revue européenne des migrations internationales*, 21(2), 135-163.

Almond, G. A. and Verba, S. 1963. *The Civic Culture: Political Attitudes and Democracy in Five Nations*. Princeton: Princeton University Press.

Banfield, E. (with Fasano Banfield, L.) 1958. *The Moral Basis of a Backward Society*. Chicago: Free Press.

Biorcio, R. 2010. *La rivincita del Nord. La Lega dalla contestazione al governo*. Rome-Bari: Laterza.

Boltanski, L. 1973. L'espace positionnel. Multiplicité des positions institutionnelles et habitus de classe. *Revue française de sociologie*, 14(1), 3-26.

Boltanski, L. 2011 (1st French edition: 2009). *On Critique. A Sociology of Emancipation*. Cambridge (UK): Polity.

Boltanski, L. and Thévenot, L. 2006 (1st French edition: 1991). *On Justification. Economies of Worth*. Princeton: Princeton University Press.

Bourdieu, P. 1991 (1st French edition: 1988). *The Political Ontology of Martin Heidegger*. Palo Alto: Stanford University Press.

Bourdieu, P. and Boltanski, L. 1976. La production de l'idéologie dominante. *Actes de la recherche en sciences sociales*, 2(2-3), 3-73.

Bourdieu, P. and de Saint-Martin, M. 1982. La sainte famille. L'épiscopat français dans le champ du pouvoir. *Actes de la recherche en sciences sociales*, 44-45, 2-53.

Cento Bull, A. 2009. Lega Nord: A Case of Simulative Politics? *South European Society and Politics*, 14(2), 129-146.

Charle, C. 1996. *Les intellectuels en Europe au XIXe siècle. Essai d'histoire comparée*. Paris: Seuil.

Cohen, S. 2004. *Folks Devils and Moral Panics*. 3rd Edition. London: Routledge.

Cousin, B. 2009. La stratification sociale en Italie et les paradoxes de la modernisation conservatrice, in *L'Italie contemporaine de 1945 à nos jours*, edited by M. Lazar. Paris: Fayard, 303-313.

Cousin, B. and Vitale, T. 2002. Oriana Fallaci ou la rhétorique matamore. *Mouvements*, 23, 146-149.

Cousin, B. and Vitale, T. 2005. Quand le racisme se fait best-seller. Pourquoi les Italiens lisent-ils Oriana Fallaci ? *La Vie des Idées*, 3, 71-77.

Cousin, B. and Vitale, T. 2006. La question migratoire et l'idéologie occidentaliste de Forza Italia. *La Vie des Idées*, 11, 27-36.

Cousin, B. and Vitale, T. 2007. Les liaisons dangereuses de l'islamophobie. Retour sur le 'moment Fallaci' du champ journalistique italien. *La Vie des Idées*, 24, 83-90.

Cousin, B. and Vitale, T. 2008. Oriana, un caso italiano. Come è nato il 'fenomeno Fallaci' sui nostri giornali. *Reset*, 105, 84-86.

Dal Lago, A. 1999. *Non-persone. L'esclusione dei migranti in una società globale*. Milan: Feltrinelli.

Della Porta, D. 1995. *Social Movements, Political Violence, and the State. A Comparative Analysis of Italy and Germany*. Cambridge: Cambridge University Press.

EU Agency for Fundamental Rights. 2009. *EU Minorities and Discrimination Survey*. Data in Focus Report 2: Muslims.

Garau, E. 2010. The Catholic Church, universal truth, and the debate on national identity and immigration: a new model of 'selective solidarity', in *Italy Today. The Sick Man of Europe*, edited by A. Mammone and G. A. Veltri. London: Routledge, 158-169.

Garland, D. 2008. On the concept of moral panic. *Crime, Media, Culture*, 4(1), 9-30.

Guolo, R. 2003. *Xenofobi e xenofili. Gli italiani e l'islam*. Rome-Bari: Laterza.

Pinotti, F. (with Viafora, G.) 2010. *La lobby di Dio*. Milan: Chiarelettere.

Poli, E. 2001. *Forza Italia. Strutture, leadership e radicamento territoriale*. Bologna: Il Mulino.

Putnam, R. D. 1993. *Making Democracy Work: Civic Traditions in Modern Italy*. Princeton: Princeton University Press.

Rivera, A. 2010. *Les dérives de l'universalisme. Ethnocentrisme et islamophobie en France et en Italie*. Paris: La Découverte.

Rohloff, A. and Wright, S. 2010. Moral Panic and Social Theory. Beyond the Heuristic. *Current Sociology*, 58(3), 403-419.

Roy, O. 2004 (1st French edition: 2002). *Globalized Islam. The Search for a New Ummah*. New York : Columbia University Press.

Sapiro, G. 2009. Modèles d'intervention politique des intellectuels. Le cas français. *Actes de la recherche en sciences sociales*, 176-177, 8-31.

Vaïsse, J. 2010. Eurabian Follies. The shoddy and just plain wrong genre that refuses to die. *Foreign Policy*, 1.

Vitale, T. and Claps, E. 2010. Not Always the Same Old Story: Spatial Segregation and Feelings of Dislike against Roma and Sinti in Large Cities and Medium-size Towns in Italy, in *Multi-disciplinary Approaches to Romany Studies*, edited by M. Stewart and M. Rövid. Budapest: CEU Press, 228-253.

Zadra, D. 1994. Comunione e Liberazione: A Fundamentalist Idea of Power, in *Accounting for Fundamentalisms. The Dynamic Character of Movements*, edited by M. E. Marty and R. S. Appleby. Chicago: The University of Chicago Press / American Academy of Arts and Sciences, 124-148.

Literature Presented in the Chapter

Adornato, F. 2003. *La nuova strada. Occidente e libertà dopo il Novecento*. Milan: Mondadori.

Adornato, F. and Fisichella, R. (with a foreword of Ruini, C.) 2007. *Fede e libertà. Dialoghi sullo spirito del tempo*. Rome: Liberal.

Allam, M. 2002a. *Diario dall'Islam. Cronache di una nuova guerra*. Milan: Mondadori.

Allam, M. 2002b. *Bin Laden in Italia. Viaggio nell'islam radicale*. Milan: Mondadori. [republished in 2003 as *Jihad in Italia. Viaggio nell'islam radicale*]

Allam, M. 2003. *Saddam. Storia segreta di un dittatore*. Milan: Mondadori.

Allam, M. 2004. *Kamikaze made in Europe. Riuscirà l'Occidente a sconfiggere i terroristi islamici?* Milan: Mondadori.

Allam, M. 2005. *Vincere la paura. La mia vita contro il terrorismo islamico e l'incoscienza dell'Occidente*. Milan: Mondadori.

Allam, M. 2006. *Io amo l'Italia. Ma gli Italiani la amano?* Milan: Mondadori.

Allam, M. 2007. *Viva Israele. Dall'ideologia della morte alla civiltà della vita: la mia storia*. Milan: Mondadori.

Allam, M. 2008. *Grazie Gesù. La mia conversione dall'islam al cattolicesimo*. Milan: Mondadori.

Allam, M. 2009. *Europa cristiana libera. La mia vita tra Verità e Libertà, Fede e Ragione, Valori e Regole*. Milan: Mondadori.

Baget Bozzo, G. 2001. *Di fronte all'Islam. Il grande conflitto*. Milan: Marietti.

Baget Bozzo, G. 2004. *L'Impero d'Occidente. La Storia ritorna*. Turin: Lindau.

Baget Bozzo, G. (with Iannuzzi, R.) 2006. *Tra nichilismo e Islam. L'Europa come colpa*. Milan: Mondadori.

Biffi, G. 2000a. *La città di San Petronio nel terzo millennio. Nota pastorale*. Bologna: EDB.

Biffi, G. 2000b. *Sull'immigrazione*. Rivoli: Elledici.

Camisasca, M. (with a foreword of Ratzinger, J.) 2001. *Comunione e Liberazione. Le origini (1954-1968)*. Cinisello Balsamo: Edizioni San Paolo.

Camisasca, M. (with a foreword of Biffi, G.) 2003. *Comunione e Liberazione. La ripresa (1969-1976)*. Cinisello Balsamo: Edizioni San Paolo.

Camisasca, M. 2006. *Comunione e Liberazione. Il riconoscimento (1976-1984). Appendice 1985-2005*. Cinisello Balsamo: Edizioni San Paolo.

Chiappa, E. and Mauro M. 2007. *Piccolo dizionario delle radici cristiane d'Europa*. Milan: Ares.

Fallaci, O. 2001. *La Rabbia e l'Orgoglio*. Milan: Rizzoli. [English translation published by Rizzoli in 2002]

Fallaci, O. 2004. *La Forza della Ragione*. Milan: Rizzoli. [English translation published by Rizzoli in 2006]

Fallaci, O. 2004. *Oriana Fallaci intervista sé stessa – L'Apocalisse*. Milan: Rizzoli.

Fisichella, R. 2007. *Nel mondo da credenti. Le ragioni dei cattolici nel dibattito politico italiano*. Milan: Mondadori.

Fisichella, R. 2009a. *Identità dissolta. Il Cristianesimo, lingua madre dell'Europa*. Milan: Mondadori.

Fisichella, R. 2009b. Foreword to D. Di Pace and R. Mazzoni, *Con Oriana*. Florence: Le Lettere.

Galli della Loggia, E. 2006. A proposito di Oriana. *Il Corriere della Sera*, 17 September.

Galli della Loggia, E. and Ruini, C. 2009. *Confini. Dialogo sul cristianesimo e il mondo contemporaneo*. Milan: Mondadori.

de Mattei, R. 2002. *Guerra Santa / Guerra Giusta. Islam e Cristianesimo in guerra*. Casale Monferrato: Piemme. [English translation published by Chronicles Press and The Rockford Institute in 2007]

de Mattei, R. 2009. *La Turchia in Europa. Beneficio o catastrofe?* Milan: Sugarco. [English translation published by Gracewing in 2009]

Mauro, M. 2004. *L'Europa sarà cristiana o non sarà*. Milan: Spirali.

Mauro, M. 2007. *Il Dio dell'Europa*. Milan: Ares.

Nirenstein, F. 1999. *I musulmani: colloquio di Fiamma Nirenstein con Bernard Lewis*. Rome: Liberal.

Nirenstein, F. 2003. *Islam: la guerra e la speranza. Intervista a Bernard Lewis*. Milan: Rizzoli.

Ostellino, P. 2011. La profezia di Oriana. Il confronto tra Islam e Occidente. *Il Corriere della Sera*, 9 March.

Palaiologos, M. 1966 (1st Byzantine edition in Greek: 1399). *Entretiens avec un musulman. 7e controverse*. Paris: Cerf.

Pera, M. and Ratzinger, J. 2004. *Senza radici. Europa, relativismo, Cristianesimo, Islam*. Milan: Mondadori. [English translation published by Basic Books in 2006]

Pera, M. (with a foreword of Pope Benedict XVI) 2008. *Perché dobbiamo dirci Cristiani. Il liberalismo, l'Europa, l'etica*. Milan: Mondadori. [English translation published by Encounter Books in 2011]

Quagliariello, G. 2006. *Cattolici, pacifisti, teocon. Chiesa e politica in Italia dopo la caduta del Muro*. Milan: Mondadori.

Romano, S. 2007. *Con gli occhi dell'Islam. Mezzo secolo di storia in una prospettiva mediorientale*. Milan: Longanesi.

Sartori, G. 2002. *Pluralismo, multiculturalismo e estranei. Saggio sulla società multietnica*. 2nd Edition. Milan: Rizzoli.

Sartori, G. (with Foschini, L.) 2008. *La democrazia in trenta lezioni*. Milan: Mondadori.

Sartori, G. 2009. L'integrazione degli islamici. *Il Corriere della Sera*, 20 December.

Sartori, G. 2010. Una replica ai pensabenisti sull'Islam. *Il Corriere della Sera*, 5 January.

Chapter 4

The Sweden Democrats, Racisms and the Construction of the Muslim Threat

Diana Mulinari and Anders Neergaard

As Sweden Democrat I see this [Islam and Muslims in Sweden] as our biggest foreign threat since World War II and I promise to do everything in my power to reverse the trend when we go to the polls next year.[1] (Jimmi Åkesson. 19 Oct 2009).

Important shifts have occurred in Sweden over the last couple of decades that have made racism and racialization of migrants more conspicuous on all levels of society (Harvey, 2005, Schierup et al., 2006). In the above quotation, the leader of the Sweden Democrats (SD), a cultural racist party with roots in the Nazi movement, cites Islam and Muslims in Sweden as 'the biggest foreign threat since World War II'.

Although the above quote was one of the few times the SD received autonomous space in the mainstream media, the Liberal Party, member of the government coalition that has been in power since 2006, also actively portrays Muslims as problematic individuals who threaten security, gender equality and freedom of speech. One of their members and chairman of Liberals for Diversity left the party, stating:

The Liberal Party (FP: Folkpartiet) ... with its harsh rhetoric against immigrants, has done more than any other parliamentary party toward legitimizing the Sweden Democrats. It is no coincidence that the Liberal Party has become the 'next best party' for the MPs of the Sweden Democrats. Establishing a policy that sends out a certain message, as party leaders have been engaged in doing by means of xenophobic launches concerning language tests and burqa bans, it is clear that the signal is also finally being picked up by the Liberals' base organization (Mikael Trolin SvD Brännpunkt[2], 9 Dec 2010).

---

1   Jimmi Åkesson, chairman of the Sweden Democrats in an opinion piece in the major Swedish tabloid *Aftonbladet*. 19 Oct 2009.

2   An opinion piece in *Svenska Dagbladet*, the second most important daily newspaper.

'Even in Sweden'[3] racism has shown its face, and so Sweden, while not in the forefront of European racism and racist policies can no longer be seen as a pillar of tolerance. Among racisms, the specific kind directed against Muslims is today the most central, visible, and normalized variety (Gardell 2010, Fekete 2009).

The Swedish Democrats doubled their percentage of the national vote in the 2010 parliamentary elections and obtained representation for the first time in the Swedish parliament, almost six per cent of the electorate, close to 350,000 votes, and 20 members of parliament (for an analysis see Hubinette and Lundström 2010). The party, while consistently espousing a radical and highly developed anti-Islam and anti-Muslim rhetoric, can in many ways be seen as the symptom of a particular kind of racism that has recently flourished in Sweden and that tends to dehumanize and collectivize Muslims as the enemy.

This article is based on the research project 'A Contradiction in Terms? The activity of Women and Migrants in Extreme Right-wing Populist Parties: a case study of Sweden Democrats'[4], exploring how such racist ideas are expressed and acted upon by female municipal politicians of SD (some of them of migrant background). Our empirical material consists of nineteen in-depth interviews with female Sweden Democrats, participant observation of four municipality parliaments' budget debates during fall 2009 and spring 2010; and text analysis of formal SD documents available on homepages and the party's bulletin *SD-Kuriren*. In the interviews, issues of ethnicity, migrants or racism were never raised by the interviewer. Such information was volunteered by informants as answers to general questions concerning parliamentary politics and gender issues in Sweden today. Our analysis of the interviews is characterized by a hermeneutically-inspired approach where the aim is to understand and interpret the statements of female SD municipal representatives, and also discuss them in relation to SD's documents and other secondary material, as well as previous research.

While there are distinctions between more explicit Nazi organizations[5] and SD, it is easy to find substantial similarities although through different wordings: Nazis speak of the white race while SD speaks of the nation, the motherland and Sweden for the Swedes (Lindberg 2010). At the same time the critique of SD, through its links to overtly racist and Nazi-inspired movements, has made the party well skilled in deflecting charges of racism. Their most basic argument here is that they focus on migration policies, the quantity of migration and in defending what

---

3   *Even in Sweden* is the title of cultural geographer Allan Pred´s book that exposes racism in Sweden.

4   We acknowledge thankfully funding from the Swedish Research Council.

5   The most known being the 'Party of the Swedes' (former National Socialist Front), but there are a number of small organizations/parties, for a more thorough discussion see Lööw 2000. These organizations are present in the public space through demonstrations, marches and violent attacks against migrants, homosexuals and leftists (see www.expo.se for detailed information).

they call Swedish culture, but not migrants themselves. This is a position that we challenge through these pages, suggesting that the SD develops and deepens racist arguments against Muslims that are already present and considered normal, natural, and right in Swedish public debates and that the figure of the Muslim Other encompasses and embodies today the location of the general Others that should be controlled, feared and preferably expelled.

Racisms and the Discursive Trap of the Muslim Other

Sweden has been a country with a relatively just welfare, gender and migration regime. While ethnic discrimination and racisms have been there, the redistributive mechanisms of the regime have prevented strong polarizations linked to class, gender or ethnicity (Schierup et al. 2006). A strong social democratic hegemony and the dominance of social democratic governments (from 1932 to 2006, with the exception of 1976 to 82 and 1991 to 94) have been seen as a bulwark against right-wing populism and extreme right-wing parties (ERP). The short-lived experience of 'New Democracy' from 1991 to 94, was the exception until SD entered the national parliament 2010. However, Sweden had already high levels of violence committed by members of Nazi and racist groups towards asylum seekers, migrants, and homosexuals (Pred 2000).

The quote cited in the introduction is an example of the SD party's consistent and self-conscious demonization of the Muslim Other. While racism towards Muslims has become a centrepiece in the politics of the Sweden Democrats, the strength of the party has been the ability to mediate and articulate already existing and established forms of racism. In a piece entitled 'War Making and State Making as Organized Crime' Charles Tilly (1985) argues that the state plays an active role in creating the same threats that it then offers itself as capable of resolving. This has similarities with what Hall et al. (1978) analyzed in *Policing the Crisis*. The themes explored in this book – state, racism, masculinity, and fear of crime – continue to be central elements in social conflicts and discourses in an era of neo-liberalism, and are well suited for analysis of contemporary racism against Muslims. Hall et al. depart from Cohen's definition of moral panic (1972) in arguing that both crime and media statistics articulate fears about crime and 'race' and prompt an authoritarian solution of 'law and order' (Clarke 2008, Jefferson 2008, Lea 1999). However, the merit of adding Tilly's perspective is to avoid viewing the state simply as reactive, a point that misses state institutions' role in process of racialization. This approach of the state as 'ringmaster' is illustrated in the treatment of Muslims in Sweden. Swedish governments, especially the right-wing government that came to power in 2006, have been central in contributing to racism directed at the Muslim Other. This racism is also apparent in the mainstream media, in academia, in the field of cultural production and in some organizations advocating forms of fundamentalist secularism (Gerle 2010, Gardell

2010, Malm 2009, Larsson 2006). The cultural racism against Muslims that SD raises in its political agenda, has already been legitimized in media ideology and mainstream political / institutional processes and practices, (such as teaching based on Christian ethics and Western humanism in schools, language tests) as well as discrimination towards and suspicion of refugees.[6]

A view often argued in research on extreme right-wing parties (ERPs) is that they introduced racism into nonracist societies and that their ideology is in fact not racism, but rather xenophobia or hostility to foreigners (Betz 1994, Mudde 2000). These analyses are contradictory (Mulinari and Neergaard 2010) and there is ample evidence to demonstrate that racisms (in this case against the Muslim Other) are a part of European history, both in relation to colonial conquests and to the internal colonialism of nation and state building (Broberg and Tiden 1991, Catomeris 2004). The SD and ERP are impossible to understand outside of what Perry (2001) defines as a node of ideas and practices that are permissible. Violence against specific categories of people, as Perry argues, must be understood as extreme or reinforced reflections of normality.

David Goldberg (2006) proposes the concept of racial regionalization (and racial Europeanization) in order to identify racisms linked to specific state formations and to specific regions. Here he is focusing on specific European countries and on Europe as a region. He suggests that the figure of the Muslim, alongside that of the Jew, has shaped and influenced popular anxieties about blackness in Europe (cf. Fekete 2009). Departing from Goldberg's concept of racial Europeanization, we hold that articulations of racism specific to time and place can be captured through two different modalities. Firstly, an exclusionary racism (that may also be termed a 'losers'' racism) that is associated with ERP despite such parties' rhetorical attempts to distance themselves from such racism. Secondly, an exploitational racism (that may also be called a winners' racism) that is central to the global reproduction of capitalism and is thereby found in the centre of society, a phenomenon that van Dijk (1993) defines as elite racism.

Exploitive racism grasps processes through which 'the Other' is constructed as inferior but 'usable' as low wage labour (especially in the service sector). Focusing on 'losers' racism' tends to conceal 'winners' racism, that is racism that is productive or even super-exploitive (Balibar 1991) in which 'the Others' are naturalized as a low-paid workforce particularly in the service and the informal sector in the Western world (Gavanas 2010, Mulinari 2007) and as a low-paid workforce in general in a global perspective (Sassen 1997). Winners' racism is relevant to understanding the geo-economic global world order. In Western European countries such a form of racism tends to be concealed because it is not only productive, but also remains unarticulated, in contrast with the racism of ERP

---

6   See the research reports commissioned by the Swedish government 'Utredningen om makt, integration och strukturell diskriminering' (The inquiry on power, integration and structural discrimination in the edited volumes SOU 2005:69 , 2005:112, 2006:21, 2006:30, 2006:37, 2006:40, 2006:52, 2006:53, 2006:59, 2006:60, 2006:73, 2006:78).

(van Dijk 1993). Thus there are two different logics that operate in and through the racism to which racialized groups are subjected. For the 'winners' racism it is central that 'the Others' are present so that the dominance and exploitation can take place while the 'losers' racism tends towards separation, exclusion and, in its extreme form, an eradication of 'the Others'. It is central to our argument that the moral indignation directed against SD in Swedish public opinion, occurs in a context where migrant women are praised by politicians for being good domestic workers (Carlbom 2004).

'Racism-as-exclusion' operates through a different process in which 'the Other' is marked as different and not belonging here, and are thereby 'undesirable', problematic and posing a threat. We argue that this distinction can be used to identify how racisms take different forms of expression in post-Fordist Europe, where the racialized serve as objects for the 'white' class struggle in the labour market, although with agreement in trying to reduce their access to welfare services. In several studies of ERP, racism based on exclusion has often been linked with young people, manual workers and poorly-educated people (Betz 1994, Kitschelt 1995), but there are grounds for broadening it to include members of other classes. Sennett (1998) shows that some managers and professionals can be regarded as losers to a certain extent, due to greater career flexibility, outsourcing and uncertainty, even if the group as a whole is not affected. Some commentators have suggested that relative (rather than absolute) deprivation can serve as the basis for recruitment to radical right-wing extremist parties (Lea and Young 1996). Racism against Muslims, the dominant trait of SD's exclusionary racism, is regulated by Orientalist fantasies (Yegenoglu 1998) and is located within forms of exclusionary racism.

The Sweden Democrats in Transition

> It is necessary to state that by 'special populations' we refer to those ethnic groups that have no natural place of residence in our country. It has now been made into an almost accepted view that democracy is equated with the right of anyone to settle in Sweden and enjoy the Swedish welfare system. It is obviously an incorrect interpretation. Sweden is the country of the Swedes, and from this it follows that, Swedish norms and values will have a special status in Sweden. (Sweden Democrats' Ideological Platform on Democratic Development)

This extract from the SD manifesto, far from being vulgar and coarse racism, is a nuanced, tactical and strategically designed ideology that nevertheless fails to distance itself from fundamental ideas of race (mediated through concepts such as ethnic groups, natural residence, nationality, ethnicity, and culture). The discourse of the SD, is in many ways culturally racist, based in an ethno-pluralist doctrine.[7]

With rare exceptions (Fryklund and Peterson 1981), there has been little research on ERP in Sweden, largely as a result of their relative lack of electoral success. The rapid rise and fall of the 'New Democracy' in the period from 1991 to 1994 did, however, attract some attention (Rydgren 2006, Westlind 1996). A second line of inquiry has focused on the remnants of Nazi and racist parties and similar organizations at the margins of political life that are strongly linked to racist and homophobic violence (Lodenius and Wikström 1997, Pred 2000). Research on SD combines these trajectories, emphasizing their background in Nazism and overt racism, the influence of populism from neighbouring countries and the short-lived history of 'New Democracy'.

The parliamentary success of SD raises questions of its links to racist movements. We look upon SD, as being like the Feminist Initiative[8] or the environment party The Greens: as a product of the institutionalization of a social movement. Political pragmatism often forces such parties to distance themselves from the social movements that have spawned them, while at the same time they are dependent on the existence of these social movements to survive. SD often argues that if they fail to be heard, people will turn to the Nazis. Those same Nazis, however, we contend, voice a more radical version of SD's own ideology. The identification of SD with liberal democracy as a field in which to carry on their cultural racist policies is one central aspect that distinguishes them from Nazis (who have rejected the electoral process).

In the gradual transformation from being a Nazi influenced and overt racist party, SD has shown its ability to transform its cultural racism. In fact, SD derives from an anti-Semitic tradition and has also targeted black migrants before Muslims became the preferred Other. An informant stated:

> After so many years, you don't need to keep talking, talking, talking, huh? It's just that, it's they who control a lot of stuff, they control some things in Sweden too, ok? The Jews control a lot, you know: it's TV and its Bonniers, and it's everything. But if you were to say that for example, then you'd go to jail.

---

7   The ethnopluralist doctrine talks about nationalities, cultures, ethnicities in a way that earlier was reserved for race, arguing that migration means the destruction of both 'our' and 'their' 'people'. It generally entails the idea that there is no hierarchy of better or worse (although hierarchy is often implicitly introduced), it is the 'mixing' that is destructive (Minkenberg 1997, Griffin 2000, Rydgren 2005).

8   Feminist Initiative emerged as a new political party in the 2006 Swedish election. A former leader of the left party was the spokesperson of the party whose profile is on women's rights and feminist issues. While the parliamentary impact of the party has been limited, it could be understood as an attempt at institutionalizing feminist movements through a political party (for a discussion see Eduards 2007).

In the interview the informant discusses integration and the problems with different religions. She then passes over to a discussion of the Germans' treatment of Jews, finally focusing on Jews in general. This example illustrates the broad repertoire within SD in matters of culture, nation, religion, showing that anti-Semitism is still present despite a more nuanced external discourse (for discussion concerning the understanding of anti-Semitism and Islamophobia see Schiffer and Wagner 2011).

SD defends itself against accusations of racism by declaring itself as opponents of certain migration and integration policies, not as racists but as upholders of Swedish culture. They say they are not Nazis, but a respectable party that has had difficulty keeping inappropriate (Nazi) people out of the party. However, the informants who express anti-Semitic views appear to be closely linked to the party's history (Lodenius and Larsson 2000), a history that the party has strongly distanced itself from with SD's new political focus: racism against Muslims.

Defending the National Body

SD defines culture as 'the surroundings of obvious facts, memories, and beliefs that we live in and that we are continuously shaping' (Sverigedemokraterna 2003/2005: 2) and highlights cultural diversity by making a parallel to biological diversity in nature as something necessary to maintain the specificity of each individual culture that must be protected and defended by nation states. SD's official documents highlight positive traits of other cultures, although there was no expression of this in the accounts of our informants.

> I think it's important that we retain our own culture in Sweden. Those who come here, they have to learn Swedish, and have to accept our culture, not just holding on to theirs. We do not want our children praying to Mecca.

The informant repeats a common argument used by SD: the notion that Swedish culture is at risk. In her narrative she inverts the power relations between majority and minority culture posing (the powerful) majority culture as weak and as a victim of migrant cultures. Second, she posits a notion of migrants resisting integration, and challenging Swedish culture. Thirdly, and as is often the case in the Sweden Democrats rhetoric, the racist targeting of Swedish Muslims appears through a dystopic vision of Swedish children being converted to Islam.

The SD approach to culture holds that it may take generations to become a member of a certain (national) culture (Sverigedemokraterna 2007: 7), an argument used to mark boundaries between 'us' and 'them' and proclaim the limitations of assimilation. Thus if the national culture is seen as strongly tied to human identity and as a force regulating all forms of solidarity and action, then any expectation that others might be able to leave 'their' culture is seen as almost impossible.

In official documents SD states that while it is possible to become a *citizen*, it may take several generations to become *Swedish,* thereby recasting assimilation from an individual into a collective process. But the question remains whether female politicians and SD would be willing to regulate the interactions between those immigrants who are doing well (despite having different cultures) and Swedes, because in an ethno-pluralist world view the coming together of the two might be seen as damaging to both cultures.

Most of our informants, while often speaking of the culture of 'the Other', avoided describing what is characteristic of Swedish culture. Instead, this generalized Swedish culture was talked about among most of the informants as threatened. In the few occurrences in which Swedish culture was mentioned more concretely, it was through references to nature and '*Den blomstertid nu kommer*' ['The flowers are coming into bloom'], a hymn often sung at the end of the school semester (paradoxically cited by two SD activists of migrant background that never went to school in Sweden). A compelling argument illustrating this can be found in the following quotation:

> We have lived in a peaceful country. It's what we've done for so many years. Our offspring also need to be able to continue living here. And we unfortunately don't have that kind of security in our society, we don't have it any more. And societies become divided because of this multiculturalism. And then, recently, we were on a visit to [neighborhood with many migrants] and met with the chief of police. . . . and he told me what the situation there is like. And he confirmed exactly what I've mentioned – that there are a lot of families who don't want anything to do with Swe. ... with Swedish society. They don't want to learn the language; they don't want anything to do with Swedish traditions or culture. They gladly accept the money and then they live in herds, you know. And then willingly bring their cousins, and live, I don't know, 15 of them living in a three-room apartment. The police don't dare enter; they don't really know who lives in the apartments and how many people live there. And he was the one who told me. He knows what he's talking about!

In the informant's story Swedish culture is embodied in the security and peace that has existed up to now, but is threatened by multiculturalism, along with fears that the previously harmonious society will shatter. The image of Swedish culture (with which the informant identifies) clashes with the notion of the Others, and the term 'herd' suggests a resemblance to animals, to a promiscuous chaos in which the police (who represent both what is authentically Swedish as well as authority) cannot identify them as individuals. The quotation above exemplifies also the kind of cultural racism especially targeting the Swedish population of Muslim background as articulated by the SD. The informant does not need to name Islam or Muslims: the identification of a suburb where many Swedish citizens of Muslim background live suffices.

Gender and Nation – The SD Agenda

There is an ongoing conceptual discussion on how to view and designate parties like the SD. Jens Rydgren has advanced a minimalist definition as those that 'share the fundamental core of ethno-nationalist xenophobia (based on the so-called "ethnopluralistic doctrine") and antipolitical establishment populism' (Rydgren, 2005: 436). While this definition covers a minimal core of ERP it fails to acknowledge the centrality of gender metaphors and symbols in the cultural racism towards Muslims. Gender and family symbols are essential elements of these parties and the social movement from which they derive (Koonz 1987, Yuval Davis 1997, Norocel 2010) for three reasons: gender is strongly related to the ethno-pluralist doctrine: the child of 'mixed' cultures conceptualized as destroying both cultures; gender mobilizes men to join the parties; and gender relations play a major role in the discourse against the Muslim Other.

Ethno-nationalist projects, feminist scholars have argued, depart from specific constructions of national/ethnic womanhood/manhood, posing men and women differently within the national project. The relationship between women and ethno-nationalism is identified by Yuval Davis (1997) through women's role in the biological reproduction of the nation, women's role as boundary making between national/ethnic groups, women's role as mediators of national/ethnic culture and women as symbolic signifiers of national/ethnic difference.

Much anti-Muslim racism is tied to images of certain urban areas with a high percentage of migrants.[9] Commissioned by the national government through the Ministry of Gender Equality and Integration, a 2009 report was presented prepared by researchers at the National Defence College described the Rosengård suburb of Malmö, which has a total population of 300 000, as an area isolated from the rest of the city, functioning through extremely patriarchal rules, and embodying a risk of Islamic terrorism (Ranstorp and Dos Santos 2009).

The report was thoroughly criticized by the scientific community as representing ideology, gossip and poor research, but was defended by the government. Representations of the Swedish Muslim population as a problem and a threat to Swedish gender equality are also commonly encountered in research and in the media (Gardell 2010). They follow a very similar discursive repertoire: Swedish culture as secular, women-friendly and fostering individuality vs. Muslims as religious, patriarchal and engendering authoritarian collectivism.

Gender as a central theme has been recast in different shapes. The SD transforms gender equality from being a political goal at the core of the Swedish Social Democratic welfare state's policies regarding family and work, to an attribute of the Swedish culture, that migrants in general and Muslims in particular, cannot

---

9   What in English is often referred to as the 'inner city' is called the 'suburb' (förorten) in Sweden (Ericsson et al. 2002, Pripp 2002) .

achieve.[10] While it could be argued that Scandinavian countries follow similar patterns in the ways racism against Muslims has been articulated globally, it may be that the focus on gender at the core of the 'cultural clashes' is specific to those countries' history of women-friendly welfare states (Razack 2004, Bredström 2003).

The policing of Muslim communities in the name of gender equality has been introduced by established centre-right parties. Notions of a cultural clash between the West and Islam regarding gender have been present in Swedish public debate (a central cause for sending troops to Afghanistan), but are at the same time further exploited by SD. The populist form involving overt aggression towards Muslims makes SD an extremely skilful actor in developing the discourse of the clash of civilizations. An interesting aspect of our study in this respect is the female migrant activists of SD that make more reference to civilizations (Christian vs Muslim; Western vs the Rest) than to national cultures. In the election campaign of 2010, SD launched a TV ad that portrayed an old Swedish lady trying to access welfare being overrun by younger women wearing black burqas, and their children. While no mention was made of Islam or Muslims, it implied that Muslim women and their families presented a threat.

SD's anti-Muslim racism is flexible, transforming itself in different context and arenas. The issue here is of Muslim women's clothing and in the following quote concerning municipal swimming pools, not as a matter of cultural collision (using SD's language), but as a matter of hygiene.

> A Muslim woman enters with her clothes and scarf into the public bath, and into the pool, you know? Is that hygienic? We don't really like that either. They and their children should be dressed normally, with bathing suits, like everybody else. They should follow our culture.

The connection between the Other, dirt and cleanliness has been highlighted by other post-colonial researchers (Broberg and Tydén 1991; McClintock 1995). The informant shifts from the question of what is clean to the question of what is normal. Muslims should follow the standards that exist for how 'ordinary' people are supposed to act in swimming pools. The critique of use of the hijab through reference to hygiene is one of the many ways through which the SD promulgates racism against Muslims.

10　　This is again an example of how racism is played out in Sweden. SD has taken the role of strengthening racist discourses. While many established parties make a similar point, they differ in acknowledging the possibility of migrants learning Swedish gender equality.

Ethno-Pluralism and Caring Racism

> The biggest thing that we as a party focus on is in fact the immigration issue and how it has undermined and eroded our country, a lot has been left undone because of the expenditures that are connected to an immigration that has been horrible, both for those who come here and those who live here. It's not humane, any of this.

According to the informant, migration is an economic burden for Sweden, a central piece of SD politics. However, in addition she argues that SD's policy is favourable to everyone because the refugee policy that Sweden had had previously is in her view inhumane both for Swedes and for migrants. This we see as another tenet of SD ideology: that of reformulating exclusionary racism into 'caring racism'. Caring racism is gendered: the men care through discipline ('The white man's burden'), and women care through comfort (as in the phrase at the end of the quotation below, 'It's not humane'. According to the position espoused, caring is provided for everyone, even (and especially) migrants. Caring racism is part of exclusionary racism, highlighting the idea of ethno-pluralism that everyone will gain by staying in their 'home'. In other words, for their own good migrants shouldn't come to Sweden.

In connection to racist arguments against Muslims, representatives or sympathizers defend themselves from the accusation of being racists by stating that they are migrants themselves, they have friends who are migrants, and the party is supported by many migrants, and thus not capable of being racist. In a number of our interviews a special 'coming out' discourse emerges that invariably begins with a description of the speaker as open and generous.

The following informant claims she has been forced to change her attitude because she was very naive and did not understand the connection between the increasing violence in Swedish society and the presence of migrants with Muslim background.

> I've always been a person who treats people equally. It makes no difference to me, so that's the way I've tried to raise my kids. But it has not been possible because they live in a completely different world, where there's been a lot of gangs, a lot of assaults, a lot . . . and it's always been [Muslim] migrants. That's probably when I started to react and I started to say to myself: Come on, your ideology doesn't work that way. It's a nice thought, but it doesn't work that way in real life.

In the above narrative the informant locates herself as a person caring, who earlier on treated everybody as equal. In her story it is the Muslims themselves who force her to change position. Migrants (or what are coded as migrant practices such as criminality) are the ones to blame for her change of values.

In their conception of the world, the informants belong to a party that wants to save Sweden from the disaster that threatens to befall it (mass immigration and the Muslim Other) while they also want to allocate resources to include the excluded 'Swedes'. The interviewee quoted above gives two reasons for changing her view of people from other backgrounds. Her egalitarianism is tested by her children's experience of 'gangs'. She explains her own racism as a reaction to the racism of the Other. It is 'they' who have come here bringing hate and prejudice, and forcing the informant to change her ideology, which, according to the informant, is not sustainable 'in real life'. According to her account, racism is a cultural product that has been brought to Sweden by immigrants and forces Swedes, who have previously followed a caring ideology, to think differently.

The self-representation of SD and activists as caring not only for the Swedes but also for the migrants is at times quickly transformed. In the quote below, the informant starts out with generosity, goes through labeling the Other as criminal and ends up with seeing them as terrorists.

> And above all we've been far too generous. ... I think it's betrayal to our own Swedish people that we let people keep coming here and coming here. Then, we demonstrate a little and, oh well, let them stay – and so you change your decision. They're so afraid that they don't dare make a proper decision, so that if someone is a terrorist, then they're out of here. I mean, we're not supposed to be risking Swedish people's lives because we receive these criminal elements. It's terrible. There is violence and stealing. Young people can't hang on to their phones and then there are robberies on the trains and violence has increased and it's been established that immigrants have done it. And then it's no wonder the Swedish people start to rebel in some way, to preserve their own country. They can't just come here and force themselves on a small country. It's wrong!

Caring racism is intrinsically linked to an ethno-pluralist discourse. It operates simultaneously in two ways. Firstly it posits that each culture is good, but should not be mixed or 'displaced'. In this sense there is an implication that laziness and reliance on benefits, criminality, patriarchy, and disrespect for the environment are cultural traits of the Others which, although bad, can be accepted elsewhere, but not here. The second discourse, connecting to 'caring racism', targets second generation migrants, suggesting that the problems faced by the young Swedish Muslim born and raised in Sweden are a result of them being uprooted from their 'authentic' culture and cultural home. Thus, Sweden Democrats succeed in converting their campaign to stop immigration and 'repatriate' immigrants into 'caring' for the (Muslim) Other.

Concluding Thoughts

We began this chapter with a quote from an article written by the SD leader. The SD is a party that lives on constructing Islam and Muslims as a threat for which they claim to supply the remedy. Mainstream scholarship conceptualizes ERP as including a xenophobic agenda in the public/political field. Our study challenges such views in several ways. We conclude that before their parliamentary success, the SD already appropriated in their rhetoric the diversified forms of racisms previously well established in discourses and practices at the everyday and the institutional level. In so doing, SD managed to articulate racism as a central signifier in a nationalist and ethno-pluralist political agenda. Despite the fact that our informants were never explicitly asked about racism, we have shown that racialization and at times explicit elements of racist ideologies were very present in their narratives.

Racisms, rather than xenophobia or right-wing populism form the core of the ideological frame of the party. We use racisms in the plural to suggest the malleability of their discourse in targeting a variety of racialized population groups. Due to its Nazi background, the SD originally had a strong anti-Semitic profile and repeated the familiar anti-Semitic themes of world domination, a threat to the nation, etc. The party has in its public representations decreased its anti-Semitic undertones, even if some of its activists carry anti-Semitic arguments and others maintain links to Nazi organizations. A central strategy of denying and obscuring anti-Semitism within SD is to locate (and to create) Muslims as anti-Semitic. One could argue that SD has successfully shifted its focus from anti-Semitism, through racism against blacks to the central task of interpellating an expanding racism against Muslims. At the same time, SD depiction of Muslims oscillates between a powerful and threatening Other (Muslim as terrorist; Muslim as well organized, Muslims overtaking Sweden) and notions of a weak and problematic Other (a burden for the welfare state and the Swedish nation). Gendered aspects are also stressed in the Swedish context. Here binary construction is often reinforced by the media and some academics: Muslim Others (religious, monolithic, patriarchal) as against a women-friendly, secular welfare state. For SD, the Muslim Other is the representation of the general Other, that negates in itself everything that is Sweden. It is a party that defines specific populations as unnatural to the Swedish nation.

References

Balibar, E. 1991. Is there a 'Neo-Racism'?, in *Race, Nation, Class: Ambiguous Identities*, edited by E. Balibar and I Wallerstein. London: Verso.

Betz, H.-G. 1994. *Radical right-wing populism in Western Europe*, New York: St. Martins Press.

Bredström, A. 2003. Gendered racism and the production of cultural difference: media representations and identity work among 'immigrant youth' in contemporary Sweden. *NORA: Nordic Journal of Women's Studies),* 11, 78-88.

Broberg, G. and Tydén, M. 1991. *Oönskade i folkhemmet: rashygien och sterilisering i Sverige,* Stockholm: Gidlund.

Carlbom, M. 2004. Ministerdebutant i blåsväder. *Dagens Nyheter,* 041031.

Catomeris, C. 2004. *Det ohyggliga arvet: Sverige och främlingen genom tiderna.* Stockholm: Ordfront.

Clarke, J. 2008. Still Policing the Crisis? *Crime, Media, Culture,* 4, 123-129.

Cohen, S. 1972. *Folk Devils and Moral Panics,* London: MacGibbon and Kee.

Eduards, M. 2007. *Kroppspolitik: om moder Svea och andra kvinnor.* Stockholm: Atlas.

Ericsson, U., Molina, I. and Ristilammi, P.-M. 2002. *Miljonprogram och media: föreställningar om människor och förorter.* Stockholm, Integrationsverket.

Fekete, L. 2009. *A suitable enemy: racism, migration and Islamophobia in Europe.* London: Pluto.

Fryklund, B. and Peterson, T. 1981. *Populism och missnöjespartier i Norden: studier av småborgerlig klassaktivitet,* Lund: Arkiv.

Gardell, M. 2010. *Islamofobi,* Stockholm: Leopard.

Gavanas, A. 2010. Who cleans the welfare state? Migration, informalization, social exclusion and domestic services in Stockholm. *Research Report.* Stockholm: Institute for Futures Studies.

Gerle, E. 2010. *Farlig förenkling: om religion och politik utifrån Sverigedemokraterna och Humanisterna,* Nora, Nya Doxa.

Goldberg, D. T. 2006. Racial Europeanization. *Ethnic and Racial Studies,* 29, 331-364.

Griffin, R. 2000. Interregnum or endgame? Radical right thought in the 'post-fascist' era. *Journal of Political Ideologies,* 5, 163-178.

Hall, S., Critcher, C., Jefferson, T., Clarke, J. and Roberts, B. 1978. *Policing the crisis: mugging, the state, and law and order,* London: Macmillan.

Harvey, D. 2005. *A brief history of neoliberalism,* Oxford: Oxford University Press.

Hubinette, T. and Lundström, C. 2010. Sweden after the Recent Election: The Double-Binding Power of Swedish Whiteness through the Mourning of the Loss of 'Old Sweden' and the Passing of 'Good Sweden'. *NORA-Nordic Journal of Feminist and Gender Research,* 19(1), 42-52.

Huntington, S. P. 1996. *The clash of civilizations and the remaking of world order,* New York: Simon and Schuster.

Jefferson, T. 2008. Policing the crisis revisited: The state, masculinity, fear of crime and racism. *Crime, Media, Culture,* 4, 113-121.

Kitschelt, H. 1995. *The radical right in Western Europe: a comparative analysis,* Ann Arbor: University of Michigan Press.

Koonz, C. 1987. *Mothers in the fatherland: women, the family, and Nazi politics,* New York: St. Martin's Press.

Larsson, G. 2006. *Muslimerna kommer: tankar om islamofobi,* Göteborg: Makadam.

Lea, J. 1999. Social Crime Revisited *Theoretical Criminology,* 3, 307-325.

Lea, J. and Young, J. 1996. Relative Deprivation,in *Criminological Perspectives – A Reader,* edited by J. Muncie, J., E. Maclaughlin and M. Langan. London: Sage Publications.

Lindberg, M. 2010. En nytänkt och parlamentarisk nationalsocialism. Analys av Sverigedemkraternas ideologi och program. *Nerikes Allehanda 111011.* Örebro.

Lodenius, A.-L. and Larsson, S. 2000. *Extremhögern,* Stockholm: Tiden.

Lodenius, A.-L. and Wikström, P. 1997. *Vit makt och blågula drömmar: rasism och nazism i dagens Sverige,* Stockholm Natur och kultur.

Lööw,H.2000.*NazismeniSverige1980-1999:denrasistiskaundergroundrörelsen: musiken, myterna, riterna.* Stockholm: Ordfront.

Malm, A. 2009. *Hatet mot muslimer,* Stockholm, Atlas.

Mcclintock, A. 1995. *Imperial leather: race, gender and sexuality in the colonial contest,* London: Routledge.

Minkenberg, M. 1997. The new right in France and Germany: Nouvelle Droite, Neue Rechte and the new right radical parties, in *The revival of right-wing extremism in the nineties,* edited by P. H. Merkl and L. Weinberg. London: Frank Cass.

Mudde, C. 2000. *The ideology of the extreme right,* Manchester: Manchester University Press.

Mulinari, D. and Neergaard, A. 2010. Sverigedemokraterna och det teoretiska fältet. *Det vita fältet: Samtida forskning om högerextremism.* Uppsala: Opuscula Historica Upsaliensia.

Mulinari, P. 2007. *Maktens fantasier & servicearbetets praktik: arbetsvillkor inom hotell- och restaurangbranschen i Malmö,* Linköping, Tema Genus, Institutionen för Tema, Linköpings universitet.

Norocel, O. C. 2010. Constructing radical right populist resistance: metaphors of heterosexist masculinities and the family question in Sweden. *Nordic Journal for Masculinity Studies,* 5, 169-183.

Perry, B. 2001. *In the Name of Hate: Understanding Hate Crimes,* London, Routledge.

Pred, A. 2000. *Even in Sweden: racisms, racialized spaces, and the popular geographical imagination,* Berkeley:University of California Press.

Pripp, O. 2002. Massmedierepresentationer av förortsinnevånare, med fokus på fittjabor, in: *Fittja, världen och vardagen,* edited by I. Ramberg and O. Pripp. Botkyrka: Mångkulturellt centrum.

Ranstorp, M. and Dos Santos, J. 2009. Hot mot demokrati och värdegrund: en lägesbild från Malmö. Stockholm: Centrum för Asymmetriska Hot och TerrorismStudier (CATS).

Razack, S. H. 2004. Imperilled Muslim Women, Dangerous Muslim Men and Civilised Europeans: Legal and Social Responses to Forced Marriages. *Feminist Legal Studies,* 12, 129-174.

Rydgren, J. 2005. Is extreme right-wing populism contagious? Explaining the emergence of a new party family *European Journal of Political Research,* 413-437.

Rydgren, J. 2006. *From tax populism to ethnic nationalism: radical right-wing populism in Sweden,* New York;Berghahn Books.

Sassen, S. 1997. Immigration and the new order. *Framtider International,* 7, 10-15.

Schierup, C.-U., Hansen, P. and Castles, S. 2006. *Migration, citizenship, and the European welfare state: a European dilemma,* Oxford: Oxford University Press.

Schiffer, S., and Wagner, C. 2011. Anti-Semitism and Islamophobia – new enemies, old patterns. *Race and Class,* 52 (3), 77-84.

Sennett, R. 1998. *The corrosion of character: the personal consequences of work in the new capitalism,* New York: W.W. Norton.

Sverigedemokraterna. 2003/2005. *Sverigedemokraternas principprogram* [Online]. Sverigedemokraterna. Available at: http://www.sverigedemokraterna. net/asikt_text.php?action=fullnews&id=317 [accessed: 9 October 2009].

Sverigedemokraterna. 2007. *Handlingsprogram – Invandringspolitiskt program* [Online]. Sverigedemokraterna. Available at: http://www.sverigedemokraterna. net/asikt_hp.php?action=fullnews&id=847 [accessed: 9 October 2009].

Tilly, C. 1985. War Making and State Making as Organized Crime,in *Bringing the State Back*, edited by P. Evans, D. Rueschemeyer and T. Skocpol. Cambridge: Cambridge University Press.

Van Dijk, T. 1993. *Elite Discourse and Racism,* London: Sage.

Westlind, D. 1996. *The politics of popular identity: understanding recent populist movements in Sweden and the United States,* Lund; Lund Univ. Press.

Yegenoglu, M. 1998. *Colonial Fantasies: Towards a Feminist Reading of Orientalism,* Cambridge; Cambridge University Press.

Yuval Davis, N. 1997. *Gender and Nation,* London: Sage Publications.

Chapter 5

The Social Construction of Iraqi Folk Devils: Post-9/11 Framing by the G.W. Bush Administration and US News Media

Scott A. Bonn

Introduction

On the morning of September 11, 2001, the United States was attacked by international terrorists. Almost immediately thereafter, US President George W. Bush declared a global 'war on terror' with Osama Bin Laden as its central target. Despite overwhelming evidence that the attacks had been solely orchestrated by Bin Laden's al Qaeda network (including its claim of responsibility), the Bush administration also sought to link 9/11 to Iraq, Saddam Hussein and his Baath Party (Scheer 2003). More specifically, the Bush administration initiated an 18-month propaganda campaign to convince the US public and the world that Iraq 1) was involved in the attacks of 9/11, 2) possessed weapons of mass destruction (WMD), and 3) represented a grave and growing threat to US security (Scheer 2003). In fact, Paul Wolfowitz, then Deputy Secretary of Defense under Donald Rumsfeld, began to link Iraq to 9/11 within 48 hours following the terrorist attacks (Clarke 2004). By the fall of 2002, President Bush was proclaiming that 'the Iraqi dictator must not be permitted to threaten America and the world with horrible poisons and diseases and gases and atomic weapons' (Scheer 2003: 1). The Bush administration's propaganda campaign convinced the majority of US citizens that Iraq was directly involved in the attacks of 9/11 by the time the US-led invasion of Iraq began on March 19, 2003 (Corn 2003).

This chapter examines the communication processes by which Iraq became socially constructed as evil by the G.W. Bush administration and the US news media after 9/11. The Iraq war was legitimized by an elite-engineered moral panic precipitated by the G.W. Bush administration and fueled by the US news media which exploited pre-existing negative stereotypes of Arabs/Muslims (Merskin 2004) and influenced public opinion on support for the invasion of Iraq (Druckman and Holmes 2004, Chomsky 2005, Gershkoff and Kushner 2005, Altheide 2006, Bonn 2010). Significantly, *Islamophobia* or an 'irrational fear of

Islam' has existed in the US since at least the late 1980s[1] and can be traced back to popular culture images of all Muslims as treacherous and blood-thirsty terrorists. In fact, a legacy of negative media framing of Muslims/Arabs predisposed the US public to punitive action toward Iraq even before the events of 9/11. The Bush administration effectively exploited that predisposition in the months following the terrorist attacks. The framing of Saddam Hussein and his followers as evildoers or 'folk devils' by President Bush and the news media after 9/11 interacted with negative stereotypes of all Arabs and Muslims in the US, so as to prime hostile and retaliatory public attitudes toward Iraq, which led to popular support for the invasion of that country.

What is Elite-engineered Moral Panic?

Developed in the late 1960s, the moral panic concept remains popular among scholars studying social problems, crime, media and collective behaviour (Welch 2006, Garland 2008). Generally, moral panic has been defined as a condition or situation in which public fears and state interventions greatly exceed the objective threat posed to society by a particular group who are claimed to be responsible for the condition (Cohen 1972, McCorkle and Miethe 1998). More specifically, elite-engineered moral panic occurs when an elite group deliberately undertakes a campaign to generate and sustain concern or fear on the part of the public over an issue or group that is not terribly threatening to society (Goode and Ben-Yehuda 1994).

Introduced by Jock Young (1971), the moral panic concept was developed and popularized by the criminologist Stanley Cohen (1972) when he described the public reaction to disturbances by youths called 'mods and rockers' at seaside resorts in England, during the 1960s. Cohen's work illustrated how those reactions influenced the enforcement and formation of social policy, law, and societal perceptions of threat posed by the youth groups. The moral panic concept has been applied to a wide range of social problems including, but not limited to, youth gangs (McCorkle and Miethe 1998), school violence (Burns and Crawford 1999), child abuse (Best 1994), Satanism (Victor 1994), 'wilding' (Welch, Price and Yankey 2002), flag burning (Welch 2000), the US war on drugs (Reinarman and Levine 1989, Hawdon 2001), illegal immigration (Welch 2004), terror (Rothe and Muzzatti 2004) and, most recently, the US war on Iraq (Bonn 2010).

It has been argued that moral panics arise when distorted mass media campaigns are used to create fear, reinforce stereotypes and exacerbate pre-existing divisions in

---

1   This argument has been made in multiple forums, including Islamophobia: A Challenge for Us All, Runnymede Trust, 1997, cited in Quraishi, Muzammil, Muslims and Crime: A Comparative Study, Ashgate Publishing Ltd., 2005, 60; Annan, Kofi, 'Secretary-General, addressing headquarters seminar on confronting Islamophobia', United Nations press release, 7 December, 2004.

the world, often based on race, ethnicity and class (Goode and Ben-Yehuda 1994). Furthermore, moral panics have three distinguishing characteristics (McCorkle and Miethe 2001:19-20). First, there is a focused attention on the behaviour (either real or imagined) of certain groups, who are in turn transformed into 'folk devils' by the mass media and 'stripped of all favorable characteristics and imparted with exclusively negative ones' (Goode and Ben-Yehuda 1994: 28). Second, there is a gap between the concern over a condition and the objective threat it poses. Typically, the objective threat is far less than popularly perceived and as presented by authorities. Third, there is a great deal of fluctuation over time in the level of public concern over a condition. The typical pattern begins with the discovery of the threat, followed by a rapid rise and then peak in public concern, and subsequently (and often abruptly) concern subsides. Perhaps most importantly, public hysteria over a perceived problem often results in the passing of legislation that is highly punitive, unnecessary, and serves to justify the agendas of those in positions of power and authority (Simon and Feeley 1995).

As originally explained by Cohen (1972), at least five sets of social actors are involved in a moral panic. These include: 1) folk devils, 2) rule or law enforcers, 3) the media, 4) politicians, and 5) the public. First, in the lexicon of moral panic scholars, folk devils are those individuals who are socially defined (alleged) to be responsible for creating a threat to society. Unlike some deviants or criminals, the folk devils are 'unambiguously unfavourable symbols' (Cohen 1972: 41). They are the embodiment of evil and the antagonists in a moral panic drama. Second, law enforcers such as the police, prosecutors or the military are vital to a moral panic as they are charged with upholding and enforcing the codes of conduct and official laws of the state. These agents of the state are expected to detect, apprehend and punish the folk devils. In addition, law enforcers present themselves as the protectors of society, without whom, chaos might well ensue. As noted by Altheide (2002), law enforcers must work to establish their legitimacy and justify their existence in society and moral panics facilitate such undertakings. Third, the media are perhaps the most influential facilitator in the creation of a moral panic (Goode and Ben-Yehuda 1994). Typically, news media coverage of certain events involving the folk devils is distorted or exaggerated. Such exaggerations make the folk devils appear to be much more threatening to society than they really are. As a result, public concern and anxiety are heightened through journalistic hyperbole which can bring the moral panic to a crescendo. Fourth, politicians are also vital actors in a moral panic drama. As elected officials, who must operate in the court of public opinion, politicians must present themselves as the protectors of the moral high ground. They often fuel a moral panic by aligning themselves with the news media and law enforcers in a moral crusade against the evils introduced by the folk devils. The fifth set of actors, the public, is perhaps the most important in a moral panic drama. Public agitation or concern over the folk devils is the central element of a moral panic. In fact, the success of politicians, law enforcers and the media in precipitating and sustaining a moral panic is ultimately contingent upon how successfully these sets of actors fuel public concern and outrage toward the folk devils (Rothe and Muzzatti 2004).

Beyond the actors in a moral panic, Cohen (2002: xxii) has also identified five criteria which define a moral panic:

(i)   *Concern* (rather than fear) about the potential or imagined threat;

(ii)   *Hostility-* moral outrage toward the actors (folk devils) who embody the problem and agencies (naïve social workers, spin-doctored politicians) who are 'ultimately' responsible (and may become folk devils themselves);

(iii)   *Consensus-* a widespread agreement (not necessarily total) that the threat exists, is serious and that 'something should be done.' The majority of elite and influential groups, especially the mass media, should share this consensus;

(iv)   *Disproportionality-* an exaggeration of the number or strength of the cases, in terms of the damage caused, moral offensiveness, potential risk if ignored. Public concern is not directly proportionate to objective harm;

(v)   *Volatility-* the panic erupts and dissipates suddenly and without warning.

Moral panic theorists distinguish between public concern and fear. From a moral panic perspective, the public reaction to a possible or alleged threat need not take the form of fear in order to qualify (Goode and Ben-Yehuda 1994). Rather, genuine felt concern about the situation is sufficient to constitute the public reaction criterion of moral panic. Felt concern demonstrates that the social condition is perceived to be a problem. The hostility criterion of moral panic involves an outraged, punitive response by society toward those allegedly responsible for the threat. According to moral panic theorists, hostility toward the folk devils that embody the threat is fueled by moral entrepreneurs (or crusaders), political elites and the news media. The consensus criterion is established when a substantial portion of society believes that the threat exists. Unanimity of opinion, however, is not required in order for a condition to constitute a moral panic. Consensus, therefore, can exist in a matter of degrees, so long as it reflects a widespread agreement that the threat is real, serious, and caused by the folk devils and their troublesome behavior. Disproportionality involves an exaggeration by elites and the news media regarding the actual threat or risk posed by the alleged folk devils. As a result, public concern is disproportionate to the objective threat posed to society by folk devils. Finally, the level of attention given to the so-called problem by elites and the news media fluctuates over time, as does the degree of public concern. Thus, there is an ebb and flow in both attention and concern about the folk devils that is positively related, i.e., more attention leads to more concern. Of particular relevance to this discussion is the 'elite engineered' model of moral panic.

According to Goode and Ben-Yehuda (1994: 135), the elite-engineered model of moral panic argues that 'an elite group deliberately and consciously undertakes a campaign to generate and sustain concern, fear, and panic on the part of the public over an issue that they recognize not to be terribly harmful to the society as a whole.' Often times, such a campaign is intended to divert public attention away from other objective or real problems in society, whose solution might jeopardize or undermine the interests of the elite group (Goode and Ben-Yehuda 1994). Moreover, an elite-engineered moral panic can play an important role in 'enabling the ruling stratum to maintain its privileged position' (Chambliss and Mankoff 1976: 15).

It has been argued that the events leading up to the invasion of Iraq in 2003, particularly the pre-war actions of the G.W. Bush administration and the US news media, constituted an elite-engineered moral panic. In particular, using the five criteria of moral panic identified by Cohen, Bonn (2010) undertakes an empirical application of the elite-engineered model of moral panic to a) the G.W. Bush administration's discourse regarding Iraq following 9/11 and b)examining the extent to which the policy rhetoric of a US president in the news media helped tolegitimate an international event—that is, war. Through analyses of Bush administration rhetoric (i.e., direct quotes concerning the alleged threat posed by Iraq) in the media and public opinion polls before and after 9/11, Bonn (2010) provides evidence that the Iraq war was indeed precipitated and rationalized by a moral panic engineered by the Bush administration with the support of a compliant and passive US news media. Those findings are discussed later in this chapter.

The first social actors in the elite-engineered moral panic over Iraq—that is, the folk devils, were personified by Saddam Hussein and his followers. These individuals were portrayed as the embodiments of evil by the G.W. Bush administration with the assistance of the news media after 9/11. Second, the law enforcers in this context were the US military which were morally and legally obligated to protect the US from all foreign threats. Third, the US news media occupied their normal role of promoter or spokesman of law enforcement and political elites. Fourth, it has been argued that sometimes a key politician actually defines the folk devils and precipitates or engineers a moral panic (Hawdon 2001). Such a key politician did exist in the moral panic over Iraq; specifically, President G.W. Bush who defined the Iraqi folk devils and presented the alleged threat to US security. Moreover, the law enforcers (i.e., US military) reported directly to President Bush who, conveniently, was also the commander-in-chief of the military. The fifth and final set of actors—that is, the public, occupied its usual and central role as audience in the moral panic drama over Iraq.

The Framing of Iraq as 'Evil' after 9/11

The moral panic concept is rooted in social constructionism which postulates that social problems do not exist objectively like a mountain or a river. Rather, they are constructed by the human mind, socially created or constituted by the definitional process (Berger and Luckmann 1966). As it applies to moral panic, the definition of 'evil' is clearly a social construction (Bromley, Shupe and Ventimiglia 1979). The word evil itself has a long linguistic history. The *Oxford English Dictionary* (1971) attributes the original derivation of the word 'evil' to the Goths of the 4th century A.D. who defined it as 'exceeding due measure' or 'overstepping proper limits.' As argued by Coyle (2004: 15), it is evident that the definitions of evil 'are all socially constructed and socially defined. Behaving evilly, producing evil and beingevil are radically social processes [which are defined] in a social context.'

Bromley and colleagues (1979) argued that societal elites and the news media often use 'atrocity tales' to amplify and support their arguments in the social construction of evil. What exactly are atrocity tales? Bromley et al. (1979: 43) stated:

> An *atrocity* may be defined as an event which is viewed as a flagrant violation of a fundamental cultural value. Accordingly, an *atrocity tale* is a presentation of that event (real or imaginary) in such a way as to (a) evoke moral outrage by specifying and detailing the value violations, (b) authorize, implicitly or explicitly, punitive sanctions, and (c) mobilize control efforts against the alleged perpetrators.

The intent of atrocity tales is not to present the complexity of an event dispassionately. Rather, the intent is to provide so-called evidence in support of a claim that the targeted group is in fact evil and thus deserving of punishment. The use of atrocity tales in the social construction of evil provides insights into to the labeling of folk devils in a moral panic. Similar to the claims used by elites to label folk devils in a moral panic, it is not important whether the allegations made in atrocity tales are actually true or false (Bromley et al. 1979). Rather, they are designed to elicit an emotional response. For example, the US military effectively integrated atrocity tales into propaganda films used to incite outrage toward Nazi Germany among new recruits during World War II (Lowery and DeFleur 1995).

Once a disvalued individual or group is socially defined as evil, those in power have the moral authority and even obligation to eliminate the evildoer(s) (Cohen 1972). This premise is central to the moral panic concept. As discussed above, the identification and labeling of folk devils is an essential step in the creation of a moral panic. Moreover, the folk devil does not necessarily exist objectively; rather, the folk devil is labeled as such by political elites and the news media (Cohen 1972). The label then becomes a self-fulfilling prophecy as public fear and media coverage both prompt and justify punitive actions by legal authorities toward the folk devils. The G.W. Bush administration's use of the term 'axis of evil' after 9/11 in reference to Iraq, Iran and North Korea provides such an example.

It has been argued that 'Tolerance and accommodation allow understanding that may grow into appreciation' between heterogeneous groups (Alimoglu 2010: x). Conversely, intolerance, lack of accommodation, and negative framing of the 'other' through propaganda promote disharmony and even hatred between heterogeneous groups. The framing of Iraqis as evil by the G.W. Bush administration after 9/11 did precisely the latter. Punitive rhetoric by the Bush administration after 9/11 promoted prejudice, fear and hatred toward Arabs/ Muslims, in general, and toward Iraqis, in particular. As previously discussed, moral panics typically arise when distorted mass media campaigns are used to create fear, reinforce stereotypes and exacerbate pre-existing divisions in the world that are often based on race, ethnicity and class (Goode and Ben-Yehuda 1994). The Bush administration's moral panic over Iraq after 9/11 did exactly that, as explained herein.

It is important to briefly discuss the communication processes of framing and priming at this point in order to fully understand how these processes can influence public perceptions. Framing refers to the way an issue is presented to the public (or 'angle' it is given) by the news media. Framing also involves calling attention to certain aspects of an issue while ignoring or obscuring other elements. In short, framing gives meaning to an issue. In her seminal work, Tuchman (1978) proposed that the news media rely on 'news frames' to determine what events to cover and how to cover them. Just as the photographer's choice of lens affects a photograph, the journalist's choice of news frame affects a story. Tuchman (1978) theorized that journalists select news frames for a story based in part on routine procedures and the organizational constraints of their particular medium. In addition, the choice of frame is influenced by prior news frames (e.g., existing templates), the power and authority of news sources, history and, central to this discussion, ideology. Thus, news frames are contested or negotiated phenomena rather than objective events (Tuchman 1978, Entman 1993). Most significantly, an audience can react very differently to an issue or story depending on how it is framed by the news media.

In contrast, priming is a psychological process whereby the news media emphasis on a particular issue not only increases the salience of the issue on the public agenda, but also activates in people's memories previously acquired information about that issue (Lowery and DeFleur 1995). The priming mechanism explains how the news frame used in a particular story can trigger an individual's pre-existing attitudes, beliefs and prejudices regarding that issue. Priming is thus an individual-level factor that can have great variability within a society given past events and news coverage. An example of priming would be the triggering of individual responses such as fear, anger or outrage by Americans to televised images of the 2005 London underground attacks, based on the US news media's prior framing of the events of 9/11 as the evil acts of madmen.

From the perspective of communication theory and research (see Lowery and DeFleur 1995), the framing of Saddam Hussein's regime as 'evildoers' and 'madmen' by President Bush after 9/11 interacted with established negative stereotypes of Arabs/Muslims, in general, so as to prime hostile and retaliatory attitudes among the US public toward the targeted group—that is, the Iraqi leadership. Significantly, in their model of enemy image construction, Spillman and Spillman (1977) explained how a standard repertoire of propagandistic words such as 'evil' can serve to dehumanize the 'other' in the popular imagination and can make a retaliatory response toward society's common enemy seem both logical and natural. The Bush administration employed such a standard repertoire in its discourse after 9/11 in order to define Iraqis as folk devils.

In an important study of post-9/11 presidential rhetoric, Merskin (2004) determined that the word choices and allusions used in the 'carefully constructed' post-9/11 speeches of G.W. Bush closely resembled the accumulation of historically, politically and culturally constructed negative words and images of Arabs/Muslims in the public domain. Merskin (2004: 122) explains:

> ...depictions of Arab enemies in popular culture and employed by the media were mobilized by the Bush administration and fed to a receptive public. These carefully cultivated stereotypes, used to justify the invasion... and occupation of Iraq, were affirmed during the months following September 11, 2001, and reified by the time troops invaded Iraq in 2003.

Simply put, the exploitation and reinforcement of negative stereotypes of Arabs and Muslims was central to the Bush administration's demonizing of Saddam Hussein and his followers after 9/11.

In addition, President Bush used atrocity tales in his post-9/11 rhetoric to exploit negative stereotypes of Arabs/Muslims and, thereby, bolster his case for invading Iraq. In his pre-invasion propaganda campaign, President Bush frequently referred to atrocities allegedly perpetrated by Saddam Hussein's army against the Iraqi people—in particular, the use of chemical weapons against the Kurds (Merskin 2004, Rothe and Muzzatti 2004). Such atrocity tales were designed to prime or trigger moral outrage among Americans by interacting with and exploiting negative stereotypes of Arabs/Muslims as cold-blooded killers. However, as noted by Kramer, Michalowski and Rothe (2005: 64):

> President Bush failed to mention that these gassings occurred more than a decade earlier. By avoiding any periodization of Hussein's attacks on Kurdish villages, Bush helped to leave the impression in the minds of many Americans that these attacks were recent, and perhaps ongoing.

Thus, President Bush misrepresented Iraqi history to the US public. By giving the impression that the attacks were recent, the atrocity tales used by the Bush administration incited anger, reinforced racial and religious stereotypes and primed prejudicial sentiments, particularly after 9/11, and helped to fuel a public fire that had been lit by the moral panic over Iraq. According to Chomsky (2005), this was part of a general and intentional misrepresentation of the case for attacking Iraq by the Bush administration in order to secure enduring public support for it.

It has been argued that the symbolic language of political elites which is dutifully reported by the news media is at the heart of setting the agenda for public discourse (Edelman 1988). Providing a powerful example of this, Rothe and Muzzatti (2004) demonstrated that the US news media unquestioningly framed the 'global war on terror' after 9/11 according to the specifications set by the G.W. Bush administration. Importantly, however, the framing of Saddam Hussein/Iraq as evil was first employed by the administration of President George H.W. Bush, and it was established by the media as the dominant news frame in the 1990-1991 Persian Gulf War (Bennett and Paletz 1994). Because the news frame of Saddam Hussein/Iraq as evil predated the events of 9/11, it was readily available to the G.W. Bush administration for exploitation after the terrorist attacks.

From the perspective of news as frame (Tuchman 1978), the news media were following normal journalistic routines after 9/11 when they relied overwhelmingly on G.W. Bush administration sources to define the Iraq issue for the US audience. The punitive, pro-war argument of the Bush administration concerning Iraq became the dominant news frame on Iraq and, as a result, that frame defined reality for the majority of the US public. As argued by Kellner (2005: xvi), the 'US corporate media enabled the Bush administration's policy [on Iraq].' Although there were occasional counterclaims in the news media to dispute the pro-war argument, the dominant news frame leading up to the invasion was the Bush administration's 'Iraq is evil' message (Gershkoff and Kushner 2005, Bonn 2010).

What was the Effect of the Bush Administration's Moral Panic over Iraq?

The implications of applying the label of 'evil' to others are grave. Once a disvalued individual or group becomes defined as evil in an elite-engineered moral panic, those in power have the moral authority and even obligation to eliminate the folk devils (Cohen 1972, Garland 2008).'This central tenet of the moral panic concept was manifested in the Bush administration's militaristic response to the socially constructed folk devils in Iraq. The US public generally believed the Bush administration's argument that Saddam Hussein and his followers were evil and, therefore, generally supported the president's choice to go to war. Furthermore, although paradoxical, many Americans even believed that the pre-emptive strike on Iraq was their own idea and were anxiously awaiting the Bush administration's declaration of war by early 2003 (Bonn 2010). Such a paradox, however, is consistent with social constructionism and the moral panic concept.

Becker (1968: 142) referred to the practice of reductionism by political elites (e.g., the Bush administration's framing of Iraqis as folk devils) combined with the absence of critical reasoning in society when presented with false universals as 'the demonic nature of 'evil' in our time.' In his writings on the structure of evil, Becker (1968: 142) warned that when 'uncritical fictions' take control of society, without either responsible dissent or review of the ends of action, then 'the world of ineluctable movement assumes its own laws.' From this perspective, the alleged threat posed by Saddam Hussein and his political regime became a socially constructed crisis and moral imperative in the US which justified ends over means. The Bush administration fulfilled its moral obligation to US society by providing a self-serving solution to its own elite-engineered crisis—that is, the invasion of Iraq and removal of Saddam Hussein from power. As discussed, the Bush administration's unnecessary war on Iraq was initially embraced by the majority of Americans. However, public support for it eroded dramatically when the quick victory promised by the Bush administration failed to materialize and the US death toll climbed.

Fish (2001) argued that the presentation of 'false universals' such as the Bush administration's 'good versus evil' foreign policy argument after 9/11 laid the foundation for annihilating an entire group of people. Fish (2001: A-19) stated:

> How many times have we heard these new mantras: 'we have seen the face of evil'; 'these are irrational madmen'; 'we are at war against international terrorism.' Each is at once inaccurate and unhelpful. We have not seen the face of evil; we have seen the face of an enemy who comes at us with a full roster of grievances, goals and strategies. If we reduce that enemy to 'evil,' we conjure up a shape-shifting demon, a wild-card moral anarchist beyond our comprehension and therefore beyond the reach of any counterstrategies.

Immediately following the attacks of 9/11, President Bush reduced the world to a dichotomy—i.e., good versus evil—and he used that dichotomy to frame the alleged threat from Iraq for the US public (Entman 2003). According to Fish (2001), when one's opponent is framed as evil that opponent is stripped of all humanity and is assumed to be without reason or morality. From this simplistic perspective, it is foolish and even futile to attempt to communicate with an enemy who is inhuman. Thus, the reductionism inherent to the social construction of evil eliminates any possibility of recourse other than the complete destruction of the enemy. By mid-2008, more than one million Iraqis had died in the US-led war and subsequent occupation (albeit not all at the hands of US soldiers and mercenaries) in contrast to 4,100-plus Americans. The tremendous death toll of the Iraq war clearly demonstrates the terrible consequences of labeling one's opponent as evil.

Just how effective was the G.W. Bush administration's propaganda campaign in demonizing Iraq after 9/11? By March 15, 2003, just four days prior to the invasion of Iraq, public support for it had peaked as 70% of the US population believed that Iraq was directly involved in the terrorist attacks of 9/11, and almost the same percentage approved of going to war. The Bush administration's propaganda campaign very successfully linked Iraq to the horrific but unrelated events of 9/11 in the minds of most of the US public—in large part by exploiting negative stereotypes of Arabs/Muslims—and triggered hostility toward Iraq in those Americans who craved revenge after the terrorist attacks.

Bonn (2010) utilized the five defining elements of moral panic to determine whether the build up to the Iraq war constituted an elite-engineered moral panic. Cohen (2002) identified *concern* as the first criterion of a moral panic. It has been argued that the concern criterion of a moral panic can be measured in the form of media attention (Goode and Ben-Yehuda 1994, Welch et al. 2002). Bonn (2010) determined that during the six months that immediately preceded the March 2003 invasion of Iraq, an average of 105 articles per month contained direct quotes regarding Iraq in *The New York Times*. This represents an average of 3.5 articles per day during the six months prior to the invasion or a 350% increase from the average of the 36-month study. This finding reveals that the volume of Bush administration policy rhetoric increased significantly as the invasion of Iraq approached. It must be remembered that these numbers, as high as they are, represent only one news source. It is contented that dramatically increased rhetoric by the Bush administration regarding Iraq after 9/11 met the essential concern criterion and thus laid the foundation for an elite engineered moral panic (Goode and Ben-Yehuda 1994, Cohen 2002). Furthermore, the Bush administration's policy rhetoric regarding Iraq as quoted in *The New York Times* became more punitive and communitarian after 9/11. In particular, the concern criterion is manifested in statements by President Bush prior to the invasion that 'the Iraqi dictator must not be permitted to threaten America and the world with horrible poisons and diseases and gases and atomic weapons' (Scheer 2003: 1). The message from the Bush administration to the public was that Iraq represented a serious and imminent threat to all Americans, and action had to be taken to eliminate that threat (Fish 2001). To do otherwise tempted disaster in the form of a 'mushroom cloud,' i.e., a nuclear attack on the US (Scheer 2003).

The second criterion of a moral panic identified by Cohen (2002) is *consensus*. It has been argued that there must be substantial or widespread agreement or consensus in society, although not necessarily universal, that the threat is real and serious, and caused by the alleged offenders and their behaviour (Goode and Ben-Yehuda 1994). The Gallup Polls used by Bonn (2010), which measured the percentage of the US public that approved of invading Iraq over time, establish the consensus criterion of moral panic. In these 24 polls, public support for invading Iraq ranged from a low of 52.5% in February, 2001, to a high of 64.1% in March, 2003 (four days before the start of the invasion). Public support for war fluctuated over the course of the 24 polls; it peaked just prior to the invasion of Iraq and climbed fairly steadily in the last few months leading up to it. Significantly, changes in presidential rhetoric regarding the alleged Iraq threat prior to each of the 24 polls significantly changed the likelihood of support for invasion in statistical (logistic regression) analyses. This indicates that public support for war was driven or manufactured by the policy rhetoric of the Bush administration. Thus, similar to the concern criterion discussed above, consensus is demonstrated in the relationship between the volume of presidential rhetoric and public opinion.

The third criterion of a moral panic identified by Cohen (2002) is *hostility* or moral outrage toward the social actors or folk devils which embody the problem.

Following the attacks of 9/11, the administration of George W. Bush framed the political regime of Saddam Hussein as folk devils which posed a serious and growing threat to the national security of the US (Scheer 2003, Clarke 2004). The findings of Bonn (2010) indicate that punitive rhetoric toward Hussein and Iraq was significantly more likely to be used after 9/11 (as determined in logistic regression analyses) and it was much more likely to be used by Bush administration sources than by non-administration sources such as UN chief weapons inspector, Hans Blix. This was true for President Bush as well as key members of his cabinet such as Defense Secretary Donald Rumsfeld. Thus, the use of punitive rhetoric, particularly such words as 'evil,' 'threat,' 'mad terrorists' and 'weapons of mass destruction,' combined with atrocity tales and racial stereotypes defined Saddam Hussein and his followers as folk devils. Such rhetorical framing of the Iraqis by the Bush administration fulfills the hostility criterion of a moral panic (Goode and Ben-Yehuda 1994, Welch et al. 2002).

The fourth criterion of a moral panic identified by Cohen (2002) is *disproportionality*. Disproportionality refers to an exaggeration of the objective threat posed to society by the folk devils. This criterion requires evidence that the alleged threat is greater than the actual possibility of harm or that attention paid to it is excessive relative to other more objectively serious problems (Welch et al. 2002). The financial cost of the Iraq war was disproportionate, for example, when compared to federal spending on other objective, life-threatening conditions facing the US. By July 2008, more than $540 billion had been spent on the war in Iraq and another $135 billion had been requested by President Bush and approved by Congress for fiscal year 2008-09. The total was increasing at a rate of more than $340 million per day, more than $10 billion per month, and approximately $130 billion annually.

As the Bush administration launched its unnecessary war of choice on Iraq, it simultaneously failed to act preemptively and proportionately to address life-threatening diseases and other social and environmental conditions that represented far greater hazards to US citizens in 2003 than did Iraq. In comparison to spending on the Iraq war, for example, only $2.5 billion is spent by the federal government each year on research on heart disease, the leading cause of death in the US. Heart disease annually claims 700,000 lives and costs the US an estimated $400 billion in medical expenses and lost productivity (www.infoplease.com 2007). Moreover, heart disease affects more than 62 million Americans! Similarly, about $3 billion is spent annually on HIV/AIDS research. Approximately 42,000 people are diagnosed and 18,000 people die each year from AIDS in the US and nearly one million Americans have died from AIDS since 1981 (www.avert.org 2007). In fact, the annual budget of the National Institute of Health (NIH) for research on all diseases is $30 billion—approximately the same as the cost of the war and occupation of Iraq every three months (www.americanheart.org 2007). Arguably, disproportionality is demonstrated by the Bush administration's massive spending on the unnecessary Iraq war relative to more objectively serious problems and health risks that were facing the US public during the Bush administration.

The fifth and final criterion of a moral panic outlined by Cohen (2002) is *volatility*. As previously explained, the 24 pre-war Gallup Polls used in the Bonn (2010) study reveal that public support for invading Iraq ranged from a low of 52.5% in February, 2001, to a high of 64.1% in March, 2003. Although the actual increase in public support was modest—12 percentage-points—it represents a +23% change in public support overall. Moreover, and consistent with the moral panic concept, public support for the invasion did not steadily increase throughout the 24 polls. In fact, public support for the invasion actually decreased in 11 of the polls relative to the one immediately preceding it. Importantly, from a moral panic perspective, public support for war mirrored the ebb and flow of news media coverage of the issue.

Similarly, President Bush's job approval rating fluctuated greatly over time. Riding the emotional tide of patriotism following the terrorist attacks of 9/11, his approval rating was 71% at the start of the Iraq war (Blow 2008). By March 2008, five years after he launched the invasion of Iraq, Bush's job approval rating had plummeted to 31%. Interestingly, the 40-point drop in popularity experienced by President G.W. Bush was almost identical to the drop experienced by President Lyndon B. Johnson during the Vietnam War (Blow 2008). In summary, the fluctuations in both presidential approval and public support for the Iraq war which mirrored fluctuations in the volume of news coverage and the news framing of the Iraq war demonstrate the volatility criterion of a moral panic.

Significantly, the findings of Bonn (2010) demonstrate that the war in Iraq was legitimized by a moral panic engineered by the Bush administration, and reinforced by the news media, which manipulated public support for the invasion of Iraq following 9/11. These findings expand on the moral panic literature concerning presidential rhetoric (Reinarman and Levine 1989, Hawdon 2001, Johnson et al. 2004, Rothe and Muzzatti 2004) which had previously demonstrated that the president of the US participates in the social construction of reality and the elite engineering of moral panics. Furthermore, the findings of Bonn (2010) support the primacy of the US President as a source of ideology and as a public agenda setter (Kieve 1994, Goode and Ben-Yehuda 1994, Hawdon 2001, Johnson et al. 2004) because other individual sources and tones of rhetoric in the author's logistic regression analyses were not associated with support for invading Iraq once the effects of quotes from President Bush were taken into account. Perhaps most importantly, the same findings demonstrate that the elite-engineered model of moral panic indeed applies to the events leading up to the invasion of Iraq after 9/11. Stated differently, Bonn (2010) demonstrates that even public support for a war of aggression can be engineered by the president of the US with the assistance of a compliant news media which simply follows routine journalistic procedures and which does not question authority.

Conclusion

In this chapter we have examined the communication processes by which Iraq became socially constructed as evil by the G.W. Bush administration and the US news media after 9/11. Islamophobia or an 'irrational fear of Islam' has existed in the US since at least the late 1980s. The Iraq war was legitimized by a moral panic engineered by the G.W. Bush administration with the assistance of a compliant US news media. The framing of the alleged Iraqi threat exploited pre-existing negative stereotypes of Arabs/Muslims which influenced public opinion on support for the invasion of Iraq. A legacy of negative media framing of Arabs/Muslims predisposed the US public to punitive action toward Iraq even before the events of 9/11, and the Bush administration effectively exploited that situation in the 18 months following the terrorist attacks. The framing of Saddam Hussein and his followers as folk devils by President Bush and the news media interacted with negative stereotypes of all Arabs and Muslims in the US after 9/11, so as to prime hostile and retaliatory public attitudes toward Iraq, leading to popular support for the invasion of that country in March of 2003.

References

Alimoglu, Y. 2010. *Deserts and Mountains*. Bloomington, IN: iUniverse.

Altheide, D. 2002. *Creating Fear: News and the Construction of Crisis*. New York: Aldine de Gruyter.

Altheide, D. 2006. Terrorism and the politics of fear. *Cultural Studies ⇔ Critical Methodologies* 6, 415-439.

Becker, E. 1968. *The Structure of Evil: An Essay on the Unification of the Science of Man*. New York: G. Braziller.

Bennett, W.L. and Paletz, D.L. 1994. *The Media, Public Opinion, and US Foreign Policy in the Gulf War*. Chicago, IL: University of Chicago Press.

Berger, P.L. and Luckmann, T. 1966. *The Social Construction of Reality: A Treatise in the Sociology of Knowledge*. New York: Anchor Books.

Best, J. 1994. *Troubling Children: Studies of Children and Social Problems*. New York: Aldine de Gruyter.

Blow, C.M. 2008. Americans move to the middle. [A17]. *The New York Times*, 26 July.

Bonn, S.A. 2010. *Mass Deception: Moral Panic and the US War on Iraq*. New Brunswick, NJ: Rutgers University Press.

Bromley, D.G., Shupe, Jr., A.D. and Ventimiglia, J.C. 1979. Atrocity tales, the Unification Church, and the social construction of evil. *Journal of Communication*, 29 (3), 42-53.

Burns, R. and Crawford, C. 1999. School shootings: The media and public fear: Ingredients for a moral panic. *Crime, Law and Social Change*, 32, 147-168.

Chambliss, W.J. and Mankoff, M. 1976. *Whose Law? What Order?* New York: John Wiley.

Chomsky, N. 2005. Global ethics, American foreign policy and the academic as activist: An interview with Noam Chomsky. *Journal of Global Ethics*, 1, 197-205.

Clarke, R.A. 2004. *Against All Enemies: Inside America's War on Terror*. Detroit: The Free Press.

Cohen, S. 1972. *Folk Devils and Moral Panics: The Creation of the Mods and Rockers*. London: MacGibbon and Key Ltd.

Cohen, S. 2002. *Folk Devils and Moral Panics: The Creation of the Mods and Rockers*. 3rd Edition. New York: Routledge.

Corn, D. 2003. *The Lies of George W. Bush: Mastering the Politics of Deception*. New York: Crown Publishers.

Coyle, M. J. 2004. *Finding and Defining Evil: The Social Construction of Crime as Evil*. Paper presented to the American Society of Criminology at the annual conference, Nashville, TN, 19 November Croft, S. 2006.

Culture, Crisis and America's War on Terror. Cambridge: Cambridge University Press.

Druckman, J.N. and Holmes, J.W. 2004. Does presidential rhetoric matter? Priming and presidential approval. *Presidential Studies Quarterly*, 34, 755-778.

Edelman, M. 1988. *Constructing the Political Spectacle*. Chicago, IL: University of Chicago Press.

Entman, R.W. 1993. Framing: Toward clarification of a fractured paradigm. *Journal of Communication*, 43 (4), 51-58.

Entman, R.W. 2003. Cascading activation: Contesting the White House's frame after 9/11. *Political Communication*, 20, 415-432.

Fish, C. 2001. Condemnation without absolutes. *The New York Times*, 15 October, Opinion.

Garland, D. 2008. On the concept of moral panic. *Crime, Media, Culture*, 4, 9-30.

Gershkoff, A. and Kushner, S. 2005. Shaping public opinion: The 9/11-Iraq connection in the Bush administration's rhetoric. *Perspectives on Politics*, 3 (3), 525-537.

Goode, E. and Ben-Yehuda, N. 1994. *Moral Panics: The Social Construction of Deviance*. Cambridge, MA: Blackwell.

Hawdon, J.E. 2001. The role of presidential rhetoric in the creation of a moral panic: Reagan, Bush, and the war on drugs. *Deviant Behavior*, 22, 419-445.

Johnson, T.J., Wanta, W. and Boudreau, T. 2004. Drug peddlers: How four presidents attempted to influence media and public concern on the drug issue. *Atlantic Journal of Communication*, 12, 177-199.

Kellner, D. 1990. *Television and the Crisis of Democracy*. Boulder, CO: Westview Press.

Kellner, D. 2005. The Bush administration's march to war, in *Bring 'Em On*, edited by L. Artz and Y.R. Kamalipour. Lanham, MD: Rowman & Littlefield, vii-xvii.

Kramer, R., Michalowski, R., and Rothe, D. 2005. The supreme international crime: How the US war in Iraq threatens the rule of law. *Social Justice*, 32 (2), 52-81.

Kieve, A. 1994. *The Modern Presidency and Crisis Rhetoric*. Westport, CT: Praeger.

Lowery, S.A. and DeFleur, M.L. 1995. *Milestones in Mass Communications Research: Media Effects*. 3rd Edition. New York: Longman.

McCorkle, R.C. and Miethe, T.D. 1998. The political and organizational response to gangs: An examination of a 'moral panic' in Nevada. *Justice Quarterly*, 15, 41-64.

McCorkle, R.C. and Miethe, T.D. 2001. *Panic: Rhetoric and Reality in the War on Street Gangs.* Saddle River, NJ: Prentice-Hall.

Merskin, D. 2004. The construction of Arabs as enemies: Post-September 11 discourse of George W. Bush. *Mass Communication & Society*, 7, 157-175.

Reinarman, C. and Levine, H. 1989. Crack in context: Politics and media in the making of a drug scare. *Contemporary Drug Problems*, 16, 535-577.

Rothe, D.L. and Muzzatti, S.L. 2004. Enemies everywhere: Terrorism, moral panic, and US civil society. *Critical Criminology*, 12, 327-350.

Scheer, C. 2003. *Ten Appalling Lies We Were Told About Iraq*. [Online: AlterNet]. Available at http://www.alternet.org/story/16274/ [accessed 18 September 2007].

Simon, J. and Feeley, M.M. 1995. True crime: The new penology and public discourse on crime, in *Punishment and Social Control: Essays in Honor of Sheldon L. Messinger*, edited by T.G. Blomberg and S. Cohen. New York: Aldine de Gruyter, 147-180.

Spillman, K.R. and Spillman, K. 1977. Some sociological and psychological aspects 'images of the enemy,' in *Enemy Images in American History*, edited by R. Fiebig-von Hase and U. Lehmkuhl. Providence, RI: Berghahn Books, 43-64.

Tuchman, G. 1978. *Making News: A Study in the Social Construction of Reality*. New York: The Free Press.

Victor, J.S. 1994. Fundamentalist religions and the moral crusade against satanism: The social construction of deviant behavior. *Deviant Behavior*, 15, 305-334.

Welch, M. 2000. *Flag Burning: Moral Panic and the Criminalization of Protest*. New York: Aldine de Gruyter.

Welch, M. 2004. Quiet constructions in the war on terror: Subjecting asylum seekers to unnecessary detention. *Social Justice*, 31, 113-129.

Welch, M. 2006. Seeking a safer society: America's anxiety in the war on terror. *Security Journal*, 19, 93-109.

Welch, M., Fenwick, M. and Roberts, M. 1997. Primary definitions of crime and moral panic: A content analysis of experts' quotes in feature newspaper articles on crime. *The Journal of Research in Crime and Delinquency*, 34, 474-494.

Welch, M., Price, E.A. and Yankey, N. 2002. Moral panic over youth violence: Wilding and the manufacture of menace in the media. *Youth & Society*, 34, 3-30.

www.americanheart.org. 2007. *Advocacy News*.

www.americanheart.org/presenter.jhtml?identifier=3011323 [accessed 30 January]

www.avert.org. 2007. *USA HIV & AIDS Cases by Deaths and Year*.

www.avert.org/usastaty.htm [accessed 30 January]

www.infoplease.com. 2007. *Ten Leading Causes of Death in the US*.

www.infoplease.com/ipa/A0005110.html [accessed 30 January]

Young, J. 1971. The role of the police as amplifiers of deviance, negotiators of drug control as seen in Notting Hill, in *Images of Deviance*, edited by S. Cohen. Harmondsworth, England: Penguin Books, 27-61.

Chapter 6

Local Islamophobia: The Islamic School Controversy in Camden, New South Wales

Ryan J. Al-Natour and George Morgan

Introduction

This chapter focuses on the 2007-09 controversy surrounding the proposed development of an Islamic school in Camden, a town settled by Europeans in the early nineteenth century that is in the process of being absorbed into the low-density sprawl to Sydney's south west. It describes the resistance that was mounted by local opponents of the proposed school in a xenophobic campaign that was vastly disproportionate to the fairly modest development application[1]. However, this was not simply a local matter. The popular reaction to the school erupted at a time in which contemporary global tensions have undermined official multiculturalism in Australia. The case is symptomatic of wider popular anxieties that alien values and morality are incubating in the space of nation under the ground cover provided by liberal tolerance. The school proposal sparked fierce local opposition and attracted the participation of right-wing nationalist political groups. To school opponents, Camden became a symbol of national traditions under threat from globalization. Pioneering narratives were central to local memory and informed the popular view that the Anglo-Australian Camden 'community' had the right to assert territorial claims against Muslim encroachments. Opponents drew on a catalogue of moral panics in recent history concerning Islam and people of Muslim backgrounds in order to gain support for their Islamophobic campaign. Further, the school was represented as a symptom of the spread of multicultural Sydney, and the demise of the bush town. From this perspective Camden was a beleaguered outpost of 'little Australia'.

Our sources included: interviews with local residents; field notes from the NSW Land and Environment Court's deliberations on the school proposal; media reports, including local and metropolitan print newspapers and online articles,

---

1   It is not our intention here to engage in discussion on the relative merits of faith-based as opposed to secular education but rather to show how this proposal became a lightning rod for the expression of Islamophobia.

television reports, and radio transcripts; anti-school flyers; Facebook discussions and postings; and letters to the local council and *Camden Advertiser* newspaper.

Camden: Communitarian Xenophobia on the Metropolitan Edge

Camden is a small town of fifty thousand that in recent times has begun to merge with suburban Sydney. With few of the restrictions on fringe land development that exist, for example, in European cities, the area is the site of a number of new master-planned estates accommodating those whom the former Labor Party leader (and local resident) Mark Latham termed members of the 'aspirational' class. Lacking the ethnic diversity of many of the inner and middle suburbs of Sydney, local real estate agents court those wishing to flee the ethnically diverse inner and middle suburbs of Western Sydney. They stress the area's rural values, an idealized bucolic retreat beyond the reach of globalized disorder. Publicity for Harrington Park, one of the most exclusive gated estates in the district, stresses the rural heritage values of the area:

> Stretching back to the colonial era, Harrington Park comprises some of the earliest land grants in Australia. Harrington Park's rich history is typified in the two old homesteads on its grounds – Harrington Park Homestead and Orielton Homestead. Both homesteads span a long history, having housed the gentry, military and farmers alike.

On 10 October 2007 the *Camden Advertiser* reported that the Quranic Society of New South Wales had applied to the local council for permission to build an Islamic school – primary and secondary – on land it owned in the town (Bowie 2007:3). The organization retained former Lord Mayor of Sydney, Jeremy Bingham, as a planning consultant. It stated the school would cater for the future growth and change of the Camden area (Correy 2007a:3), and that the local council's own projections indicated the population would grow six-fold over twenty years (Wilson 2008). In an effort to forestall Islamophobic objections[2], Geoff Corrigan, the local Labor Party representative in the New South Wales Parliament, quickly spoke in support of the proposal,

> I'm sure the majority of Camden residents will welcome additional educational facilities in our area as they welcomed all other schools in rural areas.. As I'm sure everyone knows, the establishment of schools in rural zones is allowable

---

2   In the Australian context there are numerous cases where local development applications for Islamic schools, mosques and prayer centres have triggered local hostility (see Dunn 1999, 2001, 2004; Kabir 2004; Humphrey 1987). While local anxieties arose in previous cases, the Islamophobic campaign against the school in Camden was of a much greater magnitude.

and that was shown by Macarthur Anglican School and Camden high School. I'm sure people won't let issues of religion hinder their welcoming of young children (Bowie 2007:3).

Other local representatives, however, were less sanguine and soon the Quranic Society was forced to defend the application. Public hostility was evident in numerous letters to the local press, widely-circulated text messages and the formation of social media groups opposing the proposed school (Kinsella 2007a:1, 11). Rumours circulated suggesting that Islamic groups were buying up local commercial property (Cuming & Marcus, 2007:6). The *Advertiser's* editor attempted to defuse the hostility (Senescall 2007:4) that was being expressed in numerous letters her publication had received. However, such expressions of multi-cultural openness did little to mollify the rising local concern and in November 2007 a public rally against the school was attended by two thousand people and led to the formation of Camden/Macarthur Residents' Group (Kinsella 2007b:1). At this point the national media began to cover the conflict. Speaking to *ABC* television, local resident, Kate McCulloch, who became a local figure-head in the fight against the school, claimed her opposition was not flavoured by racism, but rather by a fear of a possible terrorist attacks:

> Sure we are racist if you call it racist not accepting a community that also happens to bear, they've got terrorists amongst them, Okay? We can't say they haven't, they have! If we let them in here, they want to be here because they can go and hide in all their country little farmhouses! (*Four Corners* 2008).

McCulloch, who appeared in public wearing akubra hat and drizabone coat (iconic Australian bush garments), was represented in much of the media, as a shrill and unrefined xenophobe in the same mould as Pauline Hanson (Murphy 2008), the leader of the One Nation party which had had some limited electoral success in Australia during the 1990s. One Nation's support had been particularly high in provincial areas similar to Camden – small towns and cities, white-flight suburbs – where residents were keen to conserve the local Anglo monoculture from the perceived threat of ethnic minority invasion. Hanson herself, now no longer a parliamentary representative, used the controversy to voice her opposition to Islamic immigration (Kinsella 2007e:9). Others from fringe conservative political parties also weighed in. Godwin Goh a candidate in the 2007 Federal election from the small right-wing Christian Democrats Party, advocated a change to anti-discrimination and anti-vilification legislation to allow a ten year ban on any development applications concerning mosques or Islamic schools (Kinsella 2007c:10).

Other politicians, including the Camden mayor, were keen to avoid losing local support but also reluctant to embrace the rhetoric of Islamophobia. They sought other pretexts to justify their opposition, including that the construction would bring excessive development and car traffic to a neighbourhood that was on the edge of the town, thus compromising its rural character. Pat Farmer, a member of conservative Prime Minister John Howard's governing Liberal party insisted on the right of local people to 'play a role in what goes on in their backyard' but avoided referring to inter-communal conflict. The matter assumed such prominence that the Leader of the Opposition Kevin Rudd, commented on it during the campaign that led to him being elected the first Labor Prime Minister in over a decade. He opposed the development proposal ostensibly on 'planning grounds' but in doing so sounded the dog-whistle to local racist sentiment in a marginal seat (Kinsella 2007f:9). While some letters published in the *Camden Advertiser* immediately after the anti-school rally, indicated the presence of local supporters of liberal multiculturalism, the majority was clearly opposed to the proposal.

The hostility to the school took on an increasingly Islamophobic character indicating that this was not simply a protest against cultural difference but one which was represented as a new battlefront in the 'clash of civilizations'. A wooden crucifix was planted anonymously on the proposed site, inscribed with biblical verses – 'When the enemy comes in like a flood the spirit of the Lord will lift up a flag in victory' (Kinsella 2007d:19). On November 28 2007 anonymous protestors placed two pigs' heads on stakes at the proposed site with an Australian flag draped between them, an action which was reported in both national and international media (Correy 2007b:1, Tibbitts 2007, Johnston 2008). The NSW Premier at the time described this as 'bizarre and disgraceful' (Kinsella 2007d:19), but it was clear that an apparently minor local development was encoded with the symbolism of contemporary global anxieties

In December 2007 a group calling itself the Public Affairs Information Committee organized an open forum on Islam and the proposed school at which the key speakers were moral conservatives from the upper house of the NSW Parliament. Fred Nile, the leader of the Christian Democrats and Charlie Lynn, of the NSW Opposition Liberal Party addressed a very large crowd with the venue too small to accommodate all those who wished to attend. No Muslim speaker was present and only one news reporter was admitted to the gathering. Local police reported that fifty young people draped in 'Australia gear' had attempted to enter by breaking through windows (Senescall & Bowie 2007). Some members of the crowd wrapped themselves in Australian flags and chanted patriotic slogans, and denouncing 'raggers' [raghead]. The security guards who were 'of Middle Eastern appearance' endured racial abuse from crowd members, calling the guards 'Mohamed' (*AM* 2007). A member of the local branch of the Green Party who attended the session wrote an account for the local press:

> Charlie Lynn first declared he was neither racist nor bigoted then resolved to do all in his power to stop the infiltration of Muslims. The school, he said, would deliver 'culture shock as a means of social engineering'. The final speaker presented a rather hysterical denunciation. When a questioner suggested all Muslims were not fanatics, he insisted Islamic teaching dictates that Muslims will never live in harmony with 'us'. All in all, the forum turned out to be

an indoctrination session designed to reinforce prejudices against Muslims, bizarrely interspersed with enthusiastic audience renditions of Christmas carols and our national anthem' (Kelly 2008:16).

The gathering attracted the attention of the mainstream media. The tabloid newspaper, the *Daily Telegraph* picked up on rumours (that proved to be inaccurate) that Australia Day, 26 January 2008 would see a riot such as occurred in Cronulla in 2005 (Hildebrand 2008, Morgan 2007, Noble 2009) and which also took place in the context of tensions between Anglo Australians and those from Middle Eastern backgrounds.

The anti-school campaign certainly did not enjoy universal local support. The mainstream metropolitan media attention disturbed many locals who feared that the school's strident opponents would come to symbolize Camden, they would be tarred with the same brush and outsiders would see the area as an enclave of parochialism and xenophobia. The editor of the *Camden Advertiser* was among those to express dismay at the bad press stating that: 'the Sydney media is giving Camden the Campbelltown treatment: it only rates a mention if something has gone wrong' (Senescall 2008a:4)[3]. The *Camden Advertiser* published numerous letters decrying the school opponents as vocal bigots and Catholic leaders criticized the Reverend Fred Nile for using 'the bible to divide anything' (Bowie 2008a:3, 2008b:5).

Nevertheless, rumours and public accusations circulated suggesting that the school would represent a sort of moral fifth column, undermining educational norms and indoctrinating students. To address these the Quranic Society was forced to declare that the school would not be restricted to those from Muslim families, that girls would not be required to wear a headscarf and the school would comply with time restrictions on the teaching of religious studies that applied in state schools (Stringa 2008:1, 10). This did nothing to ease the hostility and tensions against Muslims.

In March 2008, *ABC* program *Four Corners* screened excerpts of racist opponents expressing anti-Muslim comments from the different anti-school rallies. *ABC* audiences were reminded of the Islamophobia in Camden (*Four Corners* 2008). The local newspaper editor criticized the report:

> The camera panned across the crowd as a voice-over described the people of Camden as 'God fearing' folk who opposed the school. No chance of mentioning that only some people from Camden are against the school, not all. Or that not everyone from this area can be represented by a woman in a hat and Drizabone claiming the people behind the school 'have terrorists amongst them' (Senescall 2008b:4).

---

3   Campbelltown, the region adjacent to Camden, had been the focus of a media blitz during street rioting in the Macquarie Fields district in 2005

Former Labor Leader of the Federal Opposition, Mark Latham, weighed into the debate in April 2008 in a newspaper article identifying a 'racist streak' and saying 'by any rational assessment, the school makes sense' on planning grounds (Latham 2008:16). Charlie Lynn responded by claiming that anti-Islamic hostility was the fault of the Bali Bombings, Sydney gang-rapes, 9/11 and 'radical Islamic mullahs' (Lynn 2008:18). On 27 May 2008, the Camden Council rejected the application on 'planning grounds' accepting a report compiled by staff that the school would create 'potential traffic troubles ... parking safety risks, inadequate footpaths and a high reliance on private transport' (Senescall and Bowie 2008).

The Quranic Society appealed against the decision in the NSW Land and Environment Court. In the hearing the advocate for the Quranic Society, was forced, in the face of public disquiet, to argue there was no 'evidence that Muslim schools in Sydney require an increase in police presence' (Bowie 2009b). Camden Council's position in Court included: the school was incompatible with 'rural' Camden and not 'environmentally sensitive', would create unreasonable 'uneconomic' demand of public services (interestingly, 'police' resources were mentioned as though the school would increase crime), noise and traffic, and that "Muslims would seek to dominate the public space and the world view of the Quranic Society is 'not compatible" with the Australian egalitarian culture' (Bowie 2009a). The Council attempted to argue that the Quranic Society had links with a terrorist organization. This was ruled out by the Commissioner (Bowie 2009c). On 2 June 2009, the Court rejected the Quranic Society's appeal on the grounds that the school did not 'conform' to the rural character of the proposed site, however rejected every other planning and environmental objection in the council's decision.

Popular Memory for Global Times

The Islamic school proposal elicited a popular memory of place that legitimized a particular national popular vision.. As the Popular Memory Group at the Centre for Contemporary Cultural Studies argued that: *We must include all the ways in which a sense of the past is constructed in our society. These do not necessarily take a written or literary form. Still less do they conform to academic standards or canons of truthfulness.* (1982, p.207). Popular memory is always situated and conjunctural. The past/present connection is constantly redefined, with particular narratives assuming prominence at different moments. The Camden dispute involved the mobilization of a pioneering memory of place, a localized version of the larger narrative of nation. This has long been part of the sense of Camden's local heritage but assumes a larger significance in the context of the perceived threat from outsiders.

A large sign on the main road into Camden announces that drivers are about to enter the 'Birth Place of the Nation's Wealth'. The story of Camden's founding is a microcosm of a larger national mythology of settlement. This region saw the establishment of the Australian wool industry, which was central to colonial wealth. In the early nineteenth century settler John Macarthur successfully petitioned Colonial Secretary Lord Camden, to obtain five thousand acres to the south west of Sydney to run livestock (Atkinson 1988:10). He named one of the areas 'Camden Park' and soon developed thriving business growing fine Merino wool. The town of Camden was established later and was situated within what was known as the Macarthur district.

The celebration of this pioneer legacy is central to the local sense of place. It appears the Camden 'story' told in the local museum, on the local council website and in some published histories of the district (Wringley 2001, Mylrea 2002). While in recent times the Aboriginal movement and its supporters have waged a resolute campaign against the idea of the glorious opening up of the 'uncharted spaces' of Australia – telling counter narratives of dispossession and genocide – local histories have remained resolutely impervious to this postcolonial message. If the narrative of 'peaceful settlement' has been questioned at a national level in the last thirty years (for instance, see Manne 2003), the pioneering mythology still has a peculiar local resilience in places like Camden. It served to provide the longstanding residents with the moral authority to speak on matters of development, with the prerogative to arbitrate on matters of local heritage and character.

So celebratory pioneering histories were not simply official constructions, they formed part of the lived understanding of place that informed the campaign against the Quranic society's development proposal. They echoed in the words used by opponents of the school. For example, the local council received numerous letters of opposition that invoked heritage and local character. One such letter read:

> Camden is the birth of the Australian Wool industry, and its culture has been that of a rural community. This will obviously change for the worse. Generations of families have built this town from nothing, to what they see as their idyllic living conditions now (Letter to Camden Council, henceforth LCC, received 8 November 2007).

Another wrote of the: 'Historical importance of the Camden area the birth place of Australia's wealth and agriculture. Camden and surrounds needs to be protected from over development' (LCC received 8 November 2007). This simultaneously invokes rurality and historical significance. A further correspondent wrote to the Council: 'Remember the slogan when you cross into this town. We ARE the birthplace of this nations [sic] wealth! If they [Council] cannot preserve the rest of this area, at least fight for the remaining part to which our ancestors built this country on' (LCC received 1 November 2007). Other objectors were more explicit in making the link between the local and global cultural conflict, characterizing the Islamic community as invaders: 'I may be paranoid but I think they have a hidden agenda, to take over by stealth as much of Sydney as possible and what better place to really make a statement than a heritage area and the 'Birthplace of the Nation'' (LCC received 10 November 2007).

For many locals the pioneering legacy is not just expressed in narrative form, it is observable and concrete, etched in the landscape, expressed in the architecture and objects. At the first public rally, a journalist interviewed a protestor who stated:

> ...if you want to go back to the heritage of the area, the farm that [adjoins] the property that they've [the Quranic Society] bought, I've milked there every day or something like that, there are still furrow marks from the First Fleet, there's still ploughs and things in those paddocks from the First Fleet, and they want to build this [monstrosity] ... (*Four Corners* 2008).

Another local farmer, Edgar Downs, in an interview with *The Australian* newspaper said that in the past there were approximately 100 farms, and now there are fewer than ten (Wilson 2008). Downs declared 'This is the last of a little Oasis', arguing that the local residents will move away from Camden 'if the rural character of the region keeps disappearing'. A journalist for the same publication echoed these thoughts: 'While other parts of Australia have already felt the growing pains of change, Camden represents a fault line between the old and the new, between the nation's historic character and everything that change represents' (Wilson 2008).

Islamic Folk Devils

The key theorists of moral panics argue that an episode of heightened public alarm about a particular outrage leads to demonization of those deemed responsible (frequently youth and cultural minorities). Folk devils represent the obverse of conventional moral rectitude. They are 'visible reminders of what we should not be' (Cohen 2002:2), and 'the personification of evil.. stripped of all favourable characteristics and imparted with exclusively negative ones' (Goode & Ben-Yehuda 1994:28). The events surrounding the Camden school proposal did not in themselves constitute a moral panic. The apparatus of policing and criminal justice system were not called into action, nor did the attempt to establish the Islamic school precipitate legislative or policy changes, processes that are central to the moral panic framework (Al-Natour 2010:582). However, the opponents of the school were able to gather symbolic ammunition in support of their cause from a series of past moral panics in Australia that were focused on Islam and Muslims. The education plans of the Quranic Society in south western Sydney were weighed down by this legacy of the stereotyping and silencing. The common element of these Islamophobic moral panics was that minority cultural practice is a challenge to the conventional national moral economy and threatens to impose a communal extraterritoriality.

Most of those opposing the school argued that Islam was antithetical to the Australian way of life. One Council letter stated:

Muslims are not welcome here or anywhere else in Australia. This would be a sad day for Camden if this school was allowed to be built in our community. They have blatantly stated time and time again that they do not want to have anything to do with our culture or our way of life. All other nationalities and cultures [which] have come to this country have helped to build this wonderful country to what it is today. They have no respect for western ways and their ultimate goal is to force their beliefs upon us by whatever means possible. If this school goes ahead, the next thing will be mosques followed by riots and who knows what else (LCC, received 8 November 2007)

Many of the concerns (both tacit and openly expressed) were based on the alleged threat posed by people (especially men) from Islamic backgrounds to law and order. Several of those who objected to the Islamic school referred to the stigmatized areas of relatively high Middle East immigrant communities, the middle ring of suburbs to Sydney's west. A moral panic that followed from a drive-by shooting at Lakemba Police Station in 1998 – blamed on Lebanese criminal gangs – – saw the emergence of 'the Arab Other is the pre-eminent folk devil of our time' (Poynting et al 2004:3). This along with a notorious stabbing of a young teenager around the same time encouraged the tabloid media to represent districts with high numbers of Arabs/Muslims as crime-plagued no-go zones terrorized by Lebanese youth gangs (Collins et al 2000:223). Crime reporting used ethnic identifiers like 'Lebanese' and 'of Middle Eastern appearance' (White 2007:46-8) and a Middle Eastern Gangs Squad was formed in the NSW police force. Public alarm was amplified by a range of key moral entrepreneurs – from talk-back radio hosts, to police and parliamentarians– who successfully advocated for zero-tolerance policing in the affected districts (Collins et al 2000:38).

The earlier moral panic echoed in the public debates in the Camden case. Opponents of the Quranic Society development claimed that the school would inevitably attract Islamic migration to Camden and that this would be accompanied by an epidemic of violent crime:

I have nothing against the Muslim culture, but Camden cannot logistically tolerate this invasion (LCC, received 16 December 2007)

My family & I lived peacefully in the Canterbury-Bankstown district for 15 years until the 1980's [sic]. After large numbers of Middle Eastern Muslims had moved into Campsie- Belmore – Lakemba & surrounding areas major crime escalated to an alarming degree. These Hoons had no respect for women, police or anyone else. I remember an occasion when they sprayed Lakemba police station during a night of drive by shootings in the area. A crime epidemic will erupt if this proposal is approved & there will be grave consequences (LCC received 13 November 2007)

Is Camden police force large enough to handle any more problems if any arise through the building of another high school so close to the one already there and with the knowledge that there [sic] religion is against integration (LCC, received 14 November 2007).

Some interviewees also expressed concerns about possible inter-communal conflict among youth

I haven't lived in Bankstown, or been there, but I know of places like Cabramatta and Parramatta, and they are just totally havoc, you can't walk around the streets there in broad daylight and it's just scary, I mean, gangs of foreigners everywhere (Juliet – interviewee 12/08/2009)

You know, groups of young Lebanese dickheads, you can tell by the look of them that they are out to cause trouble. But, I have had little run-ins with people like that in the past, and that's why I am against the school (Thomas – interviewee 1/10/2009)

Others catalogued the prospective crime wave more specifically and introduced the spectre of sexual violence

... there was a lot of rubbish going on at the time as well... About those rapes and all that, it's still in people's minds, it was a thought, they thought they are getting these people, they never thought "oh we are getting the good people" (Aaron - interviewee 22/07/2009)

In 2000 and 2002, two groups of young men from Islamic backgrounds were convicted of gang rape in separate cases in Sydney (Saniotis, 2004). The reporting on these crimes treated 'culture' and 'religion' as key variables, as if Islam provided the perpetrators with a patriarchal sanction for their actions (Dagistanli 2007:181). Although the perpetrators were themselves Australian-born, it was their perceived foreignness and lack of Australian values that was widely represented as producing their deviance (Dagistanli 2007:190). The events were represented in the popular media as 'inter-ethnic conflict' (Grewal 2007:131) with the implication that Islam and misogyny were synonymous. Poynting et al. similarly point out the dominant images of sexual deviancy and hyper-masculinity in their description of the Arab Other:

...depreciation of all women, oppression and subjection of their own women, denigrating 'western' women as immoral and sexually promiscuous, sexual violence towards 'white'/Caucasian/western women as a manifestation of bitterness and hatred towards the 'west'. Arab and Muslim cultures are thus ideologically represented as backward, brutal and misogynistic, and their masculinities present a problem to be firmly rectified (2004:151).

Local resident, Judith Bond, spoke in the Land and Environment Court hearing on the development application, warned that the Camden community was at risk of 'a surge in gang rapes' (*field notes* 22/04/2009).

The public fears based on moral panics around culture and criminality in Australia converged with wider concerns about global terrorism. The attacks of 9/11 and the Bali bombings of 2002 (in which 88 Australians were among the 190 who died) (*Four Corners* 2003) sharpened the sense of popular vulnerability and provided fuel to those promoting Islamophobia. In public discourse 9/11 was framed as an attack on Western civilisation, and the values of 'liberty, democracy and freedom' were at odds with a 'backward, oppressive and uncivilised Islam' (Aly & Walker 2007:206). 9/11 had adverse impacts on Australian Arab/Muslim communities, with a sharp rise in racist hate crime. It also set back the cause of multiculturalism.

In the Land and Environment Court, Kate McCulloch, unsuccessfully petitioned the Court to allow 'culture' to become a factor involved in the assessment of the application. In a convoluted speech, McCulloch claimed that the establishment of an Islamic school in Camden would attract Arab 'terrorists'.

> Over the years with the September 11th, the Bali bombings, Madrid bombings, the bombings in the Philippines, over in London bombings, I find it a deep atrocity. I turn on my television at night and I am moved by what is happened to many children and women, all because of religion (*field notes* 22/04/2009).

Although considering the prospect of terrorism and cultural conflict were well beyond the court's remit, McCulloch was not alone in using the case to peddle prejudice and to make the connection between the global and the local. Pain's concept of 'globalised fear' is helpful in explaining how the image of the international terrorist becomes domesticated. She writes:

> By 'globalized fear' I mean the powerful metanarrative that is currently popular in analyses of the relation of fear, terror and security. There are two senses in which these metanarratives of fear can be considered 'global'. The first is the idea, more often implicit than worked through, that emotions are being produced and circulate on a global scale; this has become prominent within much recent political analysis of security and terrorism, including work in human geography. The second sense in which these explanations and processes are 'global' ones is that they tend to be prioritised and discussed as though they apply to everyone all of the time (Pain 2009:468).

Further, Pain argues that globalised fear is central to discourses on whiteness. She writes: 'As they are presently construed, the subjects of rapidly moving global fear are white people living in the west, faced with fears about others harming them and their way of life from near or afar' and this leads to a development of the culture of fear (Pain 2009:473). This 'glocalisation' of fear is clearly illustrated in the hyperbolic rhetoric used by opponents of the Camden school.

Fault Lines between Global, National and Local

The Camden case demonstrates the complicated symbolic articulations of global, national and local. The events of 2007-2009 took place amidst growing popular fears about the effects of globalisation on Australian society and this is frequently played out in terms of the politics of urban space. Sassen has charted the emergence of global cities and their key role as the hubs of international capitalism and finance (Sassen 1997). She argues that economic processes can disarticulate global cities from the hinterlands and regions in which they are situated. Such cities have more in common with others around the world than with nearby towns and cities. As travel, communication and cultural infrastructure become increasingly centralised, so the bonds between metropole and province become looser. The time-space compression (Massey 2007) has produced webs of connection between distant places that begin to undermine those within the nation.

Globalization generates both metropolitan cultural diversity and social polarization. Global cities attract both a professional elite many of whose needs (childcare, services of various sorts) are provided by a class of low paid immigrant workers. Such urban settings with disparities of wealth and power can be the sites of inter-communal tensions involving cultural minorities. The immigrant minorities in Sydney, including those from Middle Eastern and Muslim backgrounds, tend to concentrate in the middle ring suburbs, beyond the gentrified inner city, areas that underwent considerable growth in the decades following World War II, areas like the Bankstown, Parramatta and Auburn, places that, as we have seen, are highly stigmatized. Much of the privately owned housing in outer suburbs is less culturally diverse, the locus of 'white-flight' of movement by those Anglo Australians who are dissatisfied with the multicultural character of the older suburbs. The attractions of new master-planned estates that are springing up in outer Western Sydney, including Camden, relate to the popular perception that they house a more monocultural population. Few members of cultural minorities can afford to purchase or rent housing in such places. As in Cronulla where race riots occurred in 2005, Camden has heretofore accommodated a largely lower middle class Anglo majority, many of whom are fiercely parochial. Their presence as a beleaguered community on the edge of an increasingly globalised city has engendered a form of 'battler parochialism' that is encoded as a rugged Australian independence, holding the line against urban multiculturalism. This is reminiscent of the version of radical Australian nationalism common in the late nineteenth and early twentieth centuries, a time in which all political parties fiercely opposed Chinese immigration.

Central to Australian national mythologies has been a disdain for and mistrust of those in positions of authority, an irreverence for the formality and pomp of nation. The central myths of nation are populist, celebrating the achievements of humble characters rather than great men – from the founding narratives of hairy-chested pioneering endeavour to the tales of military and sporting gallantry. Some of those who took part in the Camden protests embodied and represented a bellicose and revanchist representation of Australia, very much tied to the idea of White Australia, protected from competition from foreign labour. At the second major anti-school rally this was particularly apparent. Some local residents in Camden sported the Australian flag and defiantly chanted 'Aussie cheers' that are usually heard at sporting events, affirming how the local boundaries of Camden were marked simultaneously with national borders. At the 2008 Council decision to reject the school, a television journalist asked a protestor why they were wearing an Australian flag. The protestor reacted harshly and accused the journalist's network of being 'against Australia'. These various 'nationalistic' actions against a *local* development application illustrate how popular fears turn the building of a school into a national issue.

Conclusion

In the cultural politics surrounding the Islamic school proposal the locality became a battle ground in a larger global struggle. In the view of many of the school's opponents, the city had been surrendered to the forces of globalisation and multicultural disorder. Their campaign was much more than the expression of provincial racism. It was a communitarian defence of the perceived integrity of nation. The mobilization in defence of locality was based on a mistrust of governments and political process, a sense that the nation state was being rendered impotent in the face of the forces of globalisation such that it was up to *them* to defend cultural authority over space (Hage 1998), to take up the cudgels against the invaders in the neighbourhood. The formal political boundaries of nation no longer correspond with the boundaries of imagined community (Anderson 1991). The south-west edge of Sydney represented to them the tectonic plate between the space of authentic national integrity and the anarchic inter-communal disorder. The Camden case demonstrates how an apparently minor local struggle can become metaphorically connected to larger travails and can assume a much larger significance. The campaign against the school was played out as a communitarian nationalist defence of territory. The campaign by those who spoke against the school's establishment was shrill and hyperbolic, drawing on the crude vocabulary/ imagery of moral demonization and cultural belligerence. It took place against the backdrop of several recent moral panics directed against the Arab Other, the narratives of pioneering local history of Anglo-European prosperity, and the growth of a diverse global city encroaching on Camden's doorstep.

References

Al-Natour, R. 2010. Folk devils and the proposed Islamic school in Camden. *Continuum*, 24 (4), 573-85.

Aly, A., and Walker, D. 2007. Veiled Threats: Recurrent Cultural Anxieties in Australia. *Journal of Muslim Minority Affairs*, 27 (2), 203-214.

AM (2007) Islamic School Plans Fire Up Locals. Reporter Michael Vincent. ABC Radio Transcript. 20 December. [Accessed: 24 June 2011]. Available at: http://www.abc.net.au/am/content/2007/s2123570.htm

Anderson, B. 1991 *Imagined Communities: Reflections on the Origin and Spread of Nationalism.* London: Verso.

Atkinson, A1988. *Camden: Farm and Village Life in Early New South Wales.* Melbourne: Oxford University Press.

Bowie, A. 2007. Plans lodged for Islamic school. *Camden Advertiser.* 10 October, 3.

Bowie, A. 2008a. Riley slams Nile. *Camden Advertiser.* 30 January, 3

Bowie, A. 2008b. Bishop urges community to reconcile with Muslims. *Camden Advertiser.* 9 January,5.

Bowie, A. 2009a. Camden Council's case', Camden Advertiser. 29 April. [Accessed: 24 June 2011.] Available at: http://www.camdenadvertiser.com.au/news/local/news/general/camden-councils-case/1498544.aspx

Bowie, A. 2009b. Islamic school's fate up to Commissioner now. *Camden Advertiser.* 24 April. [Accessed: 24 June 2011]. Available at: http://www.camdenadvertiser.com.au/news/local/news/general/islamic-schools-fate-up-to-commissioner-now/1495763.aspx?storypage=0.

Bowie, A. 2009c Islamic terrorist link question ruled out. *Camden Advertiser.* 23 April. [Accessed: 24 June 2011]. Available at: http://www.camdenadvertiser.com.au/news/local/news/general/islamic-terrorist-link-question-ruled-out/1494639.aspx.

Cohen, S. 2002 *Folk Devils and Moral Panics.* New York: Routledge.

Collins, J., Noble, G., Poynting, S., and Tabar, P. 2000. *Kebabs, Kids, Cops and Crime: Youth, Ethnicity and Crime.* Sydney: Pluto Press.

Correy, J. 2007a. Muslim school planned. *Macarthur Chronicle.* 16 October, 3.

Correy, J. 2007b Global shame: Pig's heads incident is international news. *Macarthur Chronicle.* 4 December, 1.

Cuming, A., and Marcus, C. 2007 'A town's dirty secret', *Sydney Morning Herald.* 11 November. [Accessed: 24 June 2011]. Available at: http://www.smh.com.au/news/national/a-towns-dirty-secret/2007/11/10/1194329563801.html?page=fullpage#contentSwap1.

Dagistanli, S. 2007 'Like a pack of Wild Animals': Moral Panics Around 'Ethnic' Gang Rape in Sydney, in *Outrageous! Moral Panics in Australia* edited by Poynting, S and Morgan, G., Hobart: ACYS Publishing. 181-196.

Dunn, K. 1999 Mosques and Islamic Centres in Sydney, Representations of Islam and Multiculturalism. Doctoral Thesis: University of Newcastle, NSW.

Dunn, K. 2001. Representations of Islam in the Politics of Mosque Development in Sydney. *Tijdschrift voor Economische en Sociale Geografie.* 22 (3). 291-308.

Dunn, K. 2004. Islam in Australia: Contesting the Discourse of Absence.*Australian Geographer,.* 35(3), 333-353.

Four Corners. 2003. The Bali confessions'. Reporter Sally Neighbour. 10 Febuary. [Accessed 24 June 2011]. Available at: http://www.abc.net.au/4corners/content/2003/transcripts/s780910.htm

Four Corners. 2008. Dangerous ground' Reporter Sally Neighbour. Program transcript. 10 March. [Accessed: 24 June 2011]. Available at: http://www.abc.net.au/4corners/content/2008/s2185494.htm

Goode, E. and Ben-Yehuda, N.1994. *Moral Panics: The Social Construction of Deviance.* New York: Blackwell.

Grewal, K. 2007 Representations of the Young Muslim Man in Australian Public Discourse. *Transforming Cultures e-journal,* 2(1), 116-134.

Hage, G. 1998. *White Nation.* Sydney: Pluto Press.

Hildebrand, J. 2008. Nazis plotting Australia Day race riots', *Daily Telegraph.* 10 January. [Accessed: 24 June 2011]. Available at:http://www.news.com.au/story/0,23599,23028463-421,00.html.

Humphrey, M. 1987. Community, Mosque and Ethnic Politics. *Journal of Sociology.* 23 (2) 233-245.

Johnston, T. 2008. Islamic school proposal ignites fury in Australia. *New York Times.* 9 June. [Accessed: 24 June 2011] Available at:http://www.nytimes.com/2008/06/09/world/asia/09iht-race.1.13568460.html>

Kabir, N. 2004. *Muslims in Australia.* London: Kegan Paul.

Kelly, L. 2008. Your Say, Letters to the Editor, *Camden Advertiser.* 2 January. 16.

Kinsella, E. 2007a. Silent Campaign. *Camden Advertiser.* 31 October. 1 and 11.

Kinsella, E. 2007b. School Angst. *Camden Advertiser.* 7 November. 1 and 8.

Kinsella, E. 2007c. No-Goh policy on mosques and Islamic immigration. *Camden Advertiser.* 14 November. 10.

Kinsella, E. 2007d. Cross Citing of Bible. *Camden Advertiser.* 14 November. 19.

Kinsella, E. 2007e. Hanson Blasts School Plan. *Camden Advertiser,* 21 November. 9.

Kinsella, E. 2007f Rudd Weighs Into School Debate.*Camden Advertiser.* 28 November. 9.

Latham, M. 2008. It's All Right if its All White. *Camden Advertiser.* 9 April. 16.

Lynn, C. 2008. Fear Etched Into Our Minds, *Camden Advertiser.* 16 April. 18.

Macarthur Chronicle 2007. 'Agents Deny anti-Muslim selling tactics'. 11 December. 6.

Manne, R., 2003 Introduction, in *Whitewash*, edited by Manne, R. Melbourne: Black Inc,1-16

Massey, D. 2007 *World City.* Cambridge: Polity Press.

Morgan, G 2007 ' Not Drowning Waving. The Cronulla Riots and the Decline of Cosmopolitanism' in Faccioli, P and J.Gibbons (eds) *Framing Globalization.*

Visual Perspectives Newcastle-upon-Tyne: Cambridge Scholars' Press 144-157

Murphy, Damien., 2008 'Am I the New Pauline Hanson? I Hope So', *Sydney Morning Herald*. 31st May. [Accessed 24 June 2011]. Available at: http://www.smh.com.au/articles/2008/05/30/1211654312801.html

Mylrea, P 2002 *Camden District: A History to the 1840s.*Camden: Camden Historical Society.

Noble, G., 2009 'Where the bloody hell are we?' Multicultural manners in a world of hyperdiversity', in *Lines in the Sand: The Cronulla Riots, Multiculturalism and National Belonging*, edited by Noble, G. Sydney: Institute of Criminology Series, 1-22

Pain, R., 2009 'Globalized fear? Towards an emotional geopolitics', *Progress in Human Geography*. 33 (4), 466-486.

Popular Memory Group 1982 Popular memory: theory, politics, method, in *Making Histories. Studies in history-writing and politics*, edited by Johnson, R., McLennan, G., Schwarz, B. and D. Sutton.London: Hutchinson, 205-252.

Poynting, S., Noble, G., Tabar, P. and Collins, J., 2004 *Bin Laden in the Suburbs; Criminalising the Arab Other*. Sydney: Institute of Criminology.

Saniotis, A. 2004 Embodying ambivalence: Muslim Australians as 'other', *Journal of Australian Studies*. 82, 49-59

Sassen, S. 1997 *The Global City: New York, London, Tokyo*. Princeton University Press: Princeton.

Sassen, S. 1997 *The Global City: New York, London, Tokyo*. Princeton: Princeton University Press.

Senescall, R. and Bowie, A. 2008 Council unanimously rejects Muslim School – – listen to Mayor's speech and see slideshow, *Camden Advertiser* 27th May. [Accessed: 21 June 2011]. Available at: http://www.camdenadvertiser.com.au/news/local/news/general/council-unanimously-rejects-muslim-school-listen-to-mayors-speech-and-see-slideshow/775511.aspx

Senescall, R. and Bowie, A. 2007 'Anti-School Forum Draws Hundreds, *Camden Advertiser*. 20 December. [Accessed: 24 June 2011]. Available at: http://camden.yourguide.com.au/news/local/news/general/antischool-forum-draws-hundreds/195820.aspx.

Senescall, R. 2007.It's time we embraces openness. *Camden Advertiser*. 17 October. 4.

Senescall, R. 2008a. Fair go denied by Sydney media. *Camden Advertiser*. 30 January. 4.

Senescall, R. 2008b.Diversity's darker side our shame. *Camden Advertiser*. 12 March, 4.

Stringa, P. 2008. Muslims respond. Camden Advertiser. 6 February. 1, 10

Tibbitts, A. 2007 Pig heads left on pikes – but no one seems shocked, *Sydney Morning Herald*. 29 November. [Accessed 24 June 2011]. Available at: http://www.smh.com.au/news/national/pig-heads-left-on-pikes--but-no-one-seems-shocked/2007/11/28/1196036983979.html

White, R. 2007 Taking It to the Streets: The Larrikins and the Lebanese in *Outrageous! Moral Panics in Australia* edited by Poynting, Scott, & Morgan, George Hobart: ACYS Publishing, 40-52.

Wilson, A., 2008. Change poisons Camden's old 'oasis', *Australian*. 14 June. [Accessed 24 June 2011]. Available at: http://www.theaustralian.com.au/news/change-poisons-camdens-old-oasis/story-e6frg6o6-1111116630981

Wrigley, J. 2001.*A History of Camden, New South Wales*, Camden: Camden Historical Society.

Chapter 7

Perverse Muslim Masculinities in Contemporary Orientalist Discourse: The Vagaries of Muslim Immigration in the West

Selda Dagistanli and Kiran Grewal

This chapter explores a series of highly-publicized gang rape incidences in Australia and France which contributed to the emergence of moral panics not only in these national contexts but fed into a more globalised and globalising discourse. Through the identification of the perpetrators as young Muslim men, popular debate drew heavily on classic Orientalist scripts of the perversity of Muslim masculinity, alongside reference to current geo-political concerns around immigration, terrorism and managing ethnic diversity. From these rapes the concept of the 'tournantes' – literally translated as 'taking turns' – was appropriated by Neo-Nazi and white supremacist websites in various locations across the West and used to promote an international moral panic on the moral vagaries/evils of immigration from Islamic countries: a position that was strikingly similar to the anti-multicultural arguments presented within mainstream immigration debates in Europe and Australia.

In tracing the trajectory of localized moral panics around 'Muslim' gang rape in France and Australia into global discourses of contemporary Orientalism and Islamophobia, this chapter explores three inter-related factors. First, the local anxieties that are caused by the shrinking of borders between East and West as a result of immigration and globalisation; second, the technologically mediated associations (in racist websites, blogs and other media) that are made between gang rape and discourses of Islamophobic anti-multiculturalism; and finally, the wider orientalist connections made between Islam and violence in a post-September 11 context. Whilst the parameters of the particular discourses on the gang rapes in Australia and France differed, depending on the specific local concerns and nationalist vocabulary, a certain common discourse emerged: one in which the Muslim man is constructed as sexual and civilisational threat. Not only does this threat perform a particular function in reinforcing dominant power structures within each of these nations, as the proliferation of internet sites and their universalisation of the problem of 'Muslim gang rape' demonstrates, the figure of the 'Muslim gang rapist' has provided added justification for Islamophobic and anti-multicultural discourses across the West.

'Muslim Gang Rapes' in Sydney, Australia

In Australia, from 2001 to 2002, there was substantial media coverage of a set of group sexual assaults perpetrated, a year earlier, by 'Lebanese-Muslim' young men in Sydney's south west. Police informants had telephoned a reporter with a story about the upcoming trials of gang attacks on young women of 'Caucasian' backgrounds by Australian born youth of Lebanese background. The crimes were newsworthy for the brutal and horrific nature of the attacks. Accordingly, prominent press coverage provided sordid detail about the rapes, the ordeal of the victims, and the callous and degrading actions of the offenders. Mainstream Sydney newspapers (both tabloid and broadsheet) such as *The Daily Telegraph*, *The Sunday Telegraph*, *Sydney Morning Herald*, *The Sun-Herald* and *The Australian*, reported that on some occasions, the perpetrators – via text messages and phone calls – invited their friends to take turns sexually assaulting the victims. The fact that a majority of these men came from Lebanese Muslim backgrounds was emphasized by the intense, ideologically driven media coverage and led to widespread public outrage. This all culminated in the ringleader, Bilal Skaf, being sentenced at first instance to an unprecedented 55 years in prison with a non-parole period of 40 years (Warner 2004; Gleeson 2004).[1]

The basis for this highly publicized detail was that the perpetrators had apparently asked the young women before attacking them, whether they had 'Arabic blood'[2] or 'Arabic boyfriends', had called them 'Aussie pigs' and told them they deserved it because they were 'Australian' (Poynting 2002; Warner 2004). Conservative sections of the media and politicians exploited the comments uttered by the perpetrators to promote an overtly anti-multicultural agenda. Regarding the racial, ethnic and religious overtones of the group sexual assaults, a Sydney newspaper, *The Sun-Herald* on 29 July 2001, carried the headlines: '70 Girls Attacked by Rape Gangs', 'Police Warning on New Race Crime' and 'Caucasian women the targets' (Kidman 2001: 1). These headlines misrepresented and exaggerated the facts around the attacks: the women were not all Caucasian nor were there 70 attacks.[3] Another article in the *Daily Telegraph* read: 'In a

---

1   This sentence was subsequently reduced on appeal to a head sentence of 46 years with a non-parole period of 30 years by the NSW Court of Criminal Appeal (R v Bilal Skaf [2005] NSWCCA 297). The reduction of the sentence was based on the case not falling into the 'worst category' of aggravated sexual assault and was met with outrage for being too lenient.

2   This was significant because homogenised categories of 'Arab', 'Middle Eastern', 'Lebanese' and 'Muslim' had been conflated in the public imagination.

3   That this was an ideological description became apparent because the victims were reported as 'Australian' regardless of ethnic or racial background – in marked contrast to the perpetrators who were described as 'Lebanese', regardless of the fact that the perpetrators were all born in Australia. In fact, of the seven victims of the rapes, there were two girls of Italian background, one of Greek and one of Aboriginal parentage (Fickling 2002; ADB 2003: 82n). These were among the victims who secured convictions.

chilling racial development, some of the victims said they were being asked if they were true Australians before being attacked by the youths, believed to be of Middle-Eastern extraction' (Miranda 2000: 14). This media coverage had the effect of establishing the rapes as race hate crimes against white Australian women, notwithstanding the fact that the victims were of mixed ethnic and racial backgrounds (Fickling 2002; ADB 2003: 82n).

Other cases of gang rape committed by Muslim youth further added to the smouldering disquiet about Muslim criminality, immigration, and 'Middle Eastern gang rape' (see Poynting et al. 2004; Dagistanli 2007). A group sexual assault case involving Lebanese, Muslim background youth, *R v AEM (Snr), AEM (Jnr) & KEM* (2001), was also swept into the debate that conflated 'Muslim' crime, sexual assault and immigration, aided by the fact that the case went to trial at the same time as public outcries around 'illegal' immigrants. During the trial, conservative sections of the media reported that the crimes were racially motivated and state politicians, eager for electoral advantage, readily agreed. At the same time, the gang rapes also served to legitimate an increasingly dominant 'law and order' discourse that justified harsher and more punitive models of social control (Johns et al.: 2001). Judge Megan Latham, before whom the offenders were tried, did not succumb to the media campaign, nor did she agree that there was evidence before her that the attacks were racially motivated (Warner 2004: 347). Latham J:

> sentenced AEM, aged 19 years, to 6 years imprisonment (4 years minimum), his 16-year-old brother KEM to 5 years 7 months (3 years 6 months minimum) and a third youth to 18 months for detaining with intent to hold to advantage. Another youth, MM, a cousin of the brothers, was sentenced later to an effective sentence of 6 years with a minimum of 4 years (Warner 2004: 347).

These sentences, because of their perceived leniency, 'left the tabloids and the talkback opinion-vendors, and the politicians who are so much at their mercy... as well as the Police Commissioner, disappointed and outraged' (Poynting et al. 2004: 130). As a result the Department of Public Prosecutions (DPP) appealed and succeeded in obtaining increased sentences in the New South Wales Court of Criminal Appeal. This was followed by the introduction of legislation creating a new offence of aggravated sexual assault in company with a maximum penalty of 'life imprisonment' (Johns et al. 2001; Warner 2004). Skaf and others involved in the Bankstown cases were tried under these new laws, as were others in cases that followed.

In 2002, yet another group sexual assault was committed by four Pakistani immigrant Muslim brothers and their friend. The two eldest brothers chose to represent themselves, claiming that the courts, police and government were complicit in an anti-Muslim conspiracy of which they were the latest victims (Sheehan 2006: 161). In so doing, they unwittingly reinforced a popular link that had been made between gang rape and Muslim immigration (see Humphrey 2007). The brothers' insistence on self representation resulted in a new law being rushed through parliament preventing the accused in sexual assault trials from directly cross-examining complainants. The value of this development is not in question. However the haste with which the law was passed reflects the remarkable conversion of conservative forces to the cause of complainants' rights in sexual assault cases; in the past they were more likely to blame victims for sexual attacks – particularly if those victims were acquainted with the perpetrators, were intoxicated or behaved and dressed 'provocatively' (AGD 2006; Chung et al. 2006). Later in the trials, conservative journalists and tabloid newspapers who were infamous for their anti-feminist views mounted a 'victims' rights' campaign based on the 'Muslim gang rapes'.[4]

Meanwhile some commentators also picked up on reports of a gang rape phenomenon known as '*les tournantes*" in France and utilized them to demonstrate a cultural specificity to the crime of rape, based on its connection with Muslim immigrant populations (Albrechtsen 2002; Brearley 2002; Priest 2004; Sheehan 2001). Janet Albrechtsen, a columnist in *The Australian* went as far as to quote 'French and Danish experts' to support her claim that this was a problem of culture and religion. She was ultimately exposed by the media watchdog programme on the ABC, *MediaWatch*, as having doctored her quotes.[5] However, by this stage the connection had already been made and iterated across a range of popular and official discourses and Albrechtsen's international reference added to this broader discourse. A proliferation of web-blogs and articles appeared suggesting that the events in Australia must be seen as part of a broader mode of behaviour exhibited by Muslim men.

The French Example: Les Tournantes

While the links between Islam and gang rape were made explicitly in Australian media coverage of the Sydney rapes, in France the alleged relationship between Muslim populations and sexual violence emerged in a slightly less direct manner. The issue of '*les tournantes*' became the subject of media attention after the release of the film *La Squale* in November 2000, which portrayed a gang of young men of the *banlieue*[6] – mainly (but not only) from immigrant backgrounds who lure and

---

4   The contention that complainants' rights were suddenly a priority is not based solely on the fact that self-represented accused were no longer allowed to cross examine complainants. Indeed one of the conservative journalists, Miranda Devine, (well known for an anti-multicultural stance) who was quite vocal in her purported protection of women's rights in these cases, had, a couple of years earlier, lamented the waywardness of young women who 'showed vast tracts of flesh' and sent 'mixed messages' that men were likely to misinterpret (Devine 2004:15).

5   For full details see the Media Watch website - http://www.abc.net.au/mediawatch/rassial.htm.

6   Poor housing estates on the periphery of major French cities.

gang rape young women (also from immigrant backgrounds). The first reported criminal trials involving '*les tournantes*' followed in 2001 and in 2002 a victim of '*les tournantes*', Samira Bellil published her autobiography, *Dans L'Enfer des Tournantes* ('In the hell of the *Tournantes*'). Following the murder of a young woman called Sohane Benziane, who was set alight by young men in a cellar in the *banlieue* in which she lived, a highly publicized women's march under the banner *'Ni Putes, Ni Soumises'* ('Neither Sluts Nor Slaves') took place throughout France on 1 February 2003 with Sohane's sister and Samira Bellil the figureheads of the movement.

In his detailed study of media treatment of '*les tournantes*', Laurent Mucchielli (2004) noted a number of important features. The first was a disproportionate degree of both reporting and condemnation when compared with general attitudes to sexual violence. The second was an over-emphasis on the novelty of the phenomenon of gang rape within French society. Finally, Mucchielli noted a clear 'cultural' undertone to many of the attempts to both situate and explain the rapes.

As noted above, while Islam was specifically named in the Australian discourses as contributing to the rapists' attitudes and behaviour, such overt reference to religion was not possible in France. The language of Republicanism continues to dominate within French public discourse making identification of specific social or cultural markers unacceptable. However this is not to say that '*les tournantes*' were not associated with Islam within French public imaginary. Rather, the intermediary site of the *banlieue* served to contextualize the crimes, their perpetrators and causes.

Various researchers have demonstrated the manner in which the *banlieue* – historically a site on the periphery – has become fixed within French public discourse as a site of problematic masculinity, criminality, immigration and particularly North African immigrants (Rinaudo 1999; Peralva and Macé 2002; Mucchielli 2004; Grewal 2007b). For this reason the mainstream media's predominant use of the previously unknown *banlieue* slang term *'les tournantes'* – which literally translates as 'taking turns' – rather than the more generic '*viol collectif*' or '*viol en réunion*' (which do appear but less often) is significant. By calling them, '*tournantes*' these gang rapes became specifically located, invoking immediately the imagery of the *banlieue*.

An article in centre-left national broadsheet newspaper *Le Monde* provides a good illustration. In her coverage of the trials for a series of gang rapes committed in the Paris *banlieue* of Argenteuil, Pascale Robert-Diard provides a vivid image of the *banlieue*, a site she describes as a 'parallel' and closed-off world into which the Court had to venture:

> [The Court] followed them [the *banlieue* residents] into the stairwells of filthy basements, into underground 'squats'. It immersed itself in their daily life, punctuated by scholastic failure and the constant movement between middle school, care [temporary housing provided by social services] and the police station. The Court listened to their fathers, Algerians or Moroccans for the

most part, throwing up their arms in a demonstration of their powerlessness or incomprehension at the acts their sons were accused of. The Court tried in vain to get the mothers to speak, women often veiled who stated, 'I agree with my husband...'[7](Robert-Diard 2002)

The standard tropes can all be found in this description: the *banlieue* as site of educational failure and criminality which is ethnically/religiously coded. This is not the only article to do this. Indeed many of the media articles refer to mothers of the rapists wearing headscarves (an obvious symbol of Islam, especially in France with its history of the 'hijab affairs') or reproduce names with particular ethnic affiliations and origins (Tourancheau 2002; Santucci 2001; du Tanney 2001; Geisler 2002)[8] and, on occasion, explicitly refer to the parents being 'immigrants/Moroccan/Algerian/'Maghrébins' (North African)/ Arab' (Durand 2002; Tourancheau 2002; Pech 2002; d'Arrigo 2001) or the rapists being 'Beur'[9] (Tourancheau 2002).

Added to this, the most vocal and frequently cited *banlieue* commentators on *les tournantes* – gang rape survivor Bellil and the association *Ni Putes Ni Soumises* – were often framed as 'authentic insiders' and their (understandable) anger and resentment towards many of the men in their immediate circle became emblematic of a larger problem of Muslim gender relations. For example, in an interview with the left-wing newspaper, *Libération*, Bellil was quoted as stating she would never go out with a *Beur*: 'With anyone else, fine, but not with someone of my own culture! They're either religious (fanatics) or scumbags' (Benabdessadok 2004: 67)[10]. While completely understandable in light of her personal experiences as figurehead for the most prominent *banlieue* association since the *Beur* anti-racism movement of the 1980s, this comment inevitably provided legitimacy to those who saw the problem of misogyny and sexual violence as located within one particular (ethno-religiously marked) site.

So too, while *Ni Putes Ni Soumises* established its reputation as a feminist organisation responding to violence against women in the *banlieue*, the prominent place taken by the association in petitioning for a complete ban on the *hijab* in schools in France served to further reinforce a link between Islam, sexism and sexual violence. In an especially explicit example in *Le Monde*, an article on *'les*

---

7   ' Elle [la Cour] les a suivi de cages d'escalier en souterrains crasseux, de caves en 'squats'. Elle s'est immiscée dans leur quotidien, ponctué d'échecs scholaires et de va-et-vient entre le collège, le foyer d'accueil ou le commissariat de police. Elle a entendu les pères, Algériens ou Marocains pour la majorité, levant les bras en signe d'impuissance ou d'incompréhension devant les faits reprochés à leurs fils. Elle a tenté, vainement, de faire parler les mères, la tête souvent couverte d'un foulard: 'Je dis comme mon mari... '

8   Examples include; 'Moustapha', 'Karim', 'Ousmane', 'Mouloud, 'Kader'.

9   Another commonly used banlieue slang term: an inversion of the word 'Arabe' and used to describe young French citizens of North African heritage.

10   'Avec toute la terre d'accord, mais pas avec quelqu'un de ma culture! C'est soit un religieux soit une racaille'.

tournantes' by Pascale Krémer and Martine Laronche is accompanied by a cartoon depicting a young woman exclaiming, 'Neither the veil nor rape! Whether you like it or not!' [11] (Krémer & Laronche 2002). As French sociologist Éric Macé (2006) commented in an online forum organized by *Le Monde*, the young men of the *banlieue* emerged simultaneously as '*violeurs'* (rapists) and '*voileurs*' (veilers). A clear connection emerged in public discourse between gang rape and Islam.

The 'Muslim Gang Rapist', Moral Panic, and Deeper Anxieties

The interplay between media representations, political rhetoric and legal responses to these cases displays many of the features of the amplified social reaction that defines what Stan Cohen (1972/2002), Hall et al. (1978) and others refer to as 'moral panic' (Goode and Ben-Yehuda 1994; Thompson 1998: 16-19; Garland 2008). To elaborate on the theory, Stan Cohen (2002) most recently described a moral panic as erupting around an event that triggers significant media attention, whereby a certain group are stereotyped and condemned as threatening 'folk devils', followed by typically disproportionate action taken by the State and criminal justice agencies to contain the threat. Often this is enacted through populist law and order debates and excessively punitive measures to cast the folk devils out from society and restore the moral order. Where punitive measures are not implemented directly on the perpetrators (through excessive prison sentences and indirectly, general over-representation of the demonized cultural group in prison), they are realised symbolically through social, political and institutional marginalization or exclusion of the groups to which the perpetrators are thought to belong. Along these lines, Erich Goode and Nachman Ben-Yehuda (1994: 38) argue that 'hostility' towards the folk devils is one of the key components of a moral panic, with the result that those so identified must endure intense public scrutiny, social exclusion and excessive punishment (in comparison to less marginal groups) if they break the law.

Furthermore, the boundaries of a moral panic have been described as volatile. The public concern, media representations and official responses are swift, erupt quickly and subside suddenly (Goode and Ben-Yehuda 1994) typically resulting in hasty, undeliberated policy changes and unbalanced results. Despite their short duration, there is theoretical consensus that moral panics tend to resonate with existing and generalized moral anxieties (Cohen 1972/2002; Hall 1978; Goode and Ben-Yehuda 1994; Garland 2008) which are ongoing and often about separate issues. These are then popularly linked with the specific events that give rise to the volatile 'burst' that defines a moral panic. Goode and Ben-Yehuda refer to these generalized anxieties as "social stress" that occurs during "troubled, difficult, disturbing times" (1994: 36). David Garland refines this further to say that moral panic must have a specific *moral* dimension which results in 'introspective soul

---

11   'Ni Voile! Ni Viol! Que ça vous plaise ou non!'

searching', and that the moral panic is 'symptomatic' of a deeper, wider malaise that society's established values are being fundamentally disturbed (2008: 11).

In the Australian and French gang rape cases, social reactions and public condemnation of the perpetrators and the groups with which they were associated were obvious, volatile and disproportionate. This establishes them as moral panics in the classic sense of the term. More significantly however, the morally repugnant nature of the gang rapes, in both Australia and France, was perceived as *symptomatic* of a pre-established and culturally delineated threat to social and moral boundaries, thus resonating with deeper anxieties.

These anxieties were articulated (often overtly) through an anti-immigration , anti-multicultural and Islamophobic agenda. It was popularly expounded, in both Australian and French contexts, that immigrants from Islamic countries adhered to a moral framework that was fundamentally incompatible with the democratic, liberal values of the West. Homogenized constructions of the gang rapists' culture were represented as diametrically opposed to and aberrant to an imagined Western liberal norm. The gang rapes committed by perpetrators with 'Islamic backgrounds' were upheld as evidence of this. Furthermore, juxtaposed stereotypes of the sexually deviant rapist and the threatening Arab/Muslim invader resulted in an inextricable link between 'rapist' and 'Muslim immigrant invader' in public discourses. This provided validation for wider anxieties that Australian, French and generically 'Western' values, based on democracy and a (Judeo-)Christian framework, were under imminent threat. At the same time, additional justification of a combined anti-multicultural/Islamophobic agenda was found in the misogyny of the offenders: hence the debate could ostensibly proceed under the worthy banner of women's rights and an overarching condemnation of sexual violence.

In the Australian context, the Sydney gang rapes allowed for the creation of the young Muslim man as 'nasty migrant' against whom the 'good white nation' was not only consolidated but also revalidated (Grewal 2007a; Hage 2003). The furore over the gang rapes became entangled with debates about asylum seekers and terrorists (ADB report 2003) such that the violation of 'Australian girls' became symbolic of a much larger threat to the nation (see also Kampmark 2003). A clear dichotomy was established between white Australians as the victims and the Lebanese, Muslim rapists, through an "othering' of the perpetrators and the 'whitening' of the victims' (Poynting et al. 2004: 124). Hence a homogenized Arab/Lebanese, 'Middle Eastern' or Muslim[12] culture was associated with the misogynistic and callous nature of the offenders' actions. These actions became less about the violation of particular women and more symbolic of ethnic invasion or in the words of popular talkback radio presenter Alan Jones, 'first signs of

12   These terms became interchangeable in the public imagination and at times, came under the broad banner of 'race' (see Poynting and Mason 2007; Poynting et al. 2004). This new culturally and religiously conceptualised understanding of race and the homogenisation and discriminatory practices that arise from it, have been referred to as neo-racism (Balibar 1991). We will come back to this point.

Islamic hate against a community which has welcomed them...' (Fickling 2002: n.p.). The rapes were constructed as a powerful metaphorical (and literal) violation of 'Australian values' and, as violators of these values, the perpetrators became folk devils of Middle-Eastern and Muslim extraction and all Middle Eastern young men – Muslim or not – were firmly tarred with the same brush.

Popular anxieties were already rife about 'boat loads' of 'illegal' immigrants from the Middle East in mid-2001, paving the way for a racialized connection to be made about the deviancy of Middle-Eastern (and/or Muslim) people from abroad who were seen to be trespassing on Australian territory (Poynting et al. 2004). It made no difference that the offenders of the so called 'Lebanese gang rapes' were Australian-born (Poynting et al. 2004), the attacks became analogous to a breach of Australian borders by the Muslim Other. Immigration from the Middle East had resulted, so we were told, in a transgression of both moral and geographical boundaries. A clear example can be found in the comments of then Labor Premier of New South Wales, Bob Carr, who said that 'ethnic crime gangs [...were] causing mayhem on the streets [...] because of decisions about immigration made decades ago' (Morris 2001: 8). David Oldfield, then New South Wales Upper House MP of the extreme right-wing One Nation Party, called for the ban of 'Muslim' immigration to Australia and stated:

> Those 14 men did not come to the conclusion that Western women are 'sluts' and 'whores' by themselves, they were indoctrinated with these beliefs by Islamic leaders...The socially primitive nature of Islamic society is evident...in the way they treat their women and, surely now, in the way they treat ours...such backward practices are not acceptable to Australian society (cited in Poynting et al. 2004: 124).

Though previously marginal, extreme right-wing politics such as that espoused by the One Nation party (which was vocally anti-Muslim and against non-Western immigration), entered the mainstream because the social and political climate was already disposed to anti-Muslim and anti-immigration discourse. The idea that Muslim and Australian values are incompatible was also promoted by mainstream political parties. In what came to be known as the 'Tampa crisis' and 'children overboard affair', it was alleged that a fishing boat full of Middle Eastern asylum seekers threw their children overboard to prevent the Australian navy from turning the fishing boat back, when in fact the footage shown was that a boat was sinking and asylum seekers, including children, had to be rescued from the water. Then Liberal Prime Minister John Howard famously remarked: 'I don't want, in Australia, people who would throw their own children into the sea' (Four Corners 2002, cited in Poynting et al 2004: 27). The 'children overboard' allegation was fabricated for federal electoral advantage, and, as Poynting et al assert, 'the imputation that the asylum seekers were bad parents only served to strengthen the popular opinion that refugees would not be good and decent Australians' (2004: 27).

Appropriation of a language of women's rights lent further credibility to an anti-immigration agenda and an increasingly popular opposition to multiculturalism (see Ho 2007). It is important to note that while a heightened public awareness of victims' rights in sexual assault trials was, prima facie, a welcome development, the xenophobic foundations on which a 'women's rights' rhetoric was built was questionable and did not genuinely further the rights of women. Instead it perpetuated rape 'myths' that Australian women are attacked by (non-Australian) strangers while Muslim women (perhaps because they were not popularly perceived as Australian) did not even warrant a mention. In response to exceptional victim portrayals in the media, one academic, Paul Tabar, commented to a Melbourne publication: 'It is a shame we have to be racist to recognize the rights of raped women. It seems to me the fact that the rapists are an 'ethnic other' explains both the exceptional space given to the rape victims and the magnified outrage manifested by the dominant culture' (*The Age* 2002: 3).

Meanwhile, in the French context '*les tournantes*' also contributed to a more general anxiety already present about '*les violences urbaines*'. This term – often associated with the *banlieue* and used to refer to a vast array of issues ranging from delinquency and anti-social behaviour to physical violence – had gained currency in the 1990s (Peralva and Macé 2002; Mucchielli 2004; Schneidermann 2003). The combination of sensationalist media reporting and harsh 'law and order' political rhetoric had established '*les violences urbaines*' as a site of intense public concern into which the allegedly 'new' phenomenon of gang rape now fed. This in turn both resulted in and legitimated heavy handed state responses: most infamously illustrated by the 2005 riots across France and then Minister for the Interior Nicholas Sarkozy's suggestion that the *banlieues* be 'cleansed' using a *Kärcher* high pressure hose. [13]

Moreover, through the identification of young Muslim men as key perpetrators of both '*les violences urbaines*' more generally and '*les tournantes*' specifically, the dominant mythology of the French nation was not only reinforced, it was further legitimated as inherently morally 'good'. As Scott points out:

[The] image of France [as based on Enlightenment principles] is mythical; its power and appeal rests, to a large degree, on its negative portrayal of Islam. The objectification of Muslims as a fixed 'culture' has its counterpart in the mythologizing of France as an enduring 'republic'. Both are imagined to lie outside history – antagonists locked in eternal combat (2007: 7).

Similar to the 'Muslim folk devil' described above in the Australian context, in France the figure of the '*garçon arabe*' (Guénif-Souilamas and Macé 2004) has come to represent the antithesis of the French nation and the site of many of its problems. At the same time Éric Fassin notes a shifting understanding of the Republican value of *l'égalité*, which is no longer associated with questions of equality of race or class but which has specifically become, 'the equality of the sexes'[14] (2003: 8). This sexual equality, or *'démocratie sexuelle'* as he calls it, has become central to *l'exception française*; a form of 'exemplary democracy' (2003: 9), which must be defended at all costs. The French debates around veils and rapes became the basis for a specifically gendered reinstatement of nation and democracy. Meanwhile Nacira Guénif-Souilamas (2006) identifies the development of a form of 'virtuous racism' in France which, through utilising the language of women's rights, has reinforced old French colonial hierarchies through the control of formerly colonized subjects' bodies. The demonized figure of the *'garçon arabe'* is juxtaposed against the idealized figure of the *'beurette'* who is seen as the model of successful integration, whose only obstacle to full modern Enlightenment is the patriarchal and misogynist traditions of her culture of origin. By providing an apparent link between *banlieue* criminality and violence, immigrant (particularly Muslim) men and sexual violence *'les tournantes'* moral panic provided justification for the complete rejection of demands for greater recognition of ethnic difference within the French state.

Australia and France have not been the only nations to see the emergence of a 'Muslim gang rape' moral panic. Similar allegations of ethnically motivated gang rapes have been made in Germany, Sweden, Denmark and Norway, where the national newspaper *Tagbladet* reported that 65% of rapes committed in 2001-2002 were by non-Western immigrants and a professor from Oslo University sparked public controversy by stating that Norwegian women should also take some responsibility and adapt their style of dress, which was considered by male Muslim immigrants to be 'provocative' (Steyn 2002).

New Versions of the Same Old Discourse: 'Muslim Misogyny' and Contemporary Orientalism

Clearly, the particular form the discourses problematising the two sets of gang rapes took depended on the specific localized anxieties and particular national frameworks. Yet, similar discourses emerged in relation to both the construction of the perpetrators and the cultural determinacy of their actions. Despite the very different colonial histories of Australia and France, there was a surprisingly faithful reproduction of classic orientalist scripts.

In the Australian context, as is usual in popular perceptions of sexual assault, the Sydney gang rapes were seen as the result of a group of young men who were unable to control their sexual urges. Such popular myths around sexual assault worked in conjunction with historical Western perceptions of 'Muslim' or 'Arab' masculinity, via the tradition of Orientalism, as sexually perverse and

---

14   'l'égalité républicaine, c'est devenu l'égalité entre les sexes'.

morally bankrupt (Said 1978). Hence the themes expressed in the media coverage of the 'Muslim gang rape' cases, both involving the Lebanese background youth and the Pakistani immigrant brothers, were not entirely unfamiliar. On a broader, international level, homogenous and sexualized portrayals of 'Arab' or 'Muslim' men have been apparent in media reports of 'terrorists' who were reported as willing to die as martyrs both for the sake of 'revenge' against the Western world, and also so that they may be rewarded with 'unlimited sex with 72 virgins in the afterlife' (Kelley 2001; Manji 2003). Locally, the young Muslim perpetrators in both gang rape incidents were represented as displaying their own brand of sexual and moral perversity via calculated ploys to pack rape a number of young women in a number of different incidents (Warner 2004; Wallace 2005).

The message effectively delivered by the media saturation around these crimes was that Arab or Muslim youths are more likely to rape 'white' women because they see them as 'sluts'. The overarching presumption in mainstream media and extremist online coverage of this nature is that Muslim men think that white girls will *always* consent or that to force them to have sex is not *real* rape. The fact that some men – regardless of ethnic and religious background – hold this belief about women was obscured by the ideological storm that followed the 'Bankstown' or 'Lebanese' rapes in particular. Here, linking the rapes to an imagined 'essence' of Islamic or Middle-Eastern culture operated as a presumption of guilt by cultural association and echoed a common Orientalist theme that has been criticized by Said, who pointed out that the Western imagination describes the Arab or Muslim man as an 'impossible creature whose libidinal energy drives him to the paroxysms of over-stimulation' (1978: 312).

In this way, the crime of 'gang rape' became racialized while the minority ethnic communities to which the perpetrators belonged became criminalized, and were symbolically (and literally) removed from the realm of 'ordinary' citizens. The exclusion of Muslim Australians from the realm of 'ordinariness' – moral and otherwise – became exacerbated by the crimes of a few individuals who were identified as Muslim (Lebanese) Australians, or in the latter case, Pakistani immigrant Muslims. This theme continues in very recent political debates against Muslim immigration and multiculturalism in Australia. For example, Paul Sheehan, a vocal Sydney-based anti-Muslim and anti-multicultural commentator has drawn on conservative Dutch, British and German political utterances to assert that:

> Muslims are over-represented in welfare dependency, unemployment, crime, sexual assaults and religious intolerance in … four countries. Islamic fundamentalists now dominate the concerns of the security services in Britain, Germany, France, Holland, Belgium, Denmark and Sweden (2011: 11).

According to Sheehan, 'exactly the same pattern has repeated itself in Australia', reinforcing orientalist views of Islamic laziness and criminality.

In these examples, an unsavoury image is posited in relation to what has been homogenized in the Western world as Arab and Muslim culture. Said argues that within traditional Western thought, the Arab is sexualized: 'they are *only* capable of sexual incitement and not of Olympian (Western, modern) reason' (Said 1978: 313-314), thereby constructing Arab and Muslim culture as sub-human, animalistic. To illustrate further, Said has said that 'Islam is [seen as] an irrational herd or mass phenomenon, ruling Muslims by passions, instincts and unreflecting hatreds' (1978: 317).

In a more contemporary comparison, Connell illustrates the constructed deviancy and sexualisation of 'black' masculinity through 'the fantasy figure of the black rapist [...which] plays an important role in sexual politics among whites, a role much exploited by right-wing politics in the United States' (1995: 80). In the Australian context, Muslim men face strikingly similar circumstances of marginalisation and racist projection to that which has previously been faced by 'black' men in the United States. A figure analogous to Connell's example of the 'black rapist' emerged in Australia: the 'Muslim rapist' – particularly after the gang rapes perpetrated by young Muslim men in 2000 and 2002. Examples of this mythical figure have been most prevalent in the work of conservative journalists and commentators already mentioned, such as Sheehan and Albrechtsen – amongst many others. Two examples from these journalists illustrate the point. In a book titled *Girls Like You* about the K brothers' sexual assaults in 2002, Sheehan wrote: 'A clear pattern of sexual assault and sexual harassment by Muslim men was beginning to register in the legal system and the public consciousness' (2006: 64). Albrechtsen's commentary around the Muslim rapist and her hijacking of the term '*tournantes*', has already been outlined. Sheehan's and Albrechtsen's commentary foregrounds the representation of Muslim men as barbaric, violent and more susceptible to perpetrating sexual assault because of the popularly perceived conservativism and repressed sexuality of Islam.

In France, through the contextualising of *'les tournantes"* as a problem associated with North Africans, the media was also able to draw on a wide array of well-established colonial and Orientalist tropes. The example of Robert-Diard's above-cited description of the women as subservient (unwilling to express their own opinions, agreeing with their menfolk) and veiled, far from subtly demonstrates this through its evocation of the traditional Orientalist and colonial image of the oppressed, hidden Muslim woman. Equally, in the description of the first day of the trial, Patricia Tourancheau, writing for *Libération* quotes the victim's lawyer stating that the parents in the audience were organised according to sex: 'the mothers, veiled with religious symbols, up at the back, in the last row and, further away the old Arab fathers well integrated into France'.[15] This is paralleled with the description of the code of the *banlieue* in which, 'the 'chicks' don't mix with the 'guys', under threat of finishing up in the basement, treated like

---

15   ' Les mamans voilées avec la marque religieuse, en haut, au dernier rang, et, plus loin, les vieux pères arabes bien intégrés en France. '

a 'whore' [ie. raped]' (Tourancheau 2002).[16] Through this description an implicit link is drawn between what is seen as the traditional Muslim/Arabic practice of segregation of the sexes, the *hijab* and the young men's dysfunctional sexuality.

> Thus, even as the explicit resort to racialized arguments is rejected, the apparent 'affective deficit' described among young people of the *banlieue* becomes intimately connected with the traditional background of their parents. Similarly, the repetition of the idea, 'a girl who is seen [hanging out] in the street, is a slut' (Santucci 2001)[17] – by both media commentators and young men and women of the *banlieue* themselves, it must be noted – evokes traditional colonial images of the women of North Africa and the Orient more generally, cloistered in harems: an image both erotic and submissive (Alloula 1987). The constant reiteration of the 'mother/whore' dichotomy in articles explaining the attitudes of *banlieue* men and women towards female sexuality and identity seems to suggest that such a dichotomy has no place within French society. Just as in Australia rape myths were deflected onto the Sydney gang rapists– and, by implication, Muslim men more generally, – in France rape myths emerge as the sole possession of *banlieue* (immigrant/Muslim) men. By contrast, the Republic is envisaged as an enlightened and sexual egalitarian space (Fassin 2006).

In all of these cases, popular ideas around criminality, sexual deviancy, cultural difference and assimilation coalesced to provide a fertile ground upon which a conservative anti-multicultural and xenophobic agenda was developed and enhanced. This agenda proved to be the main driver in the Muslim gang rape moral panics both within Australia and France, and further afield. With the added horror of the September 11 attacks in 2001, the rapes became conflated in the public imagination with broader and unrelated national and international issues, which generated popular notions of a large-scale, abstract and terrifying 'Muslim problem' (ADB 2003). Through constructions of a 'Muslim problem' or 'threat', the conservative debates around the rapes, immigration and multiculturalism consistently came back to the same point: the incommensurability of Muslim, Arab or Middle Eastern cultures with Western liberal and (Judeo-)Christian values such as those upheld by Australia and other Western democratic nations (Marranci 2004). Existing xenophobic anxieties, with the additional rhetoric on Islamic terrorism, further reinforced these views which Samuel Huntington termed the 'clash of civilizations' (1993; 1996).

More significantly, political and media reinstatement of a 'clash of civilisations' argument and its combination with anti-multicultural and Islamophobic rhetoric, have made fashionable that which has previously been the subject of extreme right-wing and racist online discussions of Islam, often illustrated by graphic examples

---

16 ' Les 'meufs' ne se mélangent pas aux 'keums', sous peine de finir à la cave, traitée comme une 'pute'. '

17 ' Une fille qu'on voit dans la rue, c'est une pute. '

of stoning women, honour killings, gang rape and other generally violent and barbaric practices that are attributed to Islam. It is to these extremist new media proliferations of Islamophobia that we now turn, focusing exclusively on internet examples of an alleged 'epidemic' of 'Muslim gang rape'.

Local Fears, Global Discourses: The Role of New Media

> What I don't understand is what are the Swedish, French, German 'men' doing to protect their women? Have these Western 'men' become so emasculated that Muslim and African barbarians run amok in Europe? – Barbara, *Pan-European Arab Muslim Gang Rape Epidemic*, IRIS Blog, 2006.

> What's it going to take for Europeans to finally stand up and start attacking muslims? Don't they realize this is a barbarian invasion? They must be dealt with brutally and severely. Get your governments to act now – look at what Israel has to deal with. The world will either be Islamified or democratized. We're in for the fight of our lives – 'death2islam', *Pan-European Arab Muslim Gang Rape Epidemic*, IRIS Blog 2006.[18]

While there has been much written about the positive potentials offered by new media in linking activist communities and enhancing advocacy networks, the internet has also been identified as providing a new arena for decidedly reactionary agendas. As Gerstenfeld, Grant and Chiang (2003) demonstrate, the internet has provided a useful venue for extreme right-wing groups to propagate their messages. The popular mainstream media has been quick to identify the link between internet sites and Muslim extremist factions but what role does the internet perform as a site for promoting global Islamophobia?

Whilst the media discourses in Australia and France linked the particular gang rapes with ongoing debates about national identity, immigration and ethnic diversity, a number of online blogs and forums provided the means to turn the issue of 'Muslim gang rapes' into one of international concern. From the early 2000s on, various internet sites and web blogs have appeared seeking to draw links between the events in Australia, France and elsewhere as evidence of a 'global phenomenon' of Muslim gang rape. In Australia, blogs such as *Fortress Australia*[19] explicitly promote anti-Muslim sentiment. In the French context, websites such as *Racisme Anti-Blanc (Anti-White Racism)*[20] provide a detailed and clearly well researched database of incidences of violence committed by various different ethnic minority communities worldwide to support the claim that the problem is not white racism

---

18   http://www.iris.org.il/blog/archives/757-Pan-European-Arab-Muslim-Gang-Rape-Epidemic.html
19   http://fortressaustralia.blogspot.com
20   www.racismeantiblanc.bizland.com

but rather the victimisation of dominant populations by 'problem immigrants'. In a section of the website entitled 'Tournantes, an international phenomenon: from Paris to Sydney'[21] a table is reproduced from research conducted by a French academic demonstrating that 52% of the French '*tournantes*' were perpetrated by 'North African' men. So too are links provided to right-wing media articles discussing the relationship between Islam and the Sydney gang rapes and details of rapes also identified as involving 'Muslim men' in Denmark. The section is illustrated with a photograph of Sydney gang rape victim Tegan Wagner.

However such blogs are not restricted to France and Australia. Various, specifically Islamophobic websites in America also referred to the gang rapes in Australia, France and other parts of Europe as 'proof' of Islamic violence. An article by Sharon Lapkin on David Horowitz's US based website, *Front Page Mag*,[22] claims that 'in Australia, Norway, Sweden and other Western nations, there is a distinct race-based crime in motion being ignored by the diversity police: Islamic men are raping Western women for ethnic reasons' (2005). A related American website, *Jihad Watch*,[23] also wrote of 'Western Muslims' Racist Rape Spree' (2005) where Sharon Lapkin's article was reproduced. On yet another American blog titled *V-Dare*, extreme right-wing commentator Sam Francis wrote that 'racial gang rape' is 'another diversity disaster' and that while America had not yet witnessed this 'sport', 'in more cosmopolitan centres like Paris and Australia the game is blossoming' (2001).[24] Further east, the Israeli blog, *IRIS*, again pointed to a Muslim gang rape epidemic occurring across Europe in Germany, France, Sweden, Norway, Demark and Australia (see special feature on *Pan-European Arab Muslim Gang Rape Epidemic*, IRIS Blog, 2006), which invited a series of vehement and often obscene anti-Muslim comments - a couple of the milder remarks have been quoted above. The IRIS Blog issue on the 'Arab Muslim Gang Rape epidemic' had been supplemented by graphic and bloody imagery of a young Swedish woman who had allegedly been attacked by a Muslim gang.

The list of (in most cases) exclusively anti-Islamic blogs and right-wing websites provided here is by no means exhaustive. The extensive lists of links offered on these web-pages to other anti-Islamic and/or extreme right-wing websites are impossible to examine within the limits of this chapter. Moreover it becomes almost gratuitous to painstakingly refer to a wider range of right-wing new media as each website and attendant blog examined imparted identical messages. These messages resonate with long-standing orientalist thoughts of cultural determinism which posits Islam as a religion of violent, misogynistic and barbaric practices. These ideas are then used as leverage for the argument that Islamic values are perverse and therefore not compatible with the civilized values of the West, supporting a clash of civilisations

21   'Tournantes, phénomène international: de Paris à Sydney'
22   www.frontpagemag.com
23   http://www.jihadwatch.org/2005/12/western-muslims-racist-rape-spree.html. Also a David Horowitz initiative.
24   http://www.vdare.com/francis/gang_rape.htm

thesis and a 'common sense' agenda that multiculturalism does not work and should be abolished. Most websites went further. A dichotomy, as already apparent in local debates in France and Australia, was established between Islam and democracy. Warnings were issued, as exemplified in the quote from 'death2islam', that if West did not 'stand up to Islam' soon, 'the world will either be Islamified or democratized'. Not both. In the examples given, the gang rape cases were upheld as further proof to these arguments.

What is the significance of these websites? Many would argue that surely they represent only an extremist and marginal perspective. However, we are not so sure. In fact Göran Larsson has argued that while much attention has been paid to the negative portrayals of Muslims in Western media and popular culture, less attention has been paid to the role played by the new media technologies such as the internet in disseminating Islamophobic material and commentaries (2007: 54). Larsson adds, '[t]he study of Islamophobia on the Internet should also be analysed in relation to questions of identity processes, xenophobia, integration, multiculturalism and tensions within contemporary European societies' (2007: 56).

Islam and the West? Islam in the West? Reinforcing Borders

Through the 'common sense' linking of disparate international gang rape incidents supposedly perpetrated by 'Muslim'/'immigrant' men, online sources have provided a means of reinforcing a discourse of globalized Islamaphobia. On the one hand the particular gang rape moral panics discussed emerged as a result of a combination of local and global anxieties within each of the nation states, associated with immigration, increasingly visible ethnic diversity and crises of national identity. On the other hand, these moral panics then transcended their own localized context to provide the basis for a global moral panic. The debate about Islam's place in the West is removed from a particular national context (such as the Australian or French contexts discussed above) and turned into a globalised discourse in which Islam is constructed as the very antithesis of the West and at the same time a source of violence, racism and sexism: a construction that usefully justifies Islamophobic attitudes and anti-immigration, anti-multicultural rhetoric, as well as providing legitimacy to ever more securitarian discourses and policies.

Racism, according to Etienne Balibar (1991), no longer relies on a concept of 'race' as biological difference. Instead, what Balibar describes as 'neo-racism' is dependent on an idea of cultural difference as fixed and immutable and hence unable to fuse within a single geo-political space. Ideas such as these underpin 'the harmfulness of abolishing frontiers [and] the incompatibility of life-styles and traditions' (Balibar 1991: 21). Even so, some ideologies continue to adhere to biological notions of race and the superiority of the white race above all others. In Islamophobic perspectives, the category of 'culture' is often superimposed onto the notion of race whereby racial and cultural differences become interchangeable or at least utilized in the same ways to further an overtly racist agenda. At times this interchangeablilty is also based on a perception that Muslims are also a different colour or at least swarthy in appearance (see Semati 2010). This is seen in perceptions that most Muslims are Middle-Eastern or Arab and therefore of a different 'race' to white people. It is also seen in extreme right-wing and White Supremacist websites where biological difference is assumed alongside cultural difference. This is illustrated in the remark by 'Barbara', that 'Muslim and African barbarians run amok in Europe'.

Assumptions about the incommensurability of Western civilisation and a fixed, singular and static Muslim culture, underpin both overtly racist public opinions and more subtle debates about 'Muslim gang rape', immigration and the alleged evils of multiculturalism, whilst the internet allows for the proliferation of material used to demonstrate the globalized threat of Islam. If, as Peter Manning (2004) found, the most common representations of 'Arabs' and 'Muslims' in Sydney newspapers were those identified in the international news section as involved with terrorism, the linking on internet sites of different gang rapes in different contexts through the common feature of the 'Muslim perpetrator' provides an added justification for why Muslims cannot and should not be in the West.

This is important in a time when many commentators point to the crisis of national identity being experienced in many western liberal democracies. For example, writing about Europe, Stefano Allievi observes: 'second generation new Europeans, who can no longer be considered immigrants and in fact have become less and less 'other', are now being 'Islamized' which means that they may well become reconstructed as 'other', different and even extraneous' (2005:8). In her account of Islamophobia in Western Europe, Gabriele Marranci asserts that:

> Muslims are increasingly represented as members of a threatening 'transnational society', in which people want only to 'stone women', 'cut throats', and 'beat their wives'. Inevitably, of course some people may feel the need to defend the 'Western civilisation' against this 'enemy within' (2004: 107).

By setting Islam up as oppositional, always already on the outside, the traditional borders of the nation can in fact be reinforced. Marranci cites various Western European examples outlining an increasing tendency to defend nationhood by warning of an encroaching Islamic threat to Western civilisation. In Italy, Silvio Berlusconi appealed for a consciousness 'of the supremacy of our civilisation… which have brought us democratic institutions.' He added: 'Europe must revive on the basis of common Christian roots' (The Guardian, 2001: 15, cited in Marranci 2004: 107). More bluntly, late Dutch politician and media commentator, Pim Fortuyn stated that he saw 'Islam as an extraordinary threat, as a hostile society… If I could legally manage it, I would say: no Muslim come into this country any more' (cited in Marranci 2004: 108)

These European and Australian examples of a gendered nationalism, though expressed in varying degrees and in culturally specific ways, resurrect the murky ideas expressed in Samuel Huntington's 'clash of civilizations' argument:

Western Culture is challenged by groups within western societies. One such challenge comes from immigrants from other civilizations who reject assimilation and continue to adhere to and propagate the values, customs, and cultures of their home. This phenomenon is most notable among Muslims in Europe... In Europe, western civilization could also be undermined by the weakening of its central component, Christianity (Huntington 1996: 304-305).

Huntington's words seem to be echoed in the commentaries provided on the 'Sydney gang rapes' and '*les tournantes*': the refusal to integrate, the perpetuation of different traditional values and a rejection of those of the new host. At the same time, the gang rapes provide an added dimension to this clash. What emerges in the discourses on the rapes is that this is not just a matter of two different sets of values but one set that is *inherently* inferior (misogynistic, violent, barbaric) which further justifies the exclusion of the holders of such values.

Conclusion

As this chapter has attempted to demonstrate, the issue of gang rape has played a highly symbolic and ideologically charged role in French and Australian public discourses in recent years for a number of reasons. An ubiquitous Islamophobic sentiment and specific moral panics around Muslim masculinities has increasingly underpinned the idea of a clash of civilisations in public discourses around Muslim immigration (/'invasion'), terrorist attacks, and essentialized ideas of a religiously and culturally inscribed oppression of women. Islam is thusly constructed as 'backward' in direct opposition to the enlightened values of the West. We argue that such prevalent cultural ascriptions, following Balibar (1991), exemplify a type of 'neo-racism'- one in which cultural difference and inferiority both replaces and augments ideas about biological difference and inferiority. This neo-racism underpins moral panics and fears about Islam and its imagined resistance to civilisation, thus giving justification to arguments against immigration and multiculturalism. More crucially, there is a current trend in both Australia and Europe that elides anti-Muslim sentiment and hostility towards multiculturalism, through reducing the whole of Islam to a minority which engages in intransigent cultural practices (Semati 2010: 267). If Muslims are to immigrate at all, more 'moderate' voices suggest that they must fully assimilate and be 'Muslims in Europe' (see Marranci 2004) or 'Muslims in Australia' (see Poynting and Mason 2007). This much is reflected in the 'common sense' of public opinion, which is often underpinned by defensive violence:

I look at things like multiculturalism and think it's a big massive joke because these people [Muslims] don't mix with us people... Now when these people come to our country they should be given the rules.... We are predominantly a white Anglo-Saxon Christian-based country... My friends have basically said

that when their kids go to school if they can't sing a Christmas carol, they will
burn every Muslim house down in the areas to get the Muslims out because this
is our country... (Caller, 2GB Radio Sydney, 11 July 2002).

Current political debates in Australia and Europe reinforce these views.

As Liz Fekete notes, the way assimilation is negotiated in each national
context differs according to different social contexts, in ways that are 'consonant
with the myth upon which that nation has been built' (2004: 18). However, as the
Australian and French gang rape examples demonstrate, a certain global discourse
can also be identified and indeed, as the various new media sites demonstrate,
right-wing bloggers and increasingly mainstream media and political responses
have made such a link. Within this discourse a universal enemy is identified: the
'Muslim man' who comes to represent not only all that the West is not, but, more
importantly, all that makes the West *better*. By constructing sexual violence and
misogyny as the preserve of the Muslim man, anti-Muslim and anti-multicultural
rhetoric dominant in many Western liberal democracies is reinforced. It also
becomes legitimized as an almost ethical response to unacceptable behaviour.
The widespread and pervasive nature of this essentialized and racist discourse
demonstrates that Orientalism remains alive and well within the contemporary
global order.

References

The Age 2002, 'Crime and Punishment', Editorial, 17 August 2002, 3.
Albrechtsen, J. 2002. 'Blind spot allows criminal barbarism to flourish', *The Australian*, 17 July 2002, p.11
Allievi, S. 2005. 'How the Immigrant has become Muslim: Public Debates on Islam in Europe' *Revue Européene des Migrations Internationales*, 21(2), Available at: http://remi.revues.org/2497#text
Alloula, M. 1987. *The Colonial harem*, (translated by Myrna Godzich) Manchester: Manchester University Press
Anti-Discrimination Board of New South Wales, *Race for the Headlines: Racism and media discourse*: Report launched 13 February 2003, Available at: http://www.lawlink.nsw.gov.au/adb.nsf/pages/raceheadlines
Attorney General's Department of New South Wales (AGD) 2006. 'Responding to sexual assault: the way forward', *Criminal Justice Sexual Offences Taskforce Report*, NSW, Australia.
Balibar, E. 1991. 'Is there a 'Neo-Racism'', in E. Balibar & I. Wallerstein, *Race, Nation, Class: Ambiguous Identities*, London & New York: Verso, 17-29
Benabdessadok, C. 'Ni putes ni soumises: de la marche à l'université d'automne', *Mouvements*, 1248, March-April 2004, 67.
Brearley, D. 2002. 'Ethnicity and bad publicity a volatile mix – The Cultural Divide', *The Australian*, 9 May 2002, 12.

Chung, D, O'Learly, PJ and Hand, T 2006, 'Sexual violence offenders: Prevention and intervention approaches' *Australian Centre for the Study of Sexual Assault*, No.5, June

Cohen, S. 1972/2002. *Folk Devils and Moral Panics: The Creation of the Mods and Rockers*, 3rd Edition, London: Routledge.

Connell, R.W. 1995. *Masculinities*, Sydney: Australia, Allen and Unwin.

d'Arrigo, J. 2001. 'Tournante': le calvaire d'une jeune handicapée *Le Figaro*, 25 May 2011, 8.

Dagistanli, S. 2007. 'Like a pack of wild animals': Moral panics around 'ethnic' gang rape in Sydney in S. Poynting and G. Morgan, (eds) *Outrageous! Moral Panics in Australia* Hobart:ACYS Publishing, 181-196.

Devine, M. 2004. Stop pretending: dressing sexy comes with a price, *Sun-Herald*, 4 April 2004, 15.

Durand, J. 2002. La 'tournante' d'Argenteuil et l'incompréhension des parents: 'Pas mon fils, il n'a pas pu faire ça *Libération*, 5 November 2002, 22-23.

Fassin, É. 2006. La démocratie sexuelle et le conflit des civilisations *Multitudes*, 26(3): 123-131

Fekete, L. 2004. Anti-Muslim racism and the European security state, *Race & Class*, 46(1), 3-29.

Fickling, D. 2002. Racially motivated crime and punishment', *Guardian*, 23 September 2002. Available at: http://www.guardian.co.uk/elsewhere/journalist/story/0,7792,797463,00.htm

Garland, D. 2008. On the Concept of Moral Panic *Crime, Media, Culture* 4(1): 9-30.

Geisler, R. 2002. Sordides 'tournantes' dans le XVIIIe arrondissement. *Le Figaro*, 3 August 2002, 9.

Gerstenfeld, P. Grant, D. and Chiang, C. 2003. Hate Online: A Content Analysis of Extremist Internet Sites *Analyses of Social Issues and Public Policy*, 3(1), 29-44.

Goode, E. and Ben-Yehuda, N. 1994. *Moral Panics: The Social Construction of Deviance*. Oxford: Blackwell.

Grewal, K. 2007a. 'The Young Muslim Man' in Australian Public Discourse *Transforming Cultures ejournal*, 2(1), 116-134.

Grewal, K. 2007b., "The Threat from Within': Representations of the Banlieue in French Popular Discourse' in Killingsworth, M (ed) *Europe: New Voices, New Perspectives*, Melbourne: Contemporary Europe Research Centre, University of Melbourne, e-book.

Guénif-Souilamas, N. 2006. The Other French Exception: Virtuous Racism and the War of the Sexes in Postcolonial France, *French Politics, Culture & Society*, 24(3), 24-41.

Guénif-Souilamas, N. and Macé, É. 2004. *Les féministes et le garçon arabe*, Paris: Éditions de l'aube.

Hage, G. 2003. *Against Paranoid Nationalism: Searching for hope in a shrinking society*, Annandale, NSW: Pluto Press.

Hall, S., Jefferson, T., Clarke, J. and Roberts, B. 1978. *Policing the Crisis: Mugging, the State and Law and Order*. Basingstoke: Macmillan

Ho, C. 2007. Muslim women's new defenders: Women's rights, nationalism and Islamophobia in contemporary Australia, *Women's Studies International Forum*, 30, 290-298.

Humphrey, M. 2007. Culturalising the Abject: Islam, Law and Moral Panic in the West *Australian Journal of Social Issues*, 42(1), 9-25.

Huntington, S. 1993. 'The clash of civilizations?', *Foreign Affairs* 72 (3), pp. 22–28.

Huntington, S. 1996. *The clash of civilizations*, New York: Simon and Schuster.

Johns, R., Griffith, G., Simpson, R. 2001. Sentencing 'Gang Rapists': The Crimes Amendment (Aggravated Sexual Assault in Company) Bill 2001. *Parliamentary Briefing Paper*, 12/2001.

Available at: http://www.parliament.nsw.gov.au/prod/parlment/publications.nsf/key/ResearchBf122001

Kampmark, B. 2003. Islam, Women and Australia's cultural discourse of terror, *Hecate*, 29(1), 86-106.

Kelley, J. 2001. Devotion, desire drive youths to 'martyrdom'. *USA Today*. Available at: http://usatoday.com/news/world/june01/2001-06-26-suicide-usat.htm

Kidman, J. 2001. 70 girls attacked by rape gangs, *Sun-Herald*, 29 July, 1.

Krémer, P. and L. Martine 2002. . La condition des jeunes filles s'est dégradée dans les quartiers difficiles. *Le Monde*, 25 October 2002

Larsson, G. 2007. Cyber-Islamophobia? The case of WikiIslam *Contemporary Islam*, 1, 53-67

Manji, I. 2003. *The Trouble with Islam*. New York: Random House,.

Manning, P. 2004., *Dog whistle politics and journalism: reporting Arabic and Muslim people ein Sydney newspapers*. Sydney: Australian Centre for Independent Journalism.

Marranci, G. 2004. 'Multiculturalism, Islam and the clash of civilisations theory: rethinking Islamophobia', *Culture and Religion*, 5 (1), 105-117.

Miranda, C. 2000. Schoolgirls in fear after sex attacks. *Daily Telegraph*, 13 September 2000, 14.

Morris, R. 2001. Migrants to declare military experience, *Daily Telegraph*, 17 August 2001, 8.

Mucchielli, L. 2005. *Le scandale des 'tournantes': dérives médiatiques, contre-enquête sociologique* Paris : La Découverte.

Pech, M. 2002. Les désolants enseignements d'une tournante ordinaire. *Le Figaro*, 27 May 2002, 12.

Peralva, A. and Macé, E. 2002. *Médias et violences urbaines: Débats politiques et constructions journalistiques*. Paris : La Documentation française.

Poynting, S. 2002. Bin Laden in the suburbs: Attacks on Arab and Muslim Australians before and after 11 September. *Current Issues in Criminal Justice*, 14, 43-64.

Poynting, S., Noble, G, Tabar, P and J Collins 2004. *Bin Laden in the Suburbs: Criminalising the Arab Other*, Sydney: Sydney Institute of Criminology.

Poynting, S. and Mason, V. 2007. The resistable rise of Islamophobia: Anti-Muslim racism in the UK and Australia before September 11 2001, *Journal of Sociology*, 43(1), 61-85.

Priest, T. 2004. 'Don't turn a blind eye to terror in our midst'. *Australian*, 12 January 2004, 9.

Rinaudo, C 1999. *L'Ethnicite dans la Cite: Jeux et enjeux de la categorisation ethnique*, Paris & Montreal : L'Harmattan.

Robert-Diard, P 2002. 'Les auteurs du viol collectif d'Argenteuil condamnés à des peines allant de 5 à 12 ans de prison ' *Le Monde*, 29-30 September 2002, 11.

Runnymede Trust 1997. Islamophobia: a challenge for us all. Runnymede Trust Report.

Said, E. 1978. *Orientalism*. London: Penguin.

Santucci, F. 2001. Viols: la spirale infernale de la 'tournante'. *Libération*, 9 March 2001.

Schneidermann, D. 2003. Le Cauchemar médiatique. Paris: Éditions Denoël.

Scott, J.W. 2007. The Politics of the Veil, Princeton New Jersey: Princeton University Press

Semati, M. 2010, 'Islamphobia, Culture and Race in the Age of Empire', *Cultural Studies,* 24(2), 256-275

Sharma, S and Sharma, A 2003, 'White Paranoia: Orientalism in the Age of Empire', *Fashion Theory*, 7 (3-4), 301-318.

Sheehan, P. 2006. *Girls Like You*. Sydney: Macmillan.

Smith, C. 2002. 2GB Radio Sydney, 11 July 2002.

Steyn, M. 2002. Beware Multicultural Madness *Chicago Sun-Times*, 25 August 2002. Available at : http://www.atrueword.com/index.php/article/articleprint/13/-1/7.

Taylor, L. 2011. Morrison sees votes in anti-Muslim strategy. *Sydney Morning Herald*, 17 February, 1.

du Tanney, P. 2001. Une bande de violeurs aux assises., *Le Figaro*, 25 April 2001.

Tourancheau, P. 2002. Seule face à se dix-huit violeurs et ses deux entremetteuses: Victime de 'tournantes à Argenteuil, la jeune fille était manipulée par deux 'copines'. Procès à Pontoise *Libération*, 23 September 2002.

Wallace, N. 2005. In the open: rapists' campaign of vicious assaults, *Sydney Morning Herald*, 22 July. Available at: http://www.smh.com.au/articles/2005/07/21/1121539094208.html .

Warner, K. 2004. Gang rape in Sydney: crimes, the media, politics, race and sentencing *Australian and New Zealand Journal of Criminology*, 37 (3), 344-362.

Cases

R v AEM (Snr), AEM (Jnr) & KEM (2001)

Websites

Fortress Australia, http://fortressaustralia.blogspot.com
Front Page Mag, www.frontpagemag.com
IRIS Blog (Pan-European Arab Muslim Gang Rape Epidemic), http://www.iris.
 org.il/blog/archives/757-Pan-European-Arab-Muslim-Gang-Rape-Epidemic.
 html
Jihad Watch, http://www.jihadwatch.org/2005/12/western-muslims-racist-rape-
 spree.html
Racisme Anti-Blanc (Anti-White Racism), www.racismeantiblanc.bizland.com
V-Dare, http://www.vdare.com/francis/gang_rape.htm

Chapter 8

A Failed Political Attempt to Use Global Islamophobia in Western Sydney: The 'Lindsay Leaflet Scandal'

Kevin M. Dunn and Alanna Kamp

Introduction

This chapter reviews a failed attempt at using Islamophobia in the western suburbs of Sydney during an Australian federal election. The purveyors of the Islamophobia intended to distribute a fraudulent electoral leaflet, a few days before the election, to make residents anxious about the local development of a mosque. The pamphlet sought to link the opposing political party with Muslim organizations and suggested that there was a tolerance of Islamic terrorism. The political party targeted by the leaflet was tipped off, and they photographed and confronted the leaflet distributers that same night. Two days later, the leaflet affair was national headline news and became known as the 'Lindsay leaflet scandal'.

In this chapter we set the scandal within its global, national and local contexts. Islamophobia is global, but as we show, it is performed in locally situated ways. The spatially varied nature and costs of Islamophobia are reviewed. The contextualization we provide strengthens our argument that the leaflet developers were convinced that Islamophobia could be used for political gain in Australia. However, the Lindsay leaflet scandal was a failed attempt at using Islamophobia, and as such, a review of the affair provides some guidance on the political resources that are available for anti-racists. These resources include increasing public awareness of Islamophobia and its impacts, increasing public wariness around the political deployment of Islamophobia, the benefits of speaking-out against and naming Islamophobia, and the political merit of exposing the political use of Islamophobia as a confidence trick on the general public.

Orchestrating Islamophobia – The Lindsay Leaflet Scandal

In the early evening of 20 November 2007, four days before polling day of the Australian federal election, five men aligned with the New South Wales (NSW)

Liberal Party gathered in a house on one of Penrith's most prestigious streets[1]. The house belonged to Jackie Kelly, the retiring Liberal MP for the electorate of Lindsay, and her husband, Gary Clark (*Commonwealth Director of Prosecutions v Egan* 2009: 3). The group of men included Clark himself, Jeff Egan, member of the New South Wales (NSW) Liberal Party State Executive, and Greg Chijoff, who was at the time the husband of new Liberal Candidate for Lindsay, Karen Chijoff (*Commonwealth Director of Prosecutions v Egan* 2009: 4). It was here that Clark and Chijoff briefed the group on a letterbox drop which was to take place in North St Marys, a working class suburb of Lindsay, later that night and began a chain of events that led to the 'Lindsay leaflet scandal'[2].

This would not be a usual letter-drop characteristic of routine party advertising in pre-election campaigns. Rather, the leaflet and its distribution in North St Marys were fraudulent and unauthorized; prepared by Clark but attributed to the fictitious 'Islamic Australia Federation' (*Commonwealth Director of Prosecutions v Clark* 2009: 4, 6). The leaflet outlined the mission of the bogus Federation as follows:

> The role of the Islamic Australia Federation is to support Islamic Australians by providing a strong network within Islamic Australia. Muslims supporting Muslims within the community and assisting and showing christian [sic] Australians the glorious path to Islam (Lindsay Leaflet 2007; Figure 8.1).

Evocative rhetoric used in the pamphlet could have fomented local alarm about the prospect of 'Muslim take-over'. For example, the publishers used the term 'Islamic Australia', outlined the proselytizing role accorded to the Federation, and used the lower case when referring to Christians and Christianity. The leaflet also proclaimed electoral support for the opposition party (the Australian Labor Party (ALP)) because it claimed the ALP was supportive of the construction of a mosque in the local area (which had in reality never been proposed), and because the ALP were said to be forgiving of the Islamic terrorists who had murdered Australians in the Bali bombings:

---

1   Penrith is a town centre in far western Sydney and also the name of the surrounding Local Government Area (LGA) located at the base of the Blue Mountains (which borders Sydney's metropolitan expansion). Penrith is within the Federal Electorate of Lindsay which has been keenly contested by the major political parties in recent NSW State and Australian Federal General Elections.

2   The details of the events of 20 November 2007 that are outlined here have been sourced from publicly available material including newspaper reports published between 22 November 2007 and 20 May 2008 and formal evidence used in Court Proceedings – see references throughout. The details of the events reported here (including locations and participants) are consistent with the details reproduced in those sources.

> In the upcoming Federal Election we strongly support the ALP as our preferred
> party to govern this country and urge all other Muslims to do the same. ...
> Labor supports our new Mosque construction and we hope, with the support and
> funding by Local and State governments, to open our new Mosque in St Marys
> soon (Lindsay Leaflet 2007; Figure 8.1).

The leaflet was addressed as if it were convincing voters that the ALP should be
supported because of their pro-Muslim stance, but the suburb where the leaflet
was to be distributed was not a place where many Muslims lived at all. Indeed,
as we show later, it was a suburb where there are fewer Muslims than the Sydney
residential average. However, by linking the bogus Federation and its objectives,
as well as insinuations of increased Muslim presence to the ALP, the Liberal Party
volunteers must have assumed that fears and antipathy towards Muslims might be
leveraged for political gain in North St Marys—this was a place where voters may
be swayed by an Islamophobic fear campaign.

This clumsy political chicanery was foiled when the ALP were tipped off. At
midday that same day, a 'left-wing Liberal Party source, fed up with grubby tactics
employed by party members from the opposing right faction' (Benson 2007: 5)
called Luke Foley, the Assistant State Secretary of the ALP in NSW, and informed
him of the leaflet and where and when it would be distributed. Foley and Labor
Senator Steve Hutchins orchestrated an 'elaborate sting' from a hotel only 250
metres away from the Clark/Kelly residence (Benson 2007: 5). Even closer to
Clark and Kelly's home, an ALP volunteer, Mr Gilchrist, was observing the Liberal
group's every move from a parked car (*Commonwealth Director of Prosecutions v
Clark* 2009: 2).

At around 8.40pm the Liberal Party group got into their cars and travelled to
North St Marys, ten kilometres away. Mr Gilchrist followed the vehicles to the
corner of Boronia Road and Debrincat Avenue at the heart of the 1940s government
housing estate in North St Marys. Foley and Senator Hutchins along with a handful
of other ALP volunteers were already stationed at various locations in the North St
Marys area ready to catch the Liberal group red-handed. When they arrived, the
Liberal group split into pairs and began letter dropping. Egan was soon approached
by two of the ALP stingers—Wayne Forno (who was at that time Assistant Secretary
of the Transport Workers Union) and his son. Wayne Forno asked Egan for a copy
of the leaflet. Egan refused. A minute later the ALP sting leaders, Foley and Senator
Hutchins arrived on the scene and a scuffle ensued in which Egan was allegedly
injured and the bag of leaflets became the object of a tug-of-war. Egan managed
to flee with a bag of pamphlets and was soon reunited with his pamphlet-dropping
partner. The stingers were quick to follow and were able to photograph Egan,
leaflets in hand. Egan was the only one of the letter- droppers who later testified in
court that he was not aware of the contents of the leaflet at the time of distribution
(*Commonwealth Director of Prosecutions v Egan* 2009:7).

The Islamic Australia Federation

The role of the Islamic Australia Federation is to support Islamic Australians by providing a strong network within Islamic Australia. Muslims supporting Muslims within the community and assisting and showing christian Australians the glorious path to Islam.

In the upcoming **Federal election** we strongly **support the ALP** as our preferred party to govern this country and **urge all other Muslims to do the same**.

The leading role of the ALP in supporting our faith at both State and Local government levels has been exceptional and we look forward to further support when Kevin Rudd leads this country.

We gratefully acknowledge Labors support to forgive our Muslim brothers who have been unjustly sentenced to death for the Bali bombings.

Labor supports our **new Mosque** construction and we hope, with the support and funding by Local and State governments, to open our new Mosque in **St Marys soon**.

Labor was the **only** political **party** to **support** the entry to this country of our Grand Mufti reverend **Sheik al-Hilaly** and we thank Hon. Paul Keating for over-turning the objections of ASIO to allow our Grand Mufti to enter this country.

Figure 8.1 The Lindsay leaflet was fraudulently characterized as being made by a fictitious peak Islamic organization. The leaflet asked residents to vote for the Australian Labor Party (ALP) because they were pro-Muslim and would approve a local mosque. The leaflet was exposed as a fraud, manufactured by members of the Lindsay Branch of the Liberal Party of Australia with the intent of convincing non-Muslim residents in North St Marys not to vote for the ALP.

Source: *Daily Telegraph*, 22 November 2007.

Nearby, Gilchrist, who was scoping the area from his car, also happened upon a letter-dropper who quickly fled. Gilchrist got out of his car and chased the man to a nearby street where Clark, the creator of the leaflet, was being unwillingly photographed by yet another Labor stinger. A few days later one of the photographs of a man with 'features that are consistent of the features of Gary Clark' (*Commonwealth Director of Prosecutions v Clark* 2009: 5) carrying a bag and hiding his face with one of the fraudulent leaflets was plastered across Australian newspapers (see Figure 8.2). This image was later considered as incriminating evidence against Clark in court (*Commonwealth Director of Prosecutions v Clark* 2009: 3, 7-8). Clark and the fleeing letter-dropper quickly jumped into a parked car. The Labor stingers photographed the car's registration plate as it drove away.

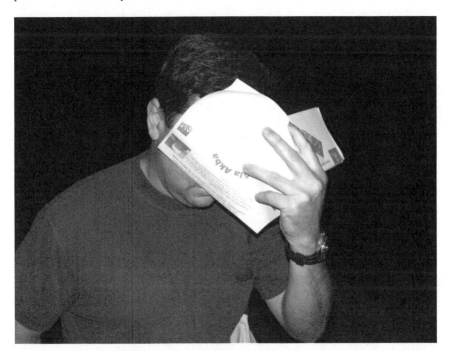

Figure 8.2   **A member of the Lindsay Branch of the Liberal Party of Australia, delivering the infamous Lindsay leaflet in North St Marys, 20 November 2007. In the Local Court of NSW, witnesses identified this as a photograph of Gary Clark of the Liberal Party of Australia (*Commonwealth Director of Prosecutions v Clark* 2009: 4-6). The picture evokes a sense of the 'sting' that evening as well as embarrassment and guilt.**

Source: David Latham

Liberal Party leaders later characterized the Lindsay leaflet scandal as an aberration. Local and national level Party leaders referred to the actions as 'silly' and 'immature', and attempted to downplay their seriousness by dismissing them as a 'prank' or as 'over-enthusiasm' (Coorey 2007). They also insisted that this was a one-off political performance but the case study itself suggests the opposite. Indeed, the political utility of Islamophobia was a taken-for-granted assumption of the leaflet manufacturers. More worryingly, the leaflet scandal has been linked to previous attempts to use Islamophobia for political gain (Commonwealth of Australia 2010: 2, 83; Dikeos 2010). In 2004, in the nearby Federal Electorate of Greenway, a fake flyer pretending to be an endorsed ALP political leaflet was distributed the day before a general election. The leaflet focused on the ALP candidate for Greenway, Ed Husic, who has a Bosnian heritage and is a non-practising Muslim. The leaflet stated that 'Ed Husic is a devout Muslim. Ed is working hard to get a better deal for Islam in Greenway' (Commonwealth of Australia 2010: 83; Hutchins 2004: 54). The leaflet was clearly intended to generate a panic among non-Muslims that the ALP was going to assist with the favouring of Muslims in the area. This demonstrates that in this region of western Sydney there was a history of stirring Islamophobia in political campaigns with the aim of delivering political injury to the ALP.

In February 2011, just over three years after the Lindsay leaflet scandal, newspapers revealed that the Liberal Party's immigration spokesman, Scott Morrison, had suggested in a Shadow Cabinet meeting in the previous December that the party could make political capital from the 'electorate's growing concerns about Muslim immigration, about Muslims in Australia and the inability of Muslim migrants to integrate' (Taylor 2011: 1). The context was later disclosed as being a hot-house session in which Shadow Cabinet members were asked to list two or three fresh ideas for improving the political stocks of the Liberal Party. Media accounts do report that other Shadow Cabinet members strongly condemned the suggestion, and clearly some had belatedly leaked the discussion to the media. Nonetheless, this is further evidence that some Australian political leaders see the inflammation of Islamophobia as politically useful. While the Lindsay leaflet scandal was a local affair, these assumptions voiced in the Shadow Cabinet also point to the importance of a national context. These local and national contexts must also be viewed against a global context to Islamophobia.

Global Islamophobia: Global Folk Devils

During March and April of 2008 the Pew Global Attitudes Project (Pew) undertook surveys across 24 countries to gather a sense of the negative or positive views held towards Muslims (n:24717) (2008: 7). Respondents in the sample countries were asked, '… please tell me if you have a very favourable, somewhat favourable, somewhat unfavourable or very unfavourable opinion of Muslims'. In Australia, 53 per cent said they had a somewhat favourable opinion and seven per cent were very favourable (Pew, 2008: 53-54). Islamophobia was high in Asian counties such as Japan (61 per cent negative), China (55 per cent) and South Korea (50 per cent). Even across the largely non-Muslim countries of the west there were considerable variations in the extent of negativity towards Muslims. In the United Kingdom (23 per cent) and United States (23 per cent) the negative feeling was a little less than that in Australia (29 per cent) and in France (32 per cent). But the rates of negative feeling towards Muslims were much higher in Germany (50 per cent), Spain (52 per cent) and Poland (46 per cent). The Pew results demonstrate two somewhat contradictory trends. First, Islamophobia is a global phenomenon. Second, there is considerable variation in the extent to which respondents in different countries said they held negative opinions towards Muslims. This variation itself is evidence of the spatially dynamic and constructed nature of Islamophobia. Global Islamophobia has no essence; it is not a natural consequence of a clash of civilizations, nor is it a structural given or a necessary outcome of (neo)liberalism. Islamophobia is a political construction with shared aspects of the stereotyping of Islam across nations (Dunn 2001; Obama 2009; Said 1981). However, Islamophobia is given life through political performances that have local relevance.

The development of Islamophobia has been conceptualized as typical of 'new racism'. It has been said that 'old racism' made overt references to 'racial groups' and to natural hierarchies in which some groups were held to be naturally superior and some inferior (Barker 1981; Cole 1997; Gilroy 1987; Hall 1992: 256-8; Jayasuriya 2002). These discourses were some of the philosophical foundations of colonialism (Anderson 2007). Another old racism discourse was that racial groups were so socially distant from each other that they were incompatible and should not share the same spaces. This discourse of racial separatism effectively ruled out cross-racial intimacy and was an ideological bulwark for apartheid. The new racism discourses elide any reference to 'race' per se, and take issue instead with cultural, ethnic or religious groups. Common to the discourse of new racism are phrases such as: 'I am not racist, but… I don't like such-and-such a group' or 'that such-and-such a group does not fit-in'. This is how contemporary anti-Muslim politics in the west can be seen as a manifestation of the new racism. Islam is characterized as incompatible with western values and Muslims are said to not fit within 'Christian-based societies' (Hopkins 2004). This reliance on asserted incompatibility helps explain the domestic inflection of Islamophobia. Islamophobia constructs Muslims as too different from the local non-Muslims, be they Australian non-Muslims, French or British non-Muslims.

Islamophobia must be performed in ways that have domestic resonance. Muslims are constructed as incompatible with the customs and values of a given place. The concept of the 'folk devil' is useful here (Cohen 1972; Goode and Ben-Yehuda 1994; Garland 2008). The folk devil group and their performances are constructed as being 'out of place' (Cresswell 1996; Sibley, 1995). This out-of-place-ness is an important component of the outcasting involved in moral panics (Hall et al. 1978). If non-Christians are said not to belong in a certain place, for example if mosques are judged to be culturally incompatible, then this implies that Christians belong there, and that the place is Christian. In other words, outcasting the folk devil involves both the construction of the Other as well as the Self (Dunn et al. 2007). The Lindsay leaflet attempted to reinforce a few key aspects of the process described above. The leaflet developers gambled that readers of the pamphlet assumed that Australia was a Christian country and were fearful that Christian hegemony was being threatened by an emerging and deviant Muslim presence. The leaflet cultivated the impression that a cultural takeover was in train, that Muslims were seeking to convert all Christians to Islam, that mosques were being built in every suburb, and that key institutions had become prisoners to Muslim demands (Figure 8.1). The latter included the argument that the Australian Labor Party (ALP) supported the cultural take-over of Australia by Muslims, were sympathetic to Muslim terrorists, and supportive of controversial Muslim clerics.

Australian Islamophobia

An examination of the demography and policy around religious diversity sheds further light on Islamophobia in Australia and the national context within which the Lindsay leaflet scandal was conducted. At the 2006 Census of Population and Housing (Census) undertaken by the Australian Bureau of Statistics (ABS) there were 340,400 Australians who said that their religious affiliation was to Islam. This constituted 1.7 per cent of the population. The total non-Christian proportion of the Australian population was less than 6.2 per cent, and those affiliating as Christian were 63 per cent (Stevenson et al. 2010). In population terms Australia is a predominantly Christian country. During 2008 and 2009, the Australian Human Rights Commission co-ordinated a year-long public consultation on freedom of religion and belief in Australia. This included the receipt of 2033 written submissions and 24 public sittings. Gary Bouma and his colleagues prepared a report, *Freedom of religion and belief in 21st century Australia*, on the content of these submissions. Their conclusion included a comment on competing definitions of the religious character of Australia:

> The self-definition and religious character of Australia has been and remains a contentious issue, with various voices advocating Australia as a Christian nation, or as a secular nation, or as a multifaith plural nation. This issue is important, because it influences the way the different voices articulate policy and practice and argue for change (Bouma et al. 2011: 80-1).

They pointed to a public tension over whether Australia was a Christian nation, a secular nation, or a multi-faith nation, and they inferred that each vision had radical implications for freedom of religion. There is evidence to support arguments that Australia is a Christian nation, such as the demographics of affiliation and the embedded nature of Christian practice in the political establishment (the Parliamentary Prayer; the presence of God within the Preamble to the *Commonwealth of Australia Constitution Act*, etc) (Fozdar 2011a; 2011b). But there is also official support for the position that Australia is a secular nation such as Section 116 of the *Commonwealth of Australia Constitution* which prohibits establishmentarianism and mandates freedom of religion. There is also official sanction for Australia as a multi-faith nation, such as in recent proclamations on the meaning of the policy of multiculturalism (Australian Multicultural Advisory Council 2010: 2). This is the shifting, contested and somewhat fraught context to Islamophobia in Australia. The official ambiguity around national definitions of the Australian religious character provided a space for Christian-centrism and Islamophobia. The Lindsay leaflet developers were able to capitalize from and cultivate this political opportunity.

There is a convincing set of evidence of the prevalence of Islamophobia in Australia, including attitudinal data as well as reports from public inquiries. The Challenging Racism Project (2011) used a Bogardus scale to test the average levels of social distance that Australians felt towards a series of minority groups. Muslims were by far the group towards which there was most discomfort, with almost half of all 12 512 respondents saying they would be concerned if a relative were to marry a Muslim (followed by 28 per cent reporting concern if a relative were to marry an Aboriginal Australian). Just over 20 per cent said they would be very (8.7 per cent) or extremely (11.7 per cent) concerned. The AHRC-supported inquiry into 'Freedom of Religion and Belief in Australia' also found strong levels of anti-Muslim sentiment through the public submissions they had received (Bouma et al. 2011: 71-2, 81-3). There is a good deal of empirically demonstrated anti-Muslim sentiment in Australia, and there is some level of official acknowledgement of that issue. Indeed, the developers of the fraudulent Lindsay leaflet were relying on the existence of anti-Muslim sentiment amongst non-Muslim Australians for the successful incitement of Islamophobia.

The consequences of the political use of Islamophobia include the degradation of community relations, heightened public unease and the undermining of social cohesion. Stereotypes about Islam, within political and media discourse, feed into personal experiences of racism, discrimination and substantive inequality (Anti-Discrimination Board of New South Wales 2003: 5; Dunn, 2001; The International Federation for Human Rights 2005; Human Rights and Equal Opportunity Commission of Australia (HREOC) 2004). There have been well-documented instances of people of Middle Eastern appearance being attacked because of their ethnicity (e.g. Dunn 2009; HREOC 2004; Poynting and Noble 2004). The Racism Monitor team at the University of Technology Sydney found that there were increases in physical and verbal attacks against Australians of Muslim and Middle Eastern background following heavily reported terror events overseas (Dreher 2005: 11-14, 20-1). The Islamic Women's Welfare Council of Victoria (IWWCV) characterized the experiences of racism by Muslim women in Australia thus: 'Racism against Muslim women has a pervasive and persistent cyclical pattern, characterized by quiet periods of everyday racisms and incivility, which are interrupted by sharp rises in racism after international incidents of Muslim-related terrorism' (El Matrah and Dimopoulos 2008: 13). These national contexts paint a quite negative picture on the bases and impacts of Islamophobia in Australia.

From their review of religious freedom in Australia, Gary Bouma and his co-authors reported on the ways in which freedom of religion was being impaired for Australian Muslims (Bouma et al. 2011: 69-70). Interestingly, they also described how many of the public submissions to the inquiry, including those from non-Muslims, recognized the problems that Muslims in Australia faced (Bouma et al. 2011: 72). These problems included stereotyping, government inaction to protect Muslims, discrimination in spheres of life like employment and education, as well as prejudicial statements from government and some organized Christian groups and leaders. This indicates some level of official acknowledgment of the impacts of Islamophobia in Australia. A telephone survey of 600 Victorians found that 84 per cent of respondents thought that media representations influenced the way Muslims were treated, and 70 per cent agreed that Australians generally needed to be more tolerant of Muslims (El Matrah and Dimopoulos 2008: 10-11). These data suggest there is a good deal of public awareness of Islamophobia and acknowledgment that Australian Muslims suffer racism, discrimination and inequality as a result of that Islamophobia. These public acknowledgments are vital political resources for challenging Islamophobia in Australia.

Local Islamophobia

Islamophobia pertains across every state and territory in Australia. This speaks to the global and ambient nature of the issue. However, there are interesting variations across states and territories. For example, the degree of social distance towards Muslims is stronger in the eastern states of NSW and Queensland, and also in South Australia (but more so in NSW) (Challenging Racism 2011). NSW is the state with the largest Muslim presence and its state capital, Sydney, is the city with the highest proportion of Muslims (3.9 per cent) in Australia. Sydney is a city where researchers have documented moral panics involving Muslims (Poynting et al. 2004). Sydney is also where there have been official condemnations of the role of both media and politicians for inflaming ethnic relations, and specifically for conjuring public distrust of Australian Muslims and those from Middle-Eastern backgrounds (Anti-Discrimination Board of New South Wales 2003). One of the clearest such condemnations was the official finding of the NSW Police inquiry into the causes of the Cronulla riots in 2005 (Strike Force Neil (hereafter *Hazzard Report*) 2006). The *Hazzard Report* found that relations between a handful of Anglo and Middle-Eastern male youth at Cronulla had been irresponsibly inflated by 'colourful, exaggerated and inaccurate' reporting in the media (2006: 7-8, 25-28). The *Hazzard Report* (2006: 7-8, 27-8, 33-34) attributed a good deal of the blame for the riot to talk radio and tabloid newspapers. The media had circulated inaccuracies about events leading up to the riot, reinforced stereotypes, and broadcast the incitement of racist violence. The stronger level of Islamophobia in NSW and Sydney is an unfortunate by-product of the racist politics in Sydney. Again, this is suggestive of the constructed nature of Islamophobia, and of how it can fade or thrive depending on political contexts.

Although Sydney's proportion of Muslim residents (3.9 per cent) is well above the national average (1.7 per cent), Muslims are still a clear minority, with Christians making up 63 per cent of Sydney's population. In some Local Government Areas (LGAs) of Sydney Muslims comprise a much higher proportion of the population, such as the 15 per cent who are resident in Bankstown. The Bankstown LGA includes the town centre of Lakemba which has become well known as a site of Muslim settlement and Islamic infrastructure (mosques, community centres, private religious schools, halal butchers and restaurants, community media, etc). But even in Bankstown the proportion of the population who are Christian is 61 per cent. Nonetheless, the perceived threat of 'Muslim take-over' of suburbs has been core to some of the moral panics that have used and reinforced Islamophobia in Sydney over the last two decades (Dunn, 2001; Dunn et al. 2007). In the Penrith LGA, where the Lindsay leaflet scandal occurred, Muslims only constituted 1.6 per cent of the population at the 2006 Census.

North St Marys, the targeted area for the Lindsay leaflet-drop, has, since World War Two, been characterized as 'a typical post-war working class Australian community' (Penrith City Council 1989 cited in Stacker 2002: 128). It is located on the eastern boundary of the electoral division of Lindsay and is 47 kilometres west of the Sydney Central Business District. North St Marys neighbours the larger suburb of St Marys proper—the second largest established town-centre (after Penrith itself) within the Penrith LGA and the only suburb in the City of Penrith to have a strong history of industrial development (Stacker 2002: 110). Beginning with the establishment of tanneries, sawmills, brick makers and wheelwrights from the 1860s, St Marys later became a site of a large munitions factory during World War Two with factory staff being housed in the residential area of North St Marys (State Heritage Inventory 2008; Stacker 2002). In the post-war period, the munitions factory was replaced by smaller industries such as those producing textiles, industrial chemicals and tools. A large industrial estate was established and the NSW Housing Commission developed North St Marys into a residential area for low income families (State Heritage Inventory 2008; Stacker 2002). Today part of this housing estate is privately owned and part continues to be retained by the Australian Government (State Heritage Inventory 2008). North St Marys remains a 'blue-collar' neighbourhood. The 2006 Census[3] recorded labourers, technicians, trade workers, machinery operators and drivers as comprising 48.7 per cent of employed persons (compared to 7.3 per cent who are professionals). The median family income was AU$883 per week compared to the national median of AU$1 171 per week, and the suburb had a high rate of unemployment (11.7 per cent

---

3   All proceeding national, North St Marys and Penrith census data were obtained from the Australian Bureau of Statistics (2006).

compared to the national rate of 5.2 per cent). In regard to cultural diversity, 21.5 per cent of residents were born overseas with the most common overseas countries of birth being England (3.3 per cent), Philippines (2.4 per cent), New Zealand (1.6 per cent) and Fiji (1.2 per cent). The majority (77.3 per cent) of residents spoke only English at home followed by a much smaller percentage of residents who spoke Arabic (2.6 per cent). North St Marys was strongly Christian with 72.5 per cent of residents belonging to a Christian faith (compared to 63 per cent of all Australian residents). The second most common religious affiliation in North St Marys was to Islam (1.4 per cent). By comparison, 3.9 per cent of the Sydney-wide population are Muslim, as discussed earlier. This was the religious and socio-economic context of the place chosen for the distribution of the 'Lindsay leaflet'.

Ten kilometres away, across the other side of the electoral division of Lindsay, is the much more affluent suburb of Penrith where the letter-drop briefing took place. Overlooking the scenic Nepean River and with the World Heritage listed Blue Mountains as a backdrop, Penrith was never an industrial town. Rather, in the decades after its original establishment as a municipality in the 1870s, it was considered a sleepy town characterized by small businesses and frequented by holiday-makers who could enjoy recreational activities provided by the Nepean River (Stacker 2002). The 1940s and 1950s saw rapid population growth in Penrith. It was during this time that Penrith and St Marys (along with surrounding settlements) were envisaged as a single 'satellite' town — the City of Penrith LGA. St Marys would provide the industrial centre (with North St Marys housing the increased numbers of factory workers), whilst the 'satellite city' would be balanced by the recreational and tourist value of Penrith (O'Brien 1950). In addition, Penrith would provide commercial, entertainment and business facilities 'of city standards' (O'Brien 1950). Today the suburb of Penrith is a commercial and business hub of the Penrith LGA. The comparable affluence of the suburb of Penrith to North St Marys is reflected in census statistics. Unlike North St Marys, unemployment in Penrith is on par with the national rate (at 5.3 per cent) and the median family income is higher than the national (at AU$1 285 per week). Again, in contrast to North St Marys, whose residents are predominantly 'blue-collar' workers, there is a much higher concentration of office and professional staff in Penrith. The most common occupations in the suburb of Penrith are clerical and administrative (19.1 per cent of employed persons), technical and trades (15.9 per cent), and professional (12.8 per cent). It was in this suburb of relative prosperity that a racist plan to influence Labor votes in the predominantly 'White', working-class suburb of North St Marys was hatched.

The selection of North St Marys for Islamophobic leafleting is unlikely to have been random. Indeed, the ALP had been tipped off on the location of the leafleting, indicating that North St Marys had been chosen by the leaflet developers long in advance. North St Marys was locally selected as a prime site at which to deploy, cultivate and benefit from Islamophobia. This is again suggestive of the spatially inflected nature of Islamophobia. We have shown earlier how global Islamophobia is varied and how it has a nationalist proclivity. Islamophobia is also locally targeted. Finally, it is worth remembering that the public exposure of this racist electoral tactic relied heavily on the tip-off from within the Liberal Party. The tip-off also demonstrates that the tolerance of racist political performances is not universal among the Liberal Party nor specifically among those in the Lindsay electorate.

The Aftermath, Lessons and Political Resources for Anti-Racism

In April of 2008, five months after the Lindsay leaflet scandal, five men appeared in Downing Centre Local Court, charged with offences against the *Commonwealth Electoral Act 1918*. Specifically, the five Liberal Party members were accused of having been in breach of Section 328 of the Act, which stipulates guidelines for the printing and distribution of electoral advertisements and notices. Three of the five pleaded guilty, two pleaded not guilty, with one of those losing his defence. The four guilty findings were associated with fines and costs ranging from AU$500 to AU$3 100. At that time, the maximum fine payable by individuals for breaching this section of the Act was AU$1 100, and for a body corporate it was AU$5 500 (Commonwealth of Australia 2010: 4-5). After inquiring into the Lindsay leaflet scandal the Joint Standing Committee on Electoral Matters recommended that the fines be increased to the equivalent of AU$6 600 for an individual and AU$33 000 for a body corporate (Commonwealth of Australia 2010: 25). In his letter of apology to the Liberal Party leadership, one of the leaflet developers, and partner of the previous sitting member for Lindsay, took the opportunity to 'particularly apologise to the Muslim community to whom I bear no malice, for the offence caused by my actions' (Clark 2007).

The developers and distributors of the Lindsay leaflet were never held to account for their attempts to incite fear and hatred, nor for their planned use and reinforcement of Islamophobia. Leaders of the Liberal Party referred to the leaflet tactic as silly and immature, although the Liberal Prime Minister at the time, John Howard, had used more condemnatory terms like 'tasteless and offensive' (Commonwealth of Australia 2010: iii). In the Court ruling of the first guilty plea, the magistrate rebuked the accused: 'You should have had the strength of character ... to simply turn your face against this reprehensible behaviour'. She lamented that there was not a usable offence of racial slander to use against the accused, and said that the leaflet scandal had arisen 'in a political climate of divisiveness and disharmony which had been generated for a number of years. ... an ugly chapter in this country's history' (O'Shane Judgement, in *The Age* 2008). For many observers the aftermath paid too little formal attention to the racist aspects of the scandal. The ALP Member for Lindsay worried that the inquiries had paid too little heed to the words that were used: 'material that was racially and religiously motivated and material that was by its nature deeply divisive and intended to cause and incite division' (Bradbury 2010: 30-39). The most despondent note in this chapter is the reticence or inability of most public authorities and commentators to condemn the racism that was at the core of this attempted deployment and cultivation of Islamophobia.

The Lindsay leaflet developers attempted to hitch the power of global Islamophobia to their own national political ambitions through a local act of skulduggery. The existence of Islamophobia in Australia is well known and it was selected as a political resource by the leaflet developers. A well-rehearsed set of stereotypes of Muslims as intolerant and militant were the repertoire of these purveyors of Islamophobia. They poured everyday understandings of Islamophobia into the Lindsay leaflet in their attempt to spread anxiety among local non-Muslims about Australian Muslims. The non-Muslim residents of North St Marys were the targets of the Lindsay scam. We have shown the potential for deep division and harm. We have also demonstrated that the injurious effects of Islamophobia are also well known, but the political benefits were too tempting for this group of Liberal Party members in Lindsay. They attempted to gain leverage from concern about a Muslim cultural take-over in Australia. Our contextualized case study starkly reveals how Islamophobia is seen as a political device even within mainstream politics.

This review of a local attempt to obtain leverage from global Islamophobia has inferred some political resources for anti-racism. First, there is a widespread acknowledgement that Muslims are portrayed poorly in political and media discourse, and there is a public acceptance that this portrayal has substantive negative impacts upon Australian Muslims. Second, there is a good deal of public wariness and cynicism towards the political use of Islamophobia. There is no better protection against the divisiveness of Islamophobia than the inculcation of public incredulity towards such tactics. Third, there is an important role for whistle blowers who can help expose calculated uses of Islamophobia. Speaking out and exposing the motivations of an attempt to deploy and cultivate Islamophobia can have a dramatic effect. If the purveyors of Islamophobia have been exposed then this must seriously undermine the credibility of subsequent deployments. Three years after the Lindsay scandal, in the contiguous Federal Electorate of Chifley, a Liberal candidate wrote on his Facebook page that 'God was on the side of the Liberal Right and accused opponents of bringing the nation closer to the hands of a Muslim country' (Dikeos 2010: 2). The Federal Liberal leadership immediately disendorsed the candidate. Through exposé, such as this review of the Lindsay Leaflet scandal, Islamophobia can be revealed as a base attempt at political hoodwinking. If it can be revealed that moral turpitude and criminality is associated with the deployment of Islamophobia, then subsequent iterations can be fundamentally undermined.

References

The Age. 2008. Lindsay leaflet was stupid: magistrate, 29 April. [online article, accessed 1 April 2010: http://news.theage.com.au].

Anderson, K. 2007. *Race and the Crisis of Humanism*. London and New York: Routledge.

Anti-Discrimination Board of New South Wales. 2003. *Race for the headlines: racism and media discourse*. Sydney: Anti-Discrimination Board of New South Wales.

Australian Bureau of Statistics. 2006. *Census of Population and Housing 2006*. Canberra: Australian Bureau of Statistics. [http://www.abs.gov.au].

Australian Multicultural Advisory Council. 2010. *The People of Australia: The Australian Multicultural Advisory Council's Statement on Cultural Diversity and Recommendations to Government*. Canberra: The Australian Multicultural Advisory Council.

Barker, M. 1981. *The New Racism: Conservatives and the Ideology of the Tribe*. London: Junction Books.

Bradbury, D. 2010. Electoral Matters Committee Report, Commonwealth of Australia. Senate. *Parliamentary Debates* (Official Hansard). Canberra, Australia, 18 March 2010. [www.aph.gov.au/hansard].

Benson, S. 2007. Lib tip-off put scam sting in motion. *The Daily Telegraph*. 23 November, 5.

Bouma, G., Cahill, D., Dellal, H. and Zwartz, A. 2011. *Freedom of religion and belief in 21st century Australia*. Canberra: The Australian Human Rights Commission.

Challenging Racism 2011. *Findings, Challenging Racism: The Anti-Racism Research Project*. [accessed 31 March 2011, last updated 22 February 2011: http://www.uws.edu.au/social_sciences/soss/research/challenging_racism/findings_by_region].

Clark, G. 2007. Letter to Graham Jaeschke, State Director The Liberal Party of Australia (NSW Division). Reproduced in Joint Standing Committee on Electoral Matters. (2010). *Report on the 2007 Federal Election – Events in the Division of Lindsay: Review of penalty provisions in the Commonwealth Electoral Act 1918*. Canberra: Commonwealth of Australia, 73.

Cohen, S. 1972. *Folk Devils and Moral Panics*. Oxford: Blackwell.

Cole, J. 1997. *The New Racism in Europe*. Cambridge: Cambridge University Press.

Commonwealth Director of Public Prosecutions V Clark (2009). Reproduced in Commonwealth of Australia. Joint Standing Committee on Electoral Matters. (2010). *Report on the 2007 Federal Election – Events in the Division of Lindsay: Review of penalty provisions in the Commonwealth Electoral Act 1918*. Canberra: Commonwealth of Australia, 45-58. [accessed online: www.aph.gov.au].

Commonwealth Director of Public Prosecutions V Egan (2009). Reproduced in Commonwealth of Australia. Joint Standing Committee on Electoral Matters. (2010). *Report on the 2007 Federal Election – Events in the Division of Lindsay: Review of penalty provisions in the Commonwealth Electoral Act*

1918. Canberra: Commonwealth of Australia, 59-72. [accessed online: www. aph.gov.au].

Commonwealth of Australia. Joint Standing Committee on Electoral Matters. 2010. *Report on the 2007 Federal Election – Events in the Division of Lindsay: Review of penalty provisions in the Commonwealth Electoral Act 1918.* Canberra: Commonwealth of Australia. [accessed online: www.aph.gov.au].

Coorey, P. with Bibby, P., Ramachandran, A. and Australian Associated Press. 2007. Liberal shame over fake pamphlet, *The Sydney Morning Herald*, 22 November. [online article, accessed 1 April 2010: www.smh.com.au].

Cresswell, T. 1996. *In Place Out of Place: Geography, Ideology, and Transgression.* London: University of Minnesota Press.

Dikeos, T. 2010. First Muslim MP, *The 7.30 Report*. Australian Broadcasting Corporation, 26 August 2010. [online transcript, accessed 3 December 2010: http://www.abc.net.au/7.30/content/2010/s2994694.htm].

Dreher, T. 2005. *Targeted: experiences of racism in NSW after September 11, 2001.* Ultimo: University of Technology Sydney Press.

Dunn, K.M. 2001. Representations of Islam in the politics of mosque development in Sydney. *Tijdschrift voor Economische en Sociale Geografie*, 92(3), 291-308.

Dunn, K.M. 2009. Performing Australian nationalisms at Cronulla. In G. Noble (ed.), *Lines in the Sand: The Cronulla riots, multiculturalism and national belonging*. 76-94. Sydney: Institute of Criminology Press.

Dunn, K.M., Klocker, N. and Salabay, T. 2007. Contemporary racism and Islamaphobia in Australia: racialising religion, *Ethnicities*, 7(4), 564-589.

El Matrah, J. and Dimopoulos, M. 2008. *Race, faith and gender: converging discriminations against Muslim women in Victoria. The ongoing impact of September 11, 2001. A summary report on racism against Muslim women*, Northcote: Islamic Women's Welfare Council of Victoria.

Fozdar, F. 2011a. The Choir Boy and the Mad Monk: Christianity, Islam, Australia's political landscape and prospects for multiculturalism. *Journal of Intercultural Studies*, in press.

Fozdar, F. 2011b. Constructing Australian citizenship as Christian; or how to exclude Muslims from the national imagining. In M. Lobo and F. Mansouri (eds.) *Migration, Citizenship and Intercultural Relations*. Surrey: Ashgate, in press.

Garland, D. 2008. On the Concept of Moral Panic. *Crime, Media, Culture*, 4 (1), 9-30.

Gilroy, P. 1987. *There Ain't No Black in the Union Jack: The Cultural Politics of Race and Nation*. London: Hutchinson.

Goode, E. and Ben-Yehuda, N. 1994. *Moral panics: The social construction of deviance*. Cambridge, MA: Blackwell.

Hall, S., Critcher, C., Jefferson, T., Clarke, J. and Roberts, B. 1978. *Policing the Crisis*. London: Macmillan.

Hall, S. 1992. New ethnicities. In J. Donald & A. Rattansi (eds.) *'Race', Culture and Difference*. London: Sage, 252-9.

Hopkins, P. 2004. Young Muslim men in Scotland: Inclusions and Exclusions. *Children's Geographies*, 2 (2), 257-72.

Human Rights and Equal Opportunity Commission (HREOC) 2004. *Ismae Listen: National consultations on eliminating prejudice against Arab and Muslim Australians*, Sydney: Human Rights and Equal Opportunity Commission.

Hutchins, S. 2004. In Commonwealth of Australia. Senate. *Parliamentary Debates* (Official Hansard). Canberra, Australia, Thursday, 18 November 2004. [www. aph.gov.au/hansard].

International Federation for Human Rights. 2005. *Intolerance and Discrimination against Muslims in the EU – Developments since September 11*. International Federation for Human Rights.

Jacobson, G. 2008. Kelly seemed involved, court told, *Sydney Morning Herald,* 30 April, 2.

Jayasuriya, L. 2002. Understanding Australian Racism, *Australian Universities Review*, 45 (1), 40-44.

Kontaminas, B. 2008. No conviction for leaflet scam volunteer, *Sydney Morning Herald*, 20 May. [online article, accessed 1 April 2010: www.smh.com.au].

Murphy, K., Ker, P. and Zwartz, B. 2007. Liberals stand firm despite race row, *The Age*, 23 November. [online article, accessed 1 April 2010: www.theage. com.au].

Obama B. 2009. Cairo Speech in the Grand Hall of Cairo University, reproduced in *Guardian*, Thursday 4 June 2009. [accessed online 3 December 2010: www. guardian.co.uk].

O'Brien, J. 1950. *Planning Australia's First Satellite City*. Penrith City Council. [www.penrithcity.nsw.gov.au].

Pew Research Centre, 2008. *Unfavorable Views of Jews and Muslims on the Increase in Europe*. The Pew Global Attitudes Project, Washington.

Poynting, S. and Noble, G. 2004. *Living with Racism: The experience and reporting by Arab and Muslim Australians of discrimination, abuse and violence since 11 September 2001*. [accessed online: http://www.humanrights.gov.au/racial_ discrimination/isma/research/index.html].

Poynting, S., Noble G., Tabar, P. and Collins, J. 2004. *Bin Laden in the Suburbs; Criminalising the Arab Other*. Sydney: Sydney Institute of Criminology.

Said, E.W. 1981. *Covering Islam*. New York: Pantheon Books.

Sibley, D. 1995. *Geographies of Exclusion*. Boston: Blackwell.

Stacker, L. 2002. *Pictorial history: Penrith and St Marys*. Sydney: Kingsclear Books.

State Heritage Inventory. 2008. *St Marys (north) Conservation Area*, SHI Number 2260821, Penrith City Council. [www.penrithcity.nsw.gov.au].

Stevenson, D., Dunn K.M., Possamai A. and Piracha, A. 2010. Sydney: An Examination of a 'Post-Secular' World City. *The Australian Geographer*, 41(3), 323-350.

Strike Force Neil. (*Hazzard Report*) 2006. *Cronulla Riots: Review of the Police Response*, Vol. 1. Sydney: NSW Police Force.

Taylor, L. 2011. Morrison sees votes in anti-Muslim strategy, *The Sydney Morning Herald*, 17 February. [online article, accessed 14 July, 2011: http://www.smh.com.au].

Chapter 9

Moral Panic and Media Representation: The Bradford Riot

Joanne Massey and Rajinder Singh Tatla

Introduction

This chapter will concentrate on the Bradford riot of 7 July 2001 and in particular how this event was represented in the media. The riots resulted in property destruction, numerous arrests and a besmirched reputation for the city of Bradford in the north of England. On 11 September of the same year the terrorist attack on the World Trade Centre occurred. Both events resulted in increasingly polarized and negative media representations of the Muslim population, not least in the United Kingdom (Spalek 2002, Abbas 2007). The riots gave rise to prejudiced media reporting, which have continued since then:

> a culture of unashamed questioning of the cultural practices and national allegiances of British Muslims has grown. These domestic troubles have since been allowed to unfold without pause into a hysterical Islamophobia since September 11th, Afghanistan, Bali and Mombasa, one that caricatures all Muslims as fatwa fanatics and enemies of the West (Amin 2003: 460).

The media often equate Islam 'with holy war and hatred, fanaticism and violence, intolerance and the oppression of women' (Esposito, 1999:3). Stan Cohen (1972) suggests that moral panic is a media-orchestrated response of fear towards some group or individual 'folk devil', based on the perception that they are dangerously deviant and pose a menace to society. The new folk devil is the Muslim extremist, scapegoated for being criminally inclined and socially problematic because of failure to 'integrate'.

Summer in 2001 Britain saw rioting in northern England: in Oldham on 26 May, Leeds on 5 June, Burnley on 23 June, and Bradford on 7 July. These were quite different from riots during the eighties and marked a new departure in Britain's racial politics (Bagguley and Hussain 2003). Bradford's Asian youths responded to the threat of a British National Party (BNP) march in a violent manner resulting in extensive property destruction, and eventually substantial prison sentences for rioters and a tarnished reputation for the city. Here a detailed content analysis of media reports of the riot looks at segregation, racism, unemployment, multiculturalism, education and extreme right-wing organizations such as the BNP and National Front (NF). This analysis will highlight collective media responses to the events in Bradford in 2001 and significant differences in newspaper reporting.

This media analysis aims to answer the question, how accurate and realistic were the media representations?

Media Representations of Race

Bagguley and Hussain (2003) argue that the British mainstream media attempted to manipulate people's perceptions towards ethnic minority groups, such as the resident Pakistani and Bengali communities in Bradford. On the whole British newspapers tend to depict issues of race and immigration in terms of a perceived 'threat' which ultimately manipulates and influences public perceptions of social events (Hall et al 1978, Morrison and Statham 2005). Arguably the Asian youth has become the 'new Asian Folk Devil' (Alexander 2000, 2004) who is newly dangerous, often a fundamentalist or associate of a 'gang' of other young Asian males (Alexander 2004). The leap from 'gang' to 'terrorist cell' is all too convenient in a world where the news media are keen to sensationalize extremism and violence connected to Islam.

Muslims in the UK were increasingly represented as fanatic fundamentalists after the Salman Rushdie Affair of 1989 that resulted from the publication of *The Satanic Verses* (Akhtar 1989, Asad 1990, Modood 1990, Jewkes 2011).

> Since then, Muslims in the UK have continued to be identified in negative contexts, even when cast as victims; a phenomenon that has increased exponentially since the terrorist attacks on the twin towers of the World Trade Center, and the rail systems in Madrid and London (Jewkes 2011: 63).

Abbas (2007) noted that the Rushdie Affair had created concerns prior to 9/11 about British South Asian Muslims. Images of the 'book burnings in Bradford' which were broadcast globally, created negative media representations of Islam and British Muslims. In addition the shift in focus from colour in the 1950s, to race in the 1960s, ethnicity in the 1980s and finally religion in current society has meant that 'religion has emerged as a major social signifier' (Abbas 2007: 289). Indeed since 9/11 'those who were once abused as 'Pakis' are now also abused as 'Muslims''' (Kundnani 2007: 127). There is a clear shift from the 1970s practice of 'Paki-bashing' (Pearson 1976) couched in terms of an economic threat posed by immigrants, to Islamophobia based on a newly dangerous and potentially terrorist Muslim folk devil. Increasingly in British politics there has been an emphasis on 'Britishness' and the right-wing press has called for the government to 'acculturate' Muslims to the British way of life, with newspapers such as the *Daily Mail* labeling multiculturalism as 'lethally divisive' (Kundnani 2007: 122).

It is thus unsurprising that reports in the media of racially aggravated crime tend to bear prejudice against non-white populations, as this report on the Bradford riot of 2001 by a local newspaper indicates: 'at the root of everything there is still a fundamental and deep-seated hatred of white people and of authority in general in the hearts of a minority of young and mainly Muslim activists and thugs' (*Bradford Telegraph and Argus* 2001 cited in Macey 2002: 33).

In a remarkable *camera obscura*, the racism here is that of Muslim populations towards whites rather than vice versa. Whilst the events of 9/11 escalated Islamophobia (Allen and Nielsen 2002, Allen 2004), the disturbances in northern England in 2001 indicate the beginning of negative press for Islam (Abbas 2007). A study carried out in The *Telegraph and Argus* newspaper questioned over 1100 Muslims and found only 4 per cent of respondents thought that media representations were fair (*Telegraph and Argus* 2007). Similarly it is arguable that the media are institutionally racist. For example, not one newspaper had given a voice to anyone who participated in the riots. The issue here is not nationality (as more than half of the Muslims in Britain are British-born) but religion. According to Abbas (2007), the low levels of economic and social improvement available to Muslim populations in deprived urban areas means they 'have had little choice but to retreat into their communities' (2007: 290).

Media misrepresentation created a stigma and indeed moral panic around Muslims, which was then legitimated by 9/11 and 7/7, resulting in increased Islamophobia (Amin 2003). Moral panics involve labeling and stereotyping (Cohen 2002: 36-7) – in this case involving a slippage from violent Asian to Islamic fundamentalist suicide bomber (Kundnani 2007). Abbas (2007) notes that the 'incessant interest and focus by the state and media on 'militant jihadi' activity in Britain potentially perpetuates the problem' (2007: 291).

Allen (2004) observes that while anti-Muslim hostility existed prior to 9/11, the attack on the twin towers served to legitimise it. From that point distrust was extended to anyone who even vaguely resembled the Muslim stereotype, paradoxically resulting in attacks on Sikh men because of their skin colour and beards. There is much debate about definitions of Islamophobia as the term implies a fear of or prejudice against the religion of Islam; however, it can also be viewed as a form of racism as the media (and popular culture) tend to conflate race and Islam (Bravo Lopez 2010).

Prior to the 9/11 terrorist attacks Islamophobia was defined as having a fear of Muslims and an 'unfounded hostility towards Islam' (Runnymede Trust 1997), though after 9/11 hostilities towards Islam were popularly viewed as somehow more 'founded'. The media fanned these perceptions by reporting on the growth of anti-western fringe Muslim groups (Allen 2004). There are few positive images of Islam in news media, thus normalizing Islamophobia[1] (Allen 2004). Indeed, stories reporting on Islam tend to focus on the recurring discourses of asylum-seekers, forced marriages, Muslim faith schools (Ahmad 2006), honour killings and Sharia law. Abbas (2007: 298) attributes Islamophobia in the media to 'a victim-blaming pathology that is saturating public opinion'. This means that the

---

1   It should be noted that whilst the media utilize stereotypes and sensationalism they are not the sole cause of Islamophobia, as other events, most notably 9/11, and politicians response to this play a role too (Allen and Nielsen 2002).

erosion of civil liberties that is being effected for all UK citizens, but in particular British Muslims, is seen as more deserved by the latter.

Race and Britain

Postwar Britain has a history of racism-related urban riots, including the 1981 and 1985 uprisings in Brixton (London), Handsworth (Birmingham), Tottenham (London) Moss Side (Manchester) and Toxteth (Liverpool), those in June 1995 in Bradford (resulting in a public inquiry[2]) and in 2001 across Lancashire and Yorkshire in Burnley, Oldham and Bradford (Kundnani 2001). Earlier that same year (June 2001) riots broke out in the Harehills area of Leeds involving hostilities between over 100 Asian youths and the heavy-handed police (Farrar 2002). The riots were a manifestation of longstanding social problems, economic deprivation and local racial tensions between white and ethnic minority communities (Ahmed et al 2001). Thus the 'riots' are 'seen as the natural, inevitable response to racial discrimination and disadvantage' (Alexander 2004). Whereas earlier riots in the 1980s had been between united communities of Black[3] and White residents against the police, later riots were attributed to communities being fragmented by 'race' (Kundnani 2001). Unemployment and exclusion from public sector service jobs which were usually given to whites resulted in 'no doubt that ethnic resentment has been fuelled by deprivation and desperation' (Amin 2003: 461). In addition, right-wing groups took advantage of the economic crisis beginning in the 1980s, in appealing to unemployed white youths 'to garner support for their racist agendas' (Poynting and Mason 2001: 73).

In the increased Islamophobia in Britain after 9/11, the emphasis has been on the need for Muslims to integrate into British culture: the Government even measured integration when it introduced 'citizenship tests' under the Nationality, Immigration and Asylum Act 2002. Kundnani (2007) argues that in the prevailing ideology it was almost as if the lack of control by the government on who was allowed to enter Britain was somehow responsible for the riots and violence in northern British towns and cities. At this time British politics was echoing with buzz-words such as 'integration', 'cohesion' and 'diversity management' which deflected any attention away from institutional racism. 'The focus had shifted from the state's upholding of human rights to the responsibility of 'Muslims' to integrate themselves into the shared values of Britishness' (Kundnani 2007: 131).

---

2   See http://www.theyworkforyou.com/debates/?id=1995-06-21a.281.0 for a transcript of the House of Commons debate on Bradford Community Relations on 21 June 1995 at 11.30 a.m.

3   In this instance Black refers to those of both African Caribbean and South Asian origin.

The City of Bradford

Before discussing the causes of the riot it is important to give a picture of Bradford as a city. In the Ouseley Report (2001), *Community Pride Not Prejudice* (published in the same month as the riot occurred), Bradford is described as

> one of the best known multi-cultural centres in Britain and represents a unique challenge to race relations. The District was once blessed with economic wealth and prosperity. But with the demise of the wool industry and the decline in manufacturing, the District has seen a slide in its fortunes. It has struggled to redefine itself as a modern, 21st century, competitive, multi-cultural area and has lost its spirit of community togetherness. As a result, the Bradford District has witnessed growing divisions among its population along race, ethnic, religious and social class lines – and now finds itself in the grip of fear (Ouseley 2001: 1).

Bradford is a city with a diverse and multicultural population with a relatively high Asian demographic. According to the 2001 census, the Black and minority ethnic (BME) population of Bradford is proportionately higher than the UK national average by a factor of 2.7'% (ONS 2011). Macey (2002) states that 'one in five people in Bradford live in areas of multiple deprivation characterized by poverty, unemployment, poor education, overcrowded housing, crime, drug dealing, firearms and prostitution' (2002: 25).

Whilst Macey draws on statistical data, it is arguable that these statistics do not represent the complex ways that social antagonisms are experienced in everyday life. According to Burnett (2009) there were two key incidents in Bradford which highlighted racial tensions there. The first was the 'Honeyford Affair' where Headteacher Ray Honeyford controversially argued that children should be taught solely in the English language, and the second the 'Rushdie Affair'. Both incidents revealed 'the contours of a 'new racism' casting Asian communities as inherently culturally inferior' (Burnett 2009: 53). A purported over-tolerance of cultural diversity has been attacked by those on the right but also the centre-left, arguing this encourages Asians in northern urban areas to 'self-segregate', resulting in a high level of racial tension (Macey 2002, Kundnani 2007). There is also a widely accepted assumption, commonly expressed in the media, that segregation leads to extremism and extremism to terrorism, though this view is inconsistent with the real biographies of terrorists (Kundnani 2007).

Bradford Riot, 7 July 2001

The riot in July 2001 was the culmination of rising racial tensions across the north-west of Britain. As early as April the media reported a fight at a Hindu wedding, leading to rumours of attacks on the Asian community by the NF. There were also riots in Oldham, Leeds, Burnley and Accrington prior to the Bradford riot on 7

July 2001. 'Thus, the violent public disturbances of 2001 started, and culminated, in Bradford in what has been described in the media as the worst urban rioting on the British mainland for 20 years' (Macey 2002: 31).

Those involved in the riot were predominantly Asian, the remaining ten per cent being white (Carling et al 2004). This was reflected in the number of sentences given for offences of which 82 per cent were of South Asians, in comparison with four per cent being of white offenders (Bagguley and Hussain 2003). The majority of the rioters were male and fit easily into the image of the 'gang' as Alexander (2004) observes: 'reports up to, during and after the riots weave a picture of angry young men, alienated from society and their own communities, entangled in a life of crime and violence' (2004: 531). The violence injured 326 police officers and 14 members of the public, with estimates of damage to property ranging up to £10 million (Benyon and Kushnick 2003). In addition there were a number of stabbings, including of police horses (Macey 2002). Researchers have argued that the riot was due to forthcoming marches planned by extreme right-wing anti-Muslim and anti-immigration organizations, the NF and BNP (Macey 2002, Bagguley and Hussain 2003, Kundnani 2007).

Macey attests that

> the immediate backdrop to the July public disturbances in Bradford centred around the NF, members of which had been banned from marching on the city. Rumours that an NF rally was planned despite the ban brought Asian youths on to the streets to 'defend the community'. An assault on an Asian youth by white drunks was the immediate catalyst for the explosion of violent disturbances (2002: 31).

Approximately 450 young Muslim men took to the streets armed with a variety of weapons (petrol bombs, baseball bats and stones) as well as using petrol bombs stored in derelict houses as missiles (Macey 2002).

When assessing the causes of the the riots politicians generally ignored the influence of the BNP and NF. The introduction of 'citizenship tests' implied the riots were due to a lack of control on immigration and failed multiculturalism. Labour Party MP from nearby Keighley, Ann Cryer, blamed the practice of arranged marriages. The publication of the White Paper 'Secure Borders, Safe Haven: Integration with Diversity in Modern Britain' in early 2002 suggested an official view that there were too many asylum seekers entering the UK . '[T]he role of the state and the media in creating a climate of racism was ignored and hostility was normalized as a natural reaction to the excessive mixing of different cultures' (Kundnani 2007: 132). The Bradford Commission Report into the earlier public disorders of 1995 and the Ouseley Report on the 2001 riots both cited ignorance and fear as major contributory factors to clashes between ethnic groups (Macey 2002). The remainder of this chapter will look at the part played by the media in the moral panic that followed the riots, which incorporated all of these ideological elements.

Methodology

This study utilizes quantitative data from content analysis of national broadsheet and national newspapers, working on the principle 'that the number of times an issue appeared on television news could be seen as an indicator of the priority given to it by broadcasters' (Philo 2007: 102). An initial textual analysis looking at each page of the sample of newspapers, allowed a broad typology of likely interpretations drawn from the texts (McKee 2003). This led to the identification of recurring themes and language in the articles. Media articles were collected for analysis directly after the riots in July 2001 from the following newspapers:*The Times, The Daily Mail, The Daily Mirror, The Sun, The Independent, The Observer, Guardian, Daily Telegraph*[4] and local newspapers. The selected newspapers allowed for analysis of a broad political and ideological spectrum..

Content Analysis

Initial analysis revealed six recurring words or concepts in the texts. These were segregation, unemployment, racism, multiculturalism, education and the British National Party/National Front. These will be examined in turn. Each newspaper gave distinct views, with the tabloid press tending to exaggerate the facts, while using concise and specific information about events. Other newspapers like *The Daily Telegraph* gave a broader view. For example, the tabloid *The Sun* may target Muslims as the cause of the Bradford riots; however *The Daily Telegraph* would suggest a social issue such as education to be the problem. Broadsheet papers such as *The Guardian* tend to focus on the failure of the existing structures to accommodate demand and social grievances: for example, social injustice, inadequate resources and lack of political representation (Benyon and Solomos, 1987). Bias is evident in much of the media and many of their arguments about issues such as segregation are unsubstantiated, thus giving an artificial and somewhat distorted version of events (Bagguley and Hussain 2003).

Segregation

The question of racial segregation has been the focus of public debate, with the suggestion that in failed multicultural societies people avoid those without the same 'racial' characteristics as them, thus creating a group identity constructed around a social, economic and political activity (Smith 1989). This discussion became more widespread after the London 7/7 bombings, which prompted Trevor

---

4   It is important to note that these newspapers include both tabloids (*The Sun*, the *Daily Mirror* and *Daily Mail*) and broadsheets (*The Times*, the *Independent*, the *Guardian*, the *Observer* (the Sunday edition of the *Guardian*) and the *Daily Telegraph*). Generally speaking, the broadsheets are aimed at a higher-brow, more educated market (Keeble 2005).

Phillips (chairman of the Commission for Racial Equality) to state Britain was 'sleepwalking towards segregation' (Kundnani 2007). Abbas (2007) argues that Muslims tend to be viewed as 'unassimilable' in terms of 'community cohesion'. Similarly Field (2007) notes Muslims are perceived as slow to integrate into mainstream society and as rejecting Western values. *The Sun* suggests that segregation may be a source of trouble and threat, stating that the then Home Secretary David Blunkett

> is concerned that some groups are isolated from the wider British community. This can lead to racial tension and riots like those earlier this year in Bradford and Oldham (27/10/01)

Other newspapers such as *The Daily Mail, The Daily Telegraph* and *The Times* suggest that the Bradford riots had their roots in segregation. They use terms like 'virtual apartheid' when referring to local schools. There is a clear implication that secondary schools are segregated along lines of race. *The Daily Mail* (14/07/01) draws on the 'Community Pride Not Prejudice' report stating, 'Lord Ouseley's report this week described Bradford as a bitterly divided city'.

There is little difference in the way that broadsheet newspapers describe Bradford. They too refer to high levels of segregation when discussing the riot: 'Segregation is a part of life. Most schools are either mostly Asian or mostly white' (*The Observer* 30/06/02). *The Independent* (10/07/01) asserts, 'Bradford is city of segregated ethnic communities in which schools are doing nothing to promote racial understanding'. *The Guardian* (23/07/01) also includes the institution of work and the space of the home, reporting, 'Bradford is a deeply divided city whose communities are segregated in home, school and workplace'.

The high Muslim population of Bradford figures in journalists' focus on 'segregation'. Muslims make up 2.78% of the UK population and 16% of the Bradford population. Muslims have settled in Bradford as a community (Valentine 2001). The media explore no causes of segregation, but offer it as a simplistic 'explanation' for the riots, suggesting that as 'outsiders' it is the Asian and Muslim population who are at fault. This observation is supported by Bagguley and Hussain (2003) who advocate that the media and others previously documenting the Bradford riots neither provide evidence nor examine the causes of the Bradford riot.

Unemployment

Another key theme was unemployment. *The Daily Mirror* (10/07/01) drew attention to the high levels of youth male unemployment in Bradford at the time of the riot. National figures indicate that more than 80 per cent of the Pakistani and Bangladeshi communities live in households whose income is below the national average (Modood et al 1997). Pakistani and Bangladeshi men are two and half times more likely to be unemployed than white men and those in work receive only two-thirds of the average earnings of white males (Modood et al 1997).

When describing young Asian males *The Daily Mail* (14/07/01) states, 'They're obsessed with designer clothes, cars, image and they want to get rich quickly, but they don't want to put the work in to gain skills'.

The Guardian and *The Observer* are less inclined towards moral panic and blaming the victim, but participate in the public worrying of the segregated communities discourse. *The Guardian* (23/07/01) observes,

> Down the years, economic decline following the mill closure has become increasingly tangled with race issues, as the mainly Pakistani ethnic community and white residents also facing unemployment and poor schooling retrenched amid mutual ignorance and suspicion.

The Observer (30/06/02) raised the issue of labour market discrimination: 'Manningham is an address that Mohammed believes that has kept him unemployed'.

Whilst some of the rioters in Bradford were unemployed, around 20 per cent of riot participants were students with better prospects than most. Indeed a short film entitled 'Bradford Riots' (2006) included a young Asian male university student with no previous record for criminal activity prior to the riot; this aspect of the reality was not highlighted in the popular mass media.

Racism

Many of the newspapers had recognized that the riots occurred because of racism and racial tension in the city. The Bradford Riots documentary (2006) also shows a group of white people abusing an Asian person which was the catalyst to the destruction of the city. Yet *The Daily Mirror* (13/07/01) puts the self-segregation slant on this, speculating, 'the politics of the men who rioted last summer in Northern England took root in the playground and parks where, as children, they no doubt grouped themselves in the most tribal way, by the colour of their skin.'

The Daily Mail, The Daily Telegraph and *The Times* also offer the folk explanation of 'reverse racism', as well as the discourse of multiculturalism-as-the-problem:

> 'White people claim they are the victims of favouritism towards ethnic minorities and Asians insist the 'Islamophobia' and racism thrive' (*The Daily Mail* 14/07/01).

> 'We need to be clear we don't tolerate the intolerable under the guise of cultural difference' *(The Times 06/09/02)*.

In this picture, racism arising from segregation, and an over-tolerance of difference, were key issues in sparking the riots, which involved the Asian community of Bradford and the white community, with the police and law enforcement authorities in the middle.

(Failed) Multiculturalism

Multiculturalism policy was often presented in media commentary as having created the divisions that led to the riots. There was widespread agreement over the failure to integrate, but some ambivalence over mutliculturalism as a remedy. T*he Sun* (27/10/01) reported that, 'Sweeping Reforms to help immigrants integrate better into society are to be unveiled by David Blunkett', echoing, 'We need to create a nation of many colours which combine to create a single rainbow'. *The Daily Mirror* (13/07/01) more negatively asserts 'The cultures have not been mixing and that creates tension'. This non-mixing is presented as either a lack or a failure of multiculturalism.

   The Times, The Daily Telegraph and *The Daily Mail* claim that the separatism inherent in multiculturalism is to blame for the Bradford riots. 'So-called community leaders' are self-appointed and guard cultural identity rather than seek a tolerably multiracial whole' (*The Times* 11/07/01). *The Daily Mail* (14/07/01) suggests too much integration of the wrong sort: 'It's as if they've taken on the worst British culture has to offer, rather than the best. As they look to the streets again, their faces masked by hoods and handkerchiefs, it was like a loss of innocence'. *The Daily Telegraph* (13/07/01) rehearses the multiculturalism-as-political-correctness argument, echoing official reports slating a supposed 'inability to talk openly about problems across cultural communities without fear of recriminations or to challenge wrong-doing'.

   Many media accounts, (which have much in common with official reports), counterpose 'social cohesion' to the supposed separatism of multiculturalism, as well as to the reality of segregation. *The Guardian* (11/11/01) claims that, 'Examining the riots in Oldham, Burnley and Bradford, the report says councillors have an obligation to promote social cohesion'. *The Observer* (30/06/02) suggests, 'Bradford council, criticized in several reports, is trying to bring the city's communities together'.

Education

Another recurring theme was education, again in connection with the failure to integrate and the failure of multiculturalism. *The Sun* (27/10/01) states 'We need to educate new immigrants in citizenship and help them develop an understanding of our language, democracy and culture'. Contradicting this, the *Daily Mirror* (13/07/01) comments 'Asian children were born and bred in the city, spoke English with a Yorkshire accent and needed a British education not a multicultural one'. Many of the newspapers argue that the cause of rioting and violent behaviour in Bradford was a lack of education among the Asian men involved . Yet given the high participation of students the Bradford riots, this is unconvincing.

   The Daily Mail (14/07/01) uses a comment from Mr Riaz, a local businessman, to connect educational and multicultural failures:'I think the education collapsed in the eighties when the emphasis was on multiculturalism'. *The Daily Telegraph* (13/07/01) contends, 'There is no reason why those schools should not be successful, both for academic achievement and in preparation for citizenship'. By this account, it is not the schools but the pupils, or more precisely Asian pupils, who are to blame. According to Valentine (2001), Bradford spent most of its budget on education. In addition in the 1970s when many Pakistanis migrated to Britain for employment, most had little formal education and could not speak English, and this certainly did not lead to riots (Bagguley and Hussain (2003). Broadsheet newspapers such as *The Independent* (10/07/01) also suggest that education is a problem. Similarly, *The Guardian* (23/07/01) complains, 'We've spent 20 years bumping along the bottom, with appalling inner city housing and schools that still turn out three times the national average of kids with absolutely zero qualifications'. This suggests the education system played a major part in the riots and is the reason why Asians in Bradford feel neglected and are labeled as social outcasts. Crucially, however, while the newspapers highlight the possible reasons for the causes of the riots, they neglect to mention what in fact causes this lack of achievements, both educationally and economically.

British National Party/National Front

One main theme identified while analyzing the texts was right-wing extreme groups such as the BNP and the NF. An undercover BBC documentary some three years after the riots, 'The Secret Agent' (BBC 2004), exposed the fanatical Islamophobia of the BNP. In language that starkly prefigures the Breivik massacre in Norway, a BNP member is filmed fantasizing about blowing up mosques and machine-gunning worshippers with 'a million bullets'. BNP party leader Nick Griffin is also recorded damning Islam as a 'vicious, wicked faith' practised by 'cranky lunatics' (*The Sun* 15/07/04).

Media opinion on right-wing extreme groups provoking the riots is mixed. 'No provocation offered last Saturday justified the orgy of violence and destruction that followed. There was no Fascist march.' (*The Daily Mirror* 10/07/01). The *Mirror* fails to mention the widely publicized *threat* of such a march, and the gatherings of racist groups in the city. The documentary 'The Bradford Riots' (2006) clearly demonstrates racial abuse being hurled at Asian men from extreme ring-wing groups, which led directly to the riot. There is further evidence of BNP presence at the riots, as undercover reporter Jason Gwynne recorded Steve Barkham, a BNP member, confessing to an attack during the 2001 Bradford riots, where he admits to beating an Asian man (*The Sun* 2007).

Whilst the *Daily Mirror* disputes the presence of fascists, *The Daily Telegraph, The Daily Mail* and *The Times* indicate that there was a presence of groups such as the BNP and The NF. *The Times* (2001:2) reports, 'Asian youths who took part in the riot said that they were sending a message to the National Front to stay away'. Similarly, *The Daily Mail* (2001:21) comments, 'By the time skinheads came along and the British National Party we'd say 'forget it''. Both of these newspapers attribute some blame to the neo-fascist presence. Bagguley and Hussain (2003) suggest that the right-wing groups can be blamed to a certain extent, but nevertheless there are other deeper rooted problems as right-wing groups have been in existence since the 1970s and riots have rarely broken out in the past. *The Guardian, The Independent* and *The Observer* also believe the BNP and The NF had contributed to the Bradford riots.

'The NF and BNP recruiters have been out on Bradford's white estates and in ethnically mixed city centre clubs' (*The Guardian* 2001:10).

'Yesterday's trouble flared after a meeting in Bradford's Centenary square organised by the Anti-Nazi League[5]', (*The Observer* 2001:2).

'The causes appeared similar to those that led to violence in Oldham, Greater Manchester, in May: The threat of National Front activity and instances of racial abuse from whites, mass protest among young Asians' (*The Independent* 2001:1).

The above examples recognize that extreme right-wing groups were a catalyst for the riots, but suggest that other issues such as multiculturalism, ('reverse') racism, unemployment, failed education and (self-)segregation in the city are also causes.

Conclusion

The content analysis identified six factors in the Bradford riot that were emphasized in the newspapers studied. They were segregation, racism, unemployment, (failed) multiculturalism, education and neo-fascist organizations (BNP and NF). There is little hard evidence offered for many of these factors. There is a measure of segregation in Bradford (Bagguley and Hussain 2003), however, the media argument is constructed in such a way as to blame the segregated minorities both for their supposed self-segregation, and for the lack of integration that is seen as a cause of the violence.

Initially this chapter posed the question of how accurate/realistic were media representations of the Bradford riot? We found that the media conflate education and multiculturalism, as education is blamed for a lack of multiculturalism and failed multiculturalism is the result of segregated schools. Academic study (Kundnani 2001, Macey 2002, Bagguley and Hussain 2003) and government reports (Ouseley 2001) evidence that Bradford was a city under economic pressure prior to the riot. This pressure was arguably experienced disproportionately by the

---

5   An anti-fascist organization that had arranged a meeting in response to the proposed march by fascist groups.

high Asian population of Bradford, who were also scapegoated for it by 'white' Bradfordians susceptible to racist 'folk explanations' offered by organizations like the BNP. These factors were accompanied by mistrust of the police among Pakistani and Bangladeshi communities, owing to a history of over-policing and institutional racism. The trigger to spark the violence was provided by the BNP; just the threat of a march (combined with previous recruitment strategies) in the city (Bagguley and Hussain 2003) in combination with shouted drunken abuse by groups of white racists (Macey 2002), was enough . Some of the media neglected to mention the threatened march but emphasized the fact that it did not take place, thus creating the impression the violence was mindless. They gave a particularly negative representation of the local Asian and especially Muslim population, creating an image of being violent, unruly, irrational but mostly threatening and criminal or deviant (Morrison and Statham 2005, Jewkes 2011).

The issue of Islamophobia is interesting here as the riot occurred before 9/11 and 7/7 which significantly fuelled fear of Islam in the UK (Amin 2003). There is evidence of the notion of wanting 'them all to go back to Pakistan' (Macey 2002) though arguably this can be attributed to anti-immigrant racism, not because they are perceived as 'fanatic fundamentalists' (Jewkes 2011). The post 9/11 rise of Islamophobia has compounded this racism, and built upon earlier Islamophobia centred on Bradford at the time of the Rushdie Affair. As Kundnani (2007: 135) observes, with both official and media responses to the riot focusing on self-segregation and the failure to integrate, 'The BNP's anti-Islam and anti-immigrant programme has been implicitly legitimized and its ambition to be seen as a 'legitimate' political party now seems close to being realized'. Islamophobic moral panic has played no small part in this mainstreaming of racist extremism.

Bibliography

Abbas, T. 2001. Media capital and the representation of South Asian Muslims in the British press: an ideological Analysis, *Journal of Muslim Minority Affairs* Vol. 21, No 2, 245-257

Abbas, T. 2007. Muslim Minorities in Britain: Integration, Multiculturalism and radicalization in the Post-7/7 Period, *Journal of Intercultural Studies,* Vol.28, No. 3, 287-300.

Ahmad, F. 2006. British Muslim Perceptions and Opinions on News Coverage of September 11,*Journal of Ethnic and Migration Studies,* Vol. 32 No. 6, 961-982.

Ahmed, N.M., Bodi, F., Kazim, R. and Shadjareh, M. 2001. *'The Oldham Riots'– Discrimination, Deprivation and Communal Tension in the United Kingdom.* Islamic Human Rights Commission.

Akhtar, S .1989. *Be Careful With Muhammad!   The Salman Rushdie Affair,* London: Bellew.

Alexander, C. 2000. *The Asian Gang,* Oxford: Berg.

Alexander, C. 2004. Imagining the Asian Gang: Ethnicity, Masculinity and Youth After 'the Riots',*Critical Social Policy,* Vol. 24, No. 4 526-549.

Allen, C. 2004. Justifying Islamophobia: A Post 9/11 Consideration of the European Union and British Contexts,*American Journal of Islamic Social Sciences,* Vol. 21, No. 3, 1-25

Allen, C. and Nielsen, J.S. 2002. *Summary Report on Islamophobia in the EU after 11 September 2001*, European Monitoring Centre on Racism and Xenophobia (EUMC), Vienna, May.

Amin, A. 2003. Unruly Strangers? The 2001 Urban Riots in Britain, *International Journal of Urban and Regional Research,* Vol. 27, No 2, 460-463

Anwar, M..1998. *Between Cultures; Continuity and change in the lives of Young Asians*, London: Routledge.

Asad, T. 1990. Multiculturalism and British Identity in the Wake of the Rushdie Affair, *Politics and Society*, Vol. 18, No. 4, 455-480.

Bagguley, P. and Hussain, Y. 2003. *The Bradford 'Riot' of 2001: A Preliminary Analysis*. Paper to the Ninth Alternative Futures and Popular Protest Conference, Manchester Metropolitan University, 22nd – 24th April 2003, Available at:http://pascalfroissart.online.fr/3-cache/2003-bagguley-hussain. pdf [accessed: 6 January 2011].

BBC news magazine 2004. Going Undercover in the BNP [Online] Available at: http://news.bbc.co.uk/1/hi/magazine/3896213.stm [accessed: 1 February 2011].

Beynon, H. and Kushnick, L. 2003. Cool Britannia or Cruel Britannia? Racism and New Labour, in *Socialist Register 2003, Fighting Identities: Race, Religion and Ethno-nationalism*, edited by L Panitch and C. Leys. London: Merlin Press.

Benyon, J. and Solomos, J. 1987. *The Roots of Urban Unrest:* Oxford: Blackwell.

Billig, M. 1978. *Fascists: A social psychological view of the National Front.* London: Academic Press.

Bravo Lopez, F. 2011. Towards a Definition of Islamophobia: Approximations of the Early Twentieth Century, *Ethnic and Racial Studies,* Vol. 34, No. 4, 556-573.

Bryman, A. 2004. *Social Research Methods*, Second edition. Oxford: Oxford University Press.

Burnett, J. 2009. Racism and the State: Authoritarianism and Coercion in *State Power Crime*, edited by R. Coleman, J. Sim, S. Tombs and D. Whyte. London: Sage.

Carling, A., Davies, D., Fernandes-Bakshi, A., Jarman, N. and Nias, P. 2004. *Fair justice for all: Programme for a Peaceful City:* Bradford: University of Bradford.

Chomsky, N. 2001. *9-11*, New York: Seven Stories Press.

Chomsky, N. 2003. *Power and Terror: Post-9/11 Talks and Interviews*, New York: Seven Stories Press.

Cohen, S. 1972. *Folk Devils and Moral Panics: The creation of the Mods and Rockers*, London: MacGibbon and Kee.

Cohen, S. 2002. *Folk Devils and Moral Panics: The creation of the Mods and Rockers* Third edition. London and New York: Routledge.

Connell, R 1995. *Masculinities.* Cambridge: Polity Press.

Copsey, N. 2007. Changing Course or Changing Clothes? Reflections on the Ideological Evolution of the British National Party 1999-2006 *Patterns of Prejudice*, Vol. 41, No. 1, 61-82.

Cumberbatch, G., McGregor, R., Brown, J. and Morrison, D. 1986. *Television and the Miners Strike.* London: BFI Broadcasting Research Unit.

Esposito, J.L. 1999. *The Islamic Threat. Myth or Reality?* New York: Oxford University Press.

Ezzy, D. 2002. *Qualitative Analysis: Practice and Innovation,* London: Routledge.

Farrar, M.2002. *The Struggle for 'Community' in a British Multi-ethnic Inner-city Area: Paradise in the Making'* Lampeter: Edwin Mellen.

Field, C.C. 2007. Islamophobia in Contemporary Britain: the Evidence of the Opinion Polls, 1988-2006 in *Islam and Christian Relations,* Vol. 18, No. 4, 447-477

Flick, U. 2006. *An Introduction to Qualitative Research.* 3rd Edition. London: Sage.

Gardner, R., Karakasoglus, Y. and Luchtenberg, S. 2008. Islamophobia in the Media: A Response From Multicultural Education *Intercultural Education* Vol. 19, No. 2, 119-136

Glasgow University Media Group 1976. *Bad News* London: Routledge and Kegan Paul.

Glasgow University Media Group 1980. *More Bad News* London: Routledge and Kegan Paul.

Glasgow University Media Group 1982. *Really Bad News* London: Writers and Readers.

Goward, P. 2006. Gender and Journalism, *Pacific Journalism Review*, vol. 12, No. 1,. 15-19.

Hall, S., Critcher, C., Jefferson, T., Clarke, J., Roberts, B. 1978 *Policing the Crisis: Mugging, the State and Law and Order*, London: Macmillan.

Home Office 2002. *Secure Borders, Safe Haven: Integration with Diversity in Modern Britain*, London: HMSO.

Home Office 2006. *The Terrorism Act 2006*, London: HMSO [Online] Available at: http://www.homeoffice.gov.uk/about-us/corporate-publications-strategy/home-office-circulars/circulars-2006/008-2006/ [accessed: 9 September 2011].

Jenkins, P. 2003. *Images of Terror: What we can and can't know about Terrorism,* New York: Aldine de Gruyter.

Jewkes, Y. 2011. *Media and Crime* (second edition), London: Sage.

Jones, A. and Singer, L. 2007. *Statistics on Race and the Criminal Justice System 2006* [Online] Available at: http://www.statewatch.org/news/2007/

oct/uk-race-and-cjs-stats-2006.pdf [accessed: 22 January 2009].

Keeble, R. 2005. *Print Journalism: A Critical Introduction.* London: Routledge.

Krippendorf, K. 1980. *Content Analysis: An Introduction to its Methodology.* London: Sage.

Kundnani, A. 2001. *From Oldham to Bradford: The Violence of the Violated, Race and Class,* Vol. 43, No. 2, 105-31 .

Kundnani, A. 2007. *The End of Tolerance: Racism in 21ˢᵗ Century Britain,* London: Pluto Press.

Lea, J. 2000. The Macpherson Report and the Question of Institutionalised Racism, *Howard Journal of Criminal Justice,* Vol. 39, No. 3, 219-233.

Macey, M. 2002. Interpreting Islam: Young Muslim Men's Involvement in Criminal Activity in Bradford,in *Islam, Crime and Criminal Justice*, edited by B. Spalek. Cullompton: Willan.

McKee, A. 2003. *Textual Analysis: A Beginner's Guide.* London: Sage.

Modood, T. 1990. *British and Asian Muslims and the Rushdie Affair* in *The Politics Quarterly,* Vol. 61, No. 2, 143-160.

Modood, T., Berthoud, R.and Lakey, J. 1997. *Ethnic Minorities in Britain: Diversity and Disadvantage* London: Policy Studies Institute.

Morrison, E. and Statham, P. 2005. *Racists Sentiments, Movements and the Mass Media: A Mediated Xenophobia?* ESRC Full Research Report [Online] Available at: www.icar.org.uk/download.php?id=250 [accessed: 20 October2008].

ONS 2011. *Ethnicity and identity: Population Size* Office for National Statistics [Online] Available at: http://www.statistics.gov.uk/cci/nugget.asp?id=455 [accessed: 13 January 2011].

Ottewekk, D. 8/06/09. Outrage as BNP Win Seat in Europe in *Manchester Evening News.*

Ouseley, H. 2001. *Community Pride not Prejudice: making Diversity Work in Bradford, Bradford: Bradford vision* [Online] Available at: http://resources.cohesioninstitute.org.uk/Publications/Documents/Document/DownloadDocumentsFile.aspx?recordId=98&file=PDFversion [accessed: 13 January 2010].

Pearson, G. 1976. 'Paki-bashing' in a North East Lancashire Cotton Town: A Case Study and its History in Mungham et al (eds) *Working Class Youth Culture,* London: Routledge.

Philips, D., Davis, C. and Ratcliffe, P. 2007. British Asian Narratives of Urban Space, *Transactions of the Institute of British Geographers,* Vol. 32, No. 2, 217-234.

Philo, G. 2007. News Content Studies, Media Group Methods and Discourse Analysis: : A Comparison of Approaches, in *Media Studies: Key Issues and Debates*, edited by E. Devereux. London: Sage.

Poynting, S. and Mason, V. 2007. The Resistible Rise of Islamophobia :Anti-Muslim racism in the UK and Australia before 11 September 2001.*Journal of Sociology*, Vol. 43, No.1, 61-86.

Price, S 1996. *Communication Studies*, Harlow: Longman.

Robinson, J. 16/04/06. Revealed: the everyday racism of life on British newspapers, *The Observer* [Online] Available at:http://www.guardian.co.uk/media/2006/apr/16/pressandpublishing.business1 [accessed: 15 March 2009].

Runnymede Trust 1997. *Islamophobia: A Challenge for Us All* Report of the Runnymede Trust Commission on British Muslims and Islamophobia [Online] Available at: http://www.cbmi.org.uk/furtherreading_assets/Islamophobia%20-%20A%20challenge%20for%20us%20all.pdf [accessed:6 January 2011].

Smith J. S. 1989. *The Politics of 'Race' and Residence*. Cambridge: Polity Press.

Spalek, B. 2002. *Islam, Crime and Criminal Justice*, Devon: Willan.

Telegraph and Argus 2001. Rioter gets three years for stoning police. [Online] Available at: http://www.thetelegraphandargus.co.uk/search/display.var.754682.0.rioter_gets_three_years_for_stoning_police.php [accessed: 21 October 2008].

Telegraph and Argus 2007. Are Muslims always cast as the movie bad guys? [Online] Available at: http://www.thetelegraphandargus.co.uk/search/1148033.Are_Muslims_always_the_bad_guys_/ [accessed: 20 October 2008].

The Daily Mirror 10/07/01. Drug lords playing the race card. [Online] Available at: http://find.galegroup.com/ips/start.do?prodId=IPS [accessed: 21 October 2008].

The Daily Mirror 13/07/01. I was right says head driven out in race row, Bradford the Aftermath_[Online] Available at: http://find.galegroup.com/ips/start.do?prodId=IPS [accessed: 15 November 2008].

The Daily Mirror 27/02/02. *Girl rioter gets 4yrs.* [Online] Available at: http://find.galegroup.com/ips/start.do?prodId=IPS [accessed: 11 November 2008].

The Daily Mail 14/07/01. A dream that turned to ashes in a week that saw some of the worst ever rioting. [Online] Available at: http://proquest.umi.com/pqdweb?did=898602601&Sid=6&Fmt=3&clientld=67318&RQT=309&VName=PQD. [accessed: 13 November 2008].

The Daily Telegraph 13/07/01. Bradford 'was already in fear before riots'. [Online] Available at: http://www.telegraph.co.uk/news/1333768/Bradford-was-already-in-fear-before-riots.html [accessed: on 21 October 2008].

The Guardian 11/11/01. Riot report blames police, minsters and communities. [Online] Available at: http://www.guardian.co.uk/uk/2001/dec/11/race.immigrationpolicy2 [accessed: 23 February 2009].

The Guardian 23/07/01. Every Silver Lining Has a Cloud [Online] http://www.guardian.co.uk/uk/2001/jul/23/race.socialsciences [accessed: 23 February 2009].

The Independent 10/07/01. 'Racism and Segregation' in Bradford. [Online] Available at: http://find.galegroup.com/ips/start.do?prodId=IPS [accessed: 23 February 2009].

The Independent 09/07/01. Bradford put on alert after night of rioting. [Online] Available at: http://find.galegroup.com/ips/start.do?prodId=IPS [accessed: 23 Febryary 2009].

The Observer 08/07/01. Bradford under siege after a day of race riots: a day of racial tensions turned into a night of fierce rioting between young Asians, police and right wing extremists. [Online] Available at: http://www.guardian.co.uk/uk/2001/jul/08/news.race [accessed: 15 March 2009].

The Observer 30/06/02. Riot city reaches boiling point: Paul Harris returns to Bradford, a year after reporting on the violence that shocked Britain, and finds little has been done to address the root problems. [Online] Available at: http://www.guardian.co.uk/uk/2002/jun/30/politics.race [accessed: 15 March 2009].

The Observer 16/04/06. Revealed: the everyday racism of life on British newspapers. [Online] Available at: http://www.guardian.co.uk/media/2006/apr/16/pressandpublishing.business1 [accessed: 15 March 2009].

The Sun 27/10/01. Learning to be Brits [Online] Available at: http://www.thesun.co.uk/sol/homepage/news/article142361.ece [accessed: 16 February 2009].

The Sun 15/07/04. Exposed: The BNP beasts. [Online] Available at:http://www.thesun.co.uk/article/0,,2-2004322117,00.html [accessed: 21 January 2009].

The Sun 19/11/05. Ghetto UK warning. [Online] Available at: http://www.thesun.co.uk/sol/homepage/features/life/article225120.ece [accessed: 22 January 2009].

The Times 09/07/01. Blunkett takes tough line on Bradford riot. [Online] Available at: http://proquest.umi.com/pqdweb?did=898602601&Sid=6&Fmt=3&client ld=67318&RQT=309&VName=PQD [accessed: 16 October 2008].

The Times 11/07/01. Only civic pride can restore civil order. [Online] Available at: http://find.galegroup.com/ips/start.do?prodId=IPS [accessed: 7 March 2009].

The Times 06/09/02. Blunkett Savages Bradford riot 'whiners' [Online] Available at: http://find.galegroup.com/ips/start.do?prodId=IPS [accessed: 7 March 2009].

Valentine, R. 2001. *Muslims in Bradford, UK*. Compass: University of Oxford

Van Dijk, A.T. 1991. *Racism and the Press*. London: Routledge

Verkaik, R. 2010. Terrorism Stop-and-search Draws Total Blank, *The Independent* 29 October 2010.

Wainwright, M. 2001. 'Police close in on Bradford riot suspects'.[Online] Available at: http://www.guardian.co.uk/uk/2001/apr/18/race.world [accessed: 20 October 2008].

Younge, G. 2002. Britain Is Again White [Online] Available at: http://www.guardian.co.uk/comment/story/0,,651971,00.html [accessed: 20 October 2008].

Films

BBC 2004. *The Secret Agent* broadcast on BBC One at 2100BST on Thursday, 15 July 2004.

Biswas, N. 2006. *Bradford Riots* Directed by Neil Biswas.UK, Channel 4. (Film: 75mm).

Chapter 10

Moral Panics, Globalization and Islamophobia: The Case of Abu Hamza in *The Sun*

Anneke Meyer

Introduction

Abu Hamza al-Masri was an imam at Finsbury Park mosque in London between 1997 and 2003. At the time of his dismissal from this position he had become a notorious figure in the UK due to outspoken views which are largely at odds with the mainstream values of a liberal western democracy. Hamza has, for instance, publicly expressed his support for the destruction of democracy, the introduction of Sharia law and the creation of a global Islamic state. After his dismissal, Hamza continued to preach outside the gates of Finsbury Park mosque which further increased his public visibility. Central to Hamza's infamy is the fact that he uses a hook to replace his missing right hand[1], which makes him an instantly recognizable iconic figure. In August 2006, Hamza was arrested under the Terrorism Act 2000 and charged with offences including encouraging racial hatred and murder of non-Muslims. Hamza's trial began on 9 January 2006 and on 7 February 2006 he was found guilty of most charges and sentenced to seven years in prison.

This chapter investigates the British tabloid *The Sun*'s portrayal of Abu Hamza in the context of moral panics about Islam. *The Sun* is by far the UK's biggest selling daily newspaper, with a circulation of around 3 million copies daily[2]. It is a tabloid marked by sensational headlines, large print, plenty of photographs and a fondness for puns. It is owned by Rupert Murdoch's *News International* and its political orientation is thoroughly populist and aligned to right-of-centre 'common sense' views. In terms of style, *The Sun* is indicative of British tabloids which command the lion's share of the British newspaper market.

---

1   In fact, both of his hands were lost, along with the use of his left eye, in injuries that he claims were sustained while working on a landmine-clearing reconstruction project in Jalalabad, Afghanistan, in about 1993
http://www.bbc.co.uk/news/uk-11701269 accessed 4 September 2011.

2   *The Sun*'s Audit Bureau of Circulation figures for June of 2006, the year of Abu Hamza's trial, were 3,148,700 (Doyle 2006).

This empirical study of *The Sun* focuses on the time period of Abu Hamza's trial, 9 January until 19 February 2006, which represents the height of media interest and outrage. Within this time frame the peak of coverage occurred immediately after the verdict, between 8 and 10 February 2006, when *The Sun* devoted several pages, including front pages, to the coverage of Abu Hamza. The research sample consists of a total of 48 articles, all of which substantially deal with Abu Hamza. Articles where his name was mentioned incidentally were excluded. The total figure comprises a wide mix of types of articles, including a large number of news articles, several opinion columns, several leading articles and a few feature articles and readers' letters. All of these were analysed with the exception of letters which represent a distinct genre in their own right and would need a separate analysis (Fowler 1991). This chapter has two aims. Firstly, it sets out to analyse how *The Sun* linguistically and visually constructs Abu Hamza as a classic folk devil (Cohen 2002). Secondly, it analyses the ways in which the case contributes to a wider, more general media-generated panic (Hall et al 1978) about dangerous Islam through *The Sun*'s systematic linking of Hamza to range of issues around Islamic terrorism.

Demonization: Abu Hamza as Folk Devil

According to Cohen's famous model (2002) one of the key features of moral panics is the creation of folk devils:individuals or groups of persons who are identified as deviant types posing a major threat to the moral fabric of society. Folk devils are portrayed in highly stereotypical and negative ways. They are stripped of any positive or neutral features and utterly demonized; they are often typically presented as evil, demonic, and wicked. The perceived moral failings of a society are projected onto folk devils, who are seen as having nothing at all in common with the 'moral majority'. *The Sun* casts Abu Hamza as a classic folk devil by portraying him as purely evil, extremely dangerous and totally removed from the norms and values of the society he lives in. Moreover, the newspaper presents him as an archetype of the Muslim terrorist, the folk devil at the heart of moral panics about dangerous Islam.

The media construction of folk devils works most basically on the level of lexis, i.e. the choice of words. *The Sun* continuously uses adjectives and nouns denoting and connoting evil to describe Abu Hamza. He is constantly referred to as 'evil', 'vile', 'menacing', or 'wicked', as for example in descriptions such as 'evil cleric' (France and Clench 9 February 2006). *The Sun*'s front page on the day after the conviction contained the headline 'As evil Hamza is finally jailed for terror crimes, we reveal.. Hook and a hooker' (Hughes 8 February 2006b). This headline, which clearly brands Hamza as evil, is so large that it spans the entire front page. The article, which focuses on the revelation that Hamza has used prostitutes in the past, continues on the inside pages where Hamza is described as 'the menacing Muslin preacher'.

Abu Hamza's evil nature is also constructed on a narrative level. *The Sun* covers several stories on a wide range of topics whose common feature is to reveal Hamza as a truly demonic person. For example, a news article entitled 'Hamza's 'gloat' at dead US seamen' (Thompson and Hughes 14 January 2006) reports

'PREACHER Abu Hamza gloated over the killing of 17 sailors in a suicide bomb attack on a US warship, the Old Bailey heard yesterday. The cleric used one of his 'sermons of hate' to celebrate deaths aboard USS Cole caused by al-Qaeda terrorists in Yemen in October 2000.'

This story presents him as evil because he laughs about and celebrates the deaths of other human beings, showing him to have no human feelings of empathy or compassion. In another news article Hamza is reported to have condoned the killing of children: 'Mr Perry[the prosecutor] told the jury that Hamza asserted that while children should not be killed deliberately, their killing was permissible if they were in the target area' (Hughes and Thompson 12 January 2006). Hamza, who is prepared to accept children as 'collateral damage', is thus represented as thoroughly wicked.

Abu Hamza is also constructed as evil on a thematic level through a discourse of religious hate and murder. Generally, media coverage in the UK has increasingly stereotyped Muslims as aggressive, violent, and full of hatred, with these negative feelings and practices being directed at Western culture (Saeed 2007). *The Sun* frequently asserts that Hamza is a religious leader who in his preaching exhorts Muslims to hate and even murder non-Muslims in the name of Islam. This message is condensed into compound nouns such as 'hate cleric' (Anon 31 January 2006) or 'hate preacher' (White 11 February 2006) which not only immediately link religion, specifically Islam, to hatred but serve as a memorable shorthand for a complex discourse (Fairclough 1989). The discourse of religion-inspired hatred and murder is repeated in *The Sun* throughout various news articles. For example, an article covering the trial features the headline 'Hamza terror trial: sermons of hate' (Hughes and Thompson 12 January 2006) and goes on to state that Hamza was responsible for 'a series of sermons preaching 'murder and hatred''. *The Sun*'s report of Hamza's conviction also reinforces the theme of religious hatred and murder by writing that 'Jurors found the ex-imam of London's Finsbury Park Mosque guilty of inciting followers to murder non-Muslims and Jews, stirring up racial hatred and possessing a terror "manual". (…) Mr Justice Hughes, left, told Hamza he encouraged disciples to believe they had a DUTY to kill.' (Hughes 8 February 2006b). This discourse not only presents Hamza as evil but makes him the symbol of religious/Islamic murder and hatred and, as a consequence, Islam as such emerges as a dangerous and violent religion.

Mass media communication heavily depends on the symbolic power of images as well as words, especially when it comes to the communication of stereotypes

(Cohen 2002). Visual imagery is crucial to the Hamza case. The hook that replaces his right hand is a significant aspect in the construction of Abu Hamza as evil. It makes him instantly recognisable and has helped fashion him into a distinct character. *The Sun* linguistically reinforces the visually built-up image of the hook by means of constant references. Hamza is frequently described as 'hook-handed Hamza' (e.g. Anon 15 February 2006; Pascoe Watson 9 February 2006; White 11 February 2006). In fact, the link between Hamza and the hook has become so sedimented that *The Sun* can also simply refer to him as 'hook', substituting the noun 'hook' for the noun 'Hamza', knowing that readers will understand who is referred to. For example, headlines during the trial included 'When Hook had hands' (Anon 8 February 2006), 'Evil Hook deserves 14 years' (Blunkett 9 February 2006), 'Hook's 'Bomb Big Ben' book' (Hughes 12 January 2006), 'Hook and a hooker' (Hughes 8 February 2006b), and 'You forced our 'masters' to put Hook behind bars' (Shanahan 10 February 2006). In the process of noun substitution, Hamza and his hook become interchangeable, a process of dehumatization (Fairclough 1989). While we might expect the loss of limbs would commonly signify victimhood, as someone marked by tragedy and loss, evoking sympathy and pity, Abu Hamza is portrayed in exactly the opposite terms: as an evil man who is the perpetrator rather than the victim of atrocities. The cultural connotations of hooks are well established: they signify crime, evil, barbarism and villains. Western folklore associates hooks with lawless, violent and primitive pirates. Captain Hook was the evil villain in J.M. Barrie's *Peter Pan*. Allen (2001: 5) has pointed out that 'his [Hamza's] hooks are the scars of warfare that evoke the archetypal stereotype of barbarism', which Western media and culture associate with Islam. In this sense the Hamza case is not just a great opportunity to demonize a person but to reinforce stereotypes about Muslims and Islam as such.

Research into the representation of Muslims and Islam in the British media has found that it is marked by a) marginalization and b) negativity and stereotyping (Saeed 2007). Content analyses show that since September 11 media coverage of Muslims and Islam has increased on a huge scale (Poole 2006; Whittaker 2002). In the case of *The Sun*, the number of articles containing the word 'Muslim' increased by 658% between 2000/2001 and 2001/2002 (Whittaker 2002). As Poole (2006: 92) argues 'the events of September 11 (..) have allowed for the construction of Muslims within a more limited and negative framework dominated by only a handful of topics such as fundamentalism/terrorism, politics, war in Iraq, education, crime. But by 2003, terrorism became *the* dominant topic by far in British news media coverage of Islam, accounting for example for 24% of all articles in *The Guardian* and 30% of all articles in *The Times* (Poole 2006). Indeed Poole (2006: 102) concludes her research by stating that 'One image dominates, that of 'Islamic terrorism'' and the threat to UK security. *The Sun* did not feature in Poole's content analysis but it is reasonable to assume that, if anything, a populist tabloid would carry an even higher percentage of articles about terrorism given the topic's fit with tabloid news values and their sensational styles. Interestingly, until 2001 the term 'terrorism' did not even feature in British news media coverage and extremism was denoted through the term 'fundamentalism' (Poole 2006). Poole (2006) argues that this linguistic shift has been accompanied by a broadening of the application of the label. The Abu Hamza case is an excellent illustration of the ways in which the media use particular figures and events to say something about Islam in general. This is what we will turn to now.

Convergence: Abu Hamza, Religious Terrorism and Islamophobia

Stuart Hall et al (1978) in their investigation of moral panics about mugging in the UK in the 1970s suggest that distinct moral panics are often mapped onto each other through a process of convergence. In this process deviant activities of very different kinds and origins are seen as essentially similar and possessing common denominators and a larger, more general moral panic emerges. Hall et al's (1978) example concerns the way in which moral panics about issues such as mugging and hooliganism converge into a general moral panic about law and order. This constitutes deviance amplification as one problem is constructed as indicative of an even wider and bigger social problem. For example, hooliganism and mugging are seen as the mere beginnings of widespread immoral behaviour and the decline of civilized society as we know it. Hence convergence is identified as one of two key mechanisms which escalate moral panics. Hall et al (1978: 226) write that 'One kind of threat or challenge to society seems larger, more menacing, if it can be mapped together with other, apparently similar, phenomena – especially if, by connecting one relatively harmless activity with a more threatening one, the scale of the danger implicit is made to appear more widespread and diffuse'. Hall et al's (1978) work is particularly useful for examining fears and panics about Islam because it recognizes and explains why moral panics tend to appear in groups.

Hall et al's (1978) ideas can be adapted to suggest that in the mid 2000s a general moral panic about dangerous Islam/Islamic terrorism appears based on smaller panics which happened in close succession: terrorist attacks such as the London bombings in 2005, or the Glasgow airport attack in 2007, the Danish cartoon episode in 2005, or the controversy around Sharia law in the UK in February 2006. They converge on the common theme of Islam's lack of fit with Western culture and consequent danger. Through the mapping together of distinct episodes, non-violent and violent, Islam emerges as a significant menace and threat to contemporary society. The Abu Hamza case is one of the smaller panics which contributes to the creation and escalation of a wider, more substantial and threatening moral panic. This section analyse how *The Sun* systematically links Abu Hamza to Islam and terrorism, with the effect that Hamza becomes a key figure representing and reinforcing the notion of dangerous Islam.

No *Sun* reader can be left in any doubt as to Abu Hamza's religion because he is constantly referred to as a 'Muslim cleric' (Hughes 25 January 2006; Hughes and Thompson 20 January 2006 – many more) or a 'Muslim preacher' (Hughes 8 February 2006). *The Sun*, like UK culture in general, makes a distinction between 'moderate' and 'extreme' Muslims and Hamza, who is often described as a 'Muslim extremist' (Anon 10 February 2006) and 'religious fanatic' (Hughes 8 February 2006) who wants to introduce Islamic Sharia law in Britain (Hughes and Thompson 12 January 2006), clearly falls into the latter category. While *The Sun* is careful not to say *directly* that all Muslims are dangerous, Islam as such becomes dangerous because it is portrayed as a religion which contains extreme teachings and attracts a large number of extreme followers. On 9 February 2006, two days after Hamza's conviction, one of the sections in *The Sun* is headed 'The Preachers who hate Britain' (Anon 9 February 2006; France and Clench 9 February 2009). One of the articles in this section carries the headline 'How many more?' and states that 'MORE than 100 Abu Hamza-style terror suspects are at large in Britain – despite Tony Blair's vow to boot them out. Spooks have compiled a danger list of UK Islamic extremists, it emerged yesterday. Some are tagged, or in jail waiting to be deported. But scores more roam free, bent on destroying the country in which they live. *The Sun* today identifies five preachers of hate, considered a threat.' (Anon 9 February 2006). Such articles, especially expressions such as 'more than 100', 'danger list', 'scores more' and 'how many more', suggest that extremists are far from a minority in Islam. These articles also reinforce the theme of religious hatred and murder by directly identifying Islam as a threat to the existence of the UK. Abu Hamza, who is labelled a terrorist and a Muslim, is used to link Islam and terrorism. He exemplifies the common-sense connection, subscribed to by *The Sun*, that Islam is a violent religion because it condones violence, murder and terrorism for religious ends. Abu Hamza's public speeches, many of them tape-recorded and played at the trial, profess exactly these views, which are summed up by *The Sun* in memorable soundbite-style headlines such as 'Get ready to sacrifice yourself for Islam' (Thompson and Hughes 13 January 2006) or 'Hamza: 'Allah loves blood'' (Thompson and Hughes 17 January 2006). The articles then go into more detail on these themes:

> 'In a video of a sermon shown to jurors he called for the killing of Jews and said: 'There is no drop of liquid is loved by Allah more than the liquid of blood.' In a private address to followers, Hamza, 47, said: 'Fight and kill the infidels wherever you find them.' 'Wherever you find them, the unbeliever is killed, take them and seize them. Any person who hinders Allah, this man must be eliminated because he is a menace. He should be killed.'

In such coverage, Abu Hamza is used to reinforce and 'prove' the dangerousness of Islam as a terrorism-inspiring religion.

Hamza was accused and convicted of crimes under the Terrorism Act 2000. These included inciting racial hatred and murder of non-Muslims. *The Sun* refers to his crimes through the shorthand expression 'terror crimes'. For example, on the day after his conviction one of *The Sun*'s 'Exclusive' sections is headed 'Hamza jailed 7 years for terror crimes' (Anon 8 February 2006; Hughes 8 February 2006a). Moreover, the front page headline on the same day reads 'As evil Hamza is finally jailed for terror crimes, we reveal.. Hook and a hooker' (Hughes 8 Feb). The expression 'terror crime' directly links Hamza to terrorism, especially Islamist terrorism. Moreover, *The Sun* cements this link by focusing the coverage of Abu Hamza onto topics which in Western culture have come to embody the very concept of terrorism, e.g. suicide bombers, 7/7, September 11 or Al-Qaeda. For example, an article with the headline 'Suicide bomb 'a war tool'' (Anon 21 January 2006) states that 'Muslim cleric Abu Hamza described suicide bombing as a legitimate tool of war yesterday. He was questioned at his Old Bailey trial about a reference to suicide bombers he made in a speech at Luton, Beds. Hamza, 47, said: 'If it is the only way to stop the enemies of Islam from attacking and you don't have other means to resist then it is your tactic of war. It will be your only tactic of war.''

Without direct evidence, *The Sun* constantly links Hamza to September 11 in the US and 7/7 in the UK:'Seven years for running a viper's nest of terror linked to every major atrocity from 9/11 to our 7/7. (..) Evil Abu Hamza connived at mass slaughter' (Leading Article 8 February 2006). Alternatively the newspaper seeks to establish a connection based on individuals involved in 9/11 and 7/7 having visited Finsbury Park mosque and/or listened to Abu Hamza's speeches. For example one article claims that 'Visitors to the mosque included the 7/7 suicide bombers' (Hughes 8 February 2006) while another elaborates further, stating:

> Killers linked to his [Hamza's] stomping ground − the Finsbury Park Mosque in North London − have claimed more than 3,100 lives. Among the maniacs are: The four London suicide bombers − led by the mastermind of the 7/7 atrocities Mohammed Siddique Khan and his cohort Shehzeed Tanweer. (..) London suicide bomber Mohammed Siddique Khan is believed to have stayed at the mosque. Detectives still probing the July 7 horror − which killed 52 people − believe his fellow killers heard Hamza preach. Would-be 9/11 hijacker Moussaoui − involved in the plot to attack New York and Washington that left more than 3,000 dead − frequented the mosque while in London (Hughes 8 February 2006).

Such connections are of course very tenuous but this does not stop *The Sun* from repeating them often and prominently, as in headlines such as 'Blame Hamza for 7/7' (France and Clench 9 February 2006).

If 7/7 and September 11 are the key events symbolizing Islamist terrorism, then Al-Qaeda and its leader Osama Bin Laden are the key symbolic figures. Abu Hamza is constantly linked to these figures. The most notable instance is an article with the headline 'Bin Laden's British HQ' (Hughes 8 February 2006) which states that

> HATE-filled Abu Hamza turned the mosque where he held court into Osama Bin Laden's British HQ, *The Sun* can reveal. The preacher − caged for seven years yesterday − was at the centre of a web of evil stretching round the world.

(..)[W]hen police raided the mosque three years ago they found a chilling haul of terrorist gear. (..) Detectives suspect the material was used in terror training camps in the UK. The mosque was used for at least four camps – which attracted more than 100 volunteers.

Hamza is here accused of running 'terrorist training camps' which recruited and trained Muslims to join Al-Qaeda as terrorist fighters. This idea is repeated in several other articles (e.g. Leading Article 8 February 2006; Hughes 8 February 2006b). It is clear that Islamist terrorism is seen as a global phenomenon in its recruitment and implementation of attacks (e.g. 'a web of evil stretching round the world'), which positions Hamza as a global player. Nevertheless, *The Sun* also focuses the threat back onto the home of its readers by emphasizing that Hamza's recruitment and training camps have hugely increased the number of Muslims terrorists in the UK. For example, a leading article states that

> Seven years for recruiting impressionable young Muslims, some of whom went on to kill or attempt murder. (..) This licence to roam was exploited by Hamza whose terrorist 'sleepers' spread like spores on the wind. Experts fear the cast of potential suicide bombers in Britain has mushroomed.(Leading Article 8 February 2006)

while a news article claims that

> Terrorism expert Neil Doyle warned: 'Abu Hamza may now be out of action but, in many ways, he's already completed his mission.' 'There's a jihad army in this country and that's thanks to Hamza and others like him.' 'This country still faces the grim prospect of more suicide bombings by people inspired by his passion for violence' (Hughes 8 February 2006).

Sensational and dramatic words and expressions such as 'spread like spores on the wind', 'mushroomed' and 'army' literally construct the terrorism threat in the UK as massive and increasing, as a direct result of Hamza's actions. This is not only a classic example of the media manufacturing fear but also constructing Hamza as the ultimate folk devil (Cohen 2002). Taken together, all these examples demonstrate that Abu Hamza is the symbol linking religion and terrorism to contribute to a general moral panic about dangerous Islam.

Us vs Them: The West vs the Rest

One of the major themes of *The Sun*'s coverage, especially after Hamza's conviction when there are few novel developments, becomes 'Britain under threat from (extreme) Islam'. This theme appeared prominently in the edition of

9 February 2006, where ex-home secretary David Blunkett publishes an opinion piece headlined 'Evil Hook deserves 14 years'. In this he writes that

> Both Muslims and non-Muslims are coming to realise that this is not a game we are in. This is about the very future of a civilised and free world. (..) From now on the message should be clear – if *you* threaten or incite the death of others, if *you* seek to destroy *our* society, *we* will act against *you*. That is *all of us*, of whatever faith and whatever background. Whether born here or overseas. This is *our* country and *we* are not prepared to tolerate the intolerable [emphasis added].

This article constructs a strong national 'we', a collective British identity, which is juxtaposed to extreme Muslims and terrorists. Blunkett is careful not to directly position all Muslims as Other and allows for the inclusion of 'moderate Muslims' in the national 'we', for example by writing, 'That is all of us, of whatever faith and whatever background'. But as Islam generally is tightly bound up with terrorism, violence, lack of civilization, and regression rather than progress in the media and wider culture (Allen 2001), it is difficult to see any Muslims fitting into the 'we' which is marked by Britain as a democratic and progressive, i.e. secular, country. In the same edition, *The Sun* responds to Blunkett's opinion piece in a leading article, picking up his accusations that British security forces have for years failed to take Hamza seriously and stop Islamic terrorism. The editorial, headlined 'Deadly error' (9 February 2006), pointedly blames these British forces for the deaths of terrorism victims, concluding with the question 'How many would be alive today if our security services had done their job?' In this context of British authority failure, Blunkett's national 'we' becomes a more narrow 'we' of 'the common British public', which really means *The Sun* and its readers. The following day, Fergus Shanahan, deputy editor of *The Sun*, wrote an opinion piece headlined '*You* forced our 'masters' to put Hook behind bars' (10 February 2006) which is worth quoting at length in this context:

> It was *People Power* that put the evil Hooky behind bars. Not the police, nor the politicians, nor the prying eyes of the security spooks. But the *sheer strength of public opinion* which became too overwhelming to be ignored any longer. Plus a *good old British jury.* If *you* were one of the hundreds of thousands of worried individuals *who backed this paper's three-year campaign* to demand action against Hooky, then *the country is in your debt.* And that is the truth about Britain today. *Our rulers are too scared to act against Muslim extremists unless the pressure from the public becomes unbearable.* David Blunkett's revelations in yesterday's Sun are deeply alarming.
>
> He says that when he was Home Secretary, he wanted Hamza arrested and the Finsbury Park mosque closed, but got no support from the Metropolitan Police, the Crown Prosecution Service, or the spy agency MI5. He says *they all claimed that seizing Hook would spark Muslim riots and refused to move against him,* despite guarantees of Government support. (..)What *we* do know is that when

Hook was finally arrested, there was a mountain of evidence against him and he
was every bit as dangerous as Blunkett feared. So why won't our politicians and
police listen to *the public* more often? Current Home Secretary Charles Clarke
said yesterday that crown prosecutors were reluctant to charge someone they
thought juries might not convict. But that is rubbish. Juries made up of *the great
British public* nearly always get it right. (..) *The public* generally DO know best
[emphasis added].

Here the juxtaposition is no longer simply between the Muslim Other and the
British nation but rather *The Sun* develops a narrative in which 'the great British
public' have stood up against Islam while British authorities failed to act because
they are 'scared' of outraging the Muslim community. While Muslim extremists
are holding British authorities to ransom, the British public refuses to bow down
and fights back, so Shanahan's story goes. It is clear that these 'common people'
with their 'common sense' do not include Muslims; the 'common people' are
directly labelled as British (e.g. 'a good old British jury', 'the great British public')
which, as far as *The Sun* and in fact most of the British media goes (Saeed 2007),
excludes Muslims. Since 2001 in particular, Muslims have been represented as
'aliens within', as living in Britain but not really belonging (Saeed 2007). They
are portrayed as 'un-British', because their faith and culture is at odds with the
mainstream norms, values and ways of life of secular Western democracies like
Britain (Allen 2001, Saeed 2007). In this portrayal, being British and being a
Muslim become increasingly incompatible.

These developments indicate that moral panics about dangerous Islam mix
elements of morality (Cohen 2002) and ideology (Hall et al 1978). In the first
instance the concern is a moral one, focused on the moral institution of religion and
the ways in which Islam breeds amoral behaviour. However, it is also ideological
as the two sides which emerge in the story are defined by strong ideological
opposition between the progressive, modern, liberal, free, democratic and Christian
nations of the West (like Britain) versus the regressive, pre-modern, illiberal, ultra-
conservative, undemocratic and dogmatic forces of the East (notably Islam). The
theme here is one of a clash of civilizations, a conflict between forces of progress
and medieval backwardness (Saeed 2007). This juxtaposition has to be criticized
on many grounds, ranging from the fact that Christianity is no less dogmatic than
Islam to the way in which Islam is essentialized and demonized. But, as Cohen
(2002) suggests, this is exactly what happens in a moral panic; the boundaries are
drawn particularly tightly and images become sharper than reality, as both groups
are symbolized in stereotypical fashions and appear as having nothing in common.
Abu Hamza, with his hooks evoking stereotypical notions of barbaric violence
(Allen 2001), becomes the ideal figure to represent Islam as Other in the sense of
backward, medieval, evil, and dangerous.

Both Cohen (2002) and Hall et al (1978) stress that moral panics are not merely
symbolic but tend to result in concrete, material practices. For Cohen, once a
moral panic has established a particular behaviour or group of people as a major

social threat, the control culture, i.e. the state and its law enforcement agencies, introduces coping mechanisms to deal with the problem. This often takes the form of new laws or regulations. Hall et al (1978) argue that moral panics reproduce conservative ideologies around law and order which, in turn, justify law and order as the foundation of a new politics. Moral panics about dangerous Islam have certainly encouraged and legitimized increasing legislative activity around terrorism. In the UK major pieces of legislation are the Terrorism Act 2000, the Anti-Terrorism, Crime and Security Act 2001, the Prevention of Terrorism Act 2005, the Terrorism Act 2006 and the Counter-Terrorism Act 2008 (Hanman 2009). Anti-terrorism legislation is not explicitly directed at Islam, however, Islamic terrorism and dangerous Islam are the underlying paradigm cases on the basis of which such legislation has been conceptualized. For instance, the stop and search powers conferred under the UK Terrorism Act 2000 allowed the police to take into account the ethnic origin of the suspect when making a decision on whether to stop and search an individual (Fekete 2006). In the absence of any visible markers of religion, the police on the street rely on ethnicity to indicate religious identity and thereby danger and terrorism. As most Muslims in Britain are of Asian origin, this group has been subjected to a major increase in the number of stop and search incidents since 2000 (Fekete 2006). A report by the Institute of Race Relations (Kundnani 2003) found that between 2002 and 2003 there had been a 28 per cent increase in the number of Asians stopped and searched by the police across the UK. Asians were two-and-a-half times more likely to be stopped and searched than Whites (Kundnani 2003). This report is corroborated by official figures from the Ministry of Justice. Between 2001 and 2008, there has been a steady increase in the disproportionality ratio of stop and search incidents of Asians compared to Whites from 1.5 in 2001/2002 to 2.3 in 2007/8 (Equality and Human Rights Commission 2010). This means that in 2007/8, 17 out of 1000 White people and 40 out of 1000 Asian people were stopped and searched. As the overall trend has been a steady, year-on-year increase in stop and searches across all ethnic groups, the actual number of Asians stopped and searched increases every year (Equality and Human Rights Commission 2010). The effectiveness of stop and search strategies in the prevention of any crime, including terrorism, has long been questioned and came under particular scrutiny recently when it emerged that not one person stopped and searched under anti-terror legislation between 2009-10 was actually arrested for a terrorism-related offence (BBC News 2010).

The practice of suspecting individuals of wrong-doing based on their ethnicity was deemed discriminatory and racist by the Race Relations Amendment Act 2000, which outlawed it for all 'ordinary' cases of stop and search. Yet stop and search under the Terrorism Act 2000 retained this special right, indicating that ethnic origin is deemed an important factor in terrorism because it allows police to guess a person's religion (Fekete 2006).

Beside stop and search practices there are many other examples of anti-terrorism initiatives and regulations being targeted especially at Muslims. As security services in the UK have become increasingly focused on Islam as a threat, places where Muslims live, gather and engage in activities have been subject to suspicion and scrutiny (Fekete 2006). For instance, significant numbers of police raids have been carried out in mosques, madrasahs, language centres for foreign students or individuals' homes. These may or may not turn up evidence of terrorist activity but certainly Muslims are the target group.

In 2006 and 2007, the Department of Education called on university lecturers to be vigilant and keep their eyes open for signs of extreme Islamic views among Asian students which may be indicators of involvement in terrorism; a request which was vigorously rejected by unions and lecturers (BBC News 2007, Taylor et al 2006). Since 2007, the government also requires foreign postgraduate students from outside the EU to be vetted prior to joining British universities. This vetting scheme, called Academic Technology Approval Scheme (ATAS), applies to those doing research in subject areas across science, technology and engineering. These subjects are classed as 'risky' in the sense that they may facilitate research into weapons of mass destruction to be used for terrorist purposes (Foreign Commonwealth Office 2011). Vetting allows the government to carry out full background checks on foreign students and refuse them visas if anything marks them out as a risk. The exemption of EU students from this mandatory scheme means that it is mostly 'Eastern' students from Asian countries who will be affected. This provides another example of the state devising strategies to monitor non-Western, Islamic individuals as they are assumed to be the source of danger.

A further example concerns the project to introduce automatic number plate recognition (ANPR) cameras to two predominantly Muslim areas of Birmingham, Washwood Heath and Sparkbrook (Lewis 2010a). These were intended to function as surveillance cameras tracking every person entering and leaving the area. Some 40 of the total 150 cameras to be installed are covert. This project was funded by a £3 million grant from the Terrorism and Allied Matters (TAM) Fund administered by the Association of Chief Police Officers. While the police justified the project as monitoring a population at risk of extremism, there was significant uproar among the community and councillors. TAM funding and the focus on predominantly Muslim areas indicate that the police consider all Muslims as a risk, as potential terrorists and that as a consequence Muslims are subjected to tighter surveillance than other ethnic or religious groups. Following public outcry, the police and Birmingham City Council have put the project on hold, yet insist it will be introduced in some form following public consultation (Lewis 2010b).

These few examples here must suffice to show how, in the case of Islamophobic moral panic, the British state has introduced strongarm measures, including new laws and regulations, to cope, in the manner analyzed by Cohen (2002), with the 'problem' constructed by the panic. Thus, as Hall et al (1978) argue in the case of the 'mugging' moral panic, right-wing ideologies of law and order are invoked, hailing strong measures by the state as the foundation of a new politics.

Conclusion

Using the case of Abu Hamza as an example, this chapter has investigated several discursive strategies through which the media create moral panics. *The Sun* produces Abu Hamza as a classic folk devil on a lexical, narrative and thematic level. But rather than being a full-blown moral panic in its own right, the real significance of this case arguably lies in its contribution to the generation of a larger, more general moral panic about dangerous Islam/Islamic terrorism. This is produced through several smaller panics converging on this topic, which is constructed across two lines of ideology. Firstly, that Islam is an inherently violent, aggressive religion, and secondly, that it is an extreme and medieval religion incompatible with modern Western civilization. These two aspects are of course inextricably linked; for instance, it is the 'extremity' of belief which makes violent tendencies so dangerous and it is the violence which makes the 'incompatibility' with Western society problematic. The Abu Hamza case lends itself to connecting these two beliefs and thereby reinforces the moral panic around dangerous Islam/Islamic terrorism. Given records of public speeches and his conviction for terrorism offences, *The Sun* can easily frame Hamza as both a Muslim and a terrorist. His declared acceptance of violence in the name of religion helps to further cement this connection. Moreover, *The Sun* continuously links Abu Hamza to key events and figures symbolizing Islamic terrorism, thereby reinforcing the connections and presenting Islam as a dangerous, terroristic religion. Hamza's hook becomes particularly useful in the context, as a visual symbol of both violence and barbarity, evil and pre-modernity. Such symbolic constructions are important, not least because they have real-life consequences. Moral panics are divisive; the net is cast widely as figures like Hamza are used to make points about Islam as such. As a consequence, they facilitate and legitimize practices which discriminate against all Muslims in everyday life.

References

Allen, C. 2001. *Islamophobia in the Media since September 11th*. Paper to the *Exploring Islamophobia* conference, Westminster University, London, 29 September. Available at http://www.fairuk.org/docs/islamophobia-in-the-media-since-911-christopherallen.pdf [accessed: 12 December 2010].

Anon 21 January 2006. Suicide bomb 'a war tool', *The Sun*.

Anon 25 January 2006. Israel 'in control', *The Sun*.

Anon 28 January 2006. Hamza 'the recruit king', *The Sun*.

Anon 31 January 2006. Hamza's jury brief, *The Sun*.

Anon 1 February 2006) 'Hamza's jury alert', *The Sun*.

Anon (8 February 2006. When Hook had hands, *The Sun*.

Anon 9 February 2006. How many more?, *The Sun*.

Anon 10 February 2006. Abu Hamza, *The Sun*.

Anon 15 February 2006. PM call on terror, *The Sun*.

BBC News 2007. Lecturers 'must block extremism', [Online, 17 September] Available at: http://news.bbc.co.uk/1/hi/6998418.stm [accessed: 23 February 2011].

BBC News 2010. No terror arrests from stop-and-search, says government [Online, 28 October] Available at: http://www.bbc.co.uk/news/uk-11642649 [accessed: 23 February 2011].

Blunkett, D. 9 February 2006. Evil Hook deserves 14 years, *The Sun*.

Cohen, S. 2002. *Folk Devil and Moral Panics: The Creation of the Mods and Rockers*. 3rd Edition. London: Routledge.

Doyle, S. 2006. Monthly national newspaper circulation figures, M*edia Week* [Online, 14 July] Available at: http://www.mediaweek.co.uk/news/rss/569846/ Monthly-national-newspaper-circulation-figures/ [accessed: 25 July 2011].

Equality and Human Rights Commission 2010. *Stop and Think: A Critical Review of the Use of Stop and Search Powers In England and Wales*. London: Equality and Human Rights Commission [Online] Available at: http://www. equalityhumanrights.com/uploaded_files/raceinbritain/ehrc_stop_and_ search_report.pdf [accessed: 23 February 2011].

Fairclough, N. 1989. *Language and Power*. London: Longman.

Fekete, L. 2006. Racial profiling and the war on terror, in *Muslims and the News Media*, edited by E. Poole and J.E. Richardson. London: IB Tauris.

Foreign Commonwealth Office 2011. Academic Technology Approval Scheme [Online] Available at: http://www.fco.gov.uk/en/about-us/what-we-do/ services-we-deliver/atas/ [accessed: 25 February 2011].

Fowler, R. 1991. *Language in the News: Discourse and Ideology in the Press*. London: Routledge.

France, A. and Clench, J. 9 February 2006. Blame Hamza for 7/7, *The Sun*.

Hall, S., Critcher, C., Jefferson, T., Clarke, J. and Roberts, B. 1978. *Policing the Crisis: Mugging, the State, and Law and Order*. Houndmills: Macmillan.

Hanman, N. 2009. Explainer: Terrorism Legislation, *The Guardian* [Online, 22 January] Available at: http://www.guardian.co.uk/commentisfree/ libertycentral/2009/jan/22/explainer-terrorism-legislation [accessed: 23 February 2011].

Hughes, S. 12 January 2006. Hook's 'Bomb Big Ben' book, *The Sun*.

Hughes, S. 25 January 2006. Hamza in new slur on Israel, *The Sun*.

Hughes, S. 8 February 2006. Bin Laden's British HQ, *The Sun*.

Hughes, S. 8 February 2006a. He had an eye for the ladies, *The Sun*.

Hughes, S. 8 February 2006b. Hook and a hooker, *The Sun*.

Hughes, S. and Thompson, P. 12 January 2006. Hamza terror trial: sermons of hate, *The Sun*.

Hughes, S. and Thompson, P. 20 January 2006. Hamza's plans of Wills and Harry HQ, *The Sun*.

Kelly, L. 11 February 2006. David Blunkett, *The Sun*.

Kundnani, A. 2003. Stop and Search: Police Step up Targeting of Blacks and Asians, Institute of Race Relations, [Online] Available at: http://www.irr.org.uk/2003/march/ak000015.html [accessed 23 February 2011].

Leading Article 8 February 2006. Justice.. what took so long?, *The Sun*.

Leading Article 9 February 2006. Deadly Error, *The Sun*.

Leading Article 11 February 2006. Rebels beware, *The Sun*.

Leading Article 13 February 2006. Time for calm, *The Sun*.

Leading Article 15 February 2006. Get tough now, *The Sun*.

Lewis, P. 2010a. Surveillance cameras in Birmingham track Muslims' every move, The Guardian [Online, 4 June] Available at: http://www.guardian.co.uk/uk/2010/jun/04/surveillance-cameras-birmingham-muslims[accessed: 25 February 2011].

Lewis, P. 2010b. Birmingham stops camera surveillance in Muslim areas, The Guardian [Online, 17 June] Available at: http://www.guardian.co.uk/uk/2010/jun/17/birmingham-stops-spy-cameras-project [accessed: 25 February 2011].

Meyer, A. 2007. *The Child at Risk: Paedophiles, Media Reponses and Public Opinion*. Manchester: Manchester University Press.

Pascoe-Watson, G. 9 February 2006. Blunkett Blast at Hamza hold-up, *The Sun*.

Phillips, M. 11 February 2006. Crack down on protests of hate, *The Sun*.

Poole, E. 2006. The Effects of September 11 and the War in Iraq on British Newspaper Coverage, in *Muslims and the News Media*, edited by E. Poole and J.E. Richardson. London: IB Tauris.

Saeed, A. 2007. Media, Racism and Islamophobia: The Representation of Islam and Muslims in the Media, *Sociology Compass*, vol. 1/2: 443-462.

Shanahan, F. 10 February 2006. You forced our 'masters' to put Hook behind bars, *The Sun*.

Taylor, M., Dodd, V. and Woodward, W. 2006. Anger over plans to spy on student, *The Guardian* [Online, 17 October] Available at: http://www.guardian.co.uk/uk/2006/oct/17/highereducation.politics [accessed: 23 February 2006].

Thompson, P. and Hughes, S. 13 January 2006. Get ready to sacrifice yourself for Islam, *The Sun*.

Thompson, P. and Hughes, S. 14 January 2006. Hamza's 'gloat' at dead US seamen, *The Sun*.

Thompson, P. and Hughes, S. 17 January 2006. Hamza: 'Allah loves blood', *The Sun*.

Thompson, P. 18 January 2006. Hamza's warning: Don't read *The Sun*, *The Sun*.

White, R. 11 February 2006. Exposed: The mad hatter, *The Sun*.

Whittaker, B. 2002. Islam and the British Press after September 11 [Online] Available at: http://www.al-bab.com/media/articles/bw020620.htm [accessed: 3 November 2010].

Chapter 11

Criminalizing Dissent in the 'War on Terror': The British State's Reaction to the Gaza War Protests of 2008-2009[1]

Joanna Gilmore

Nadifa, Hakim, Yusuf and Mohammed

On the evening of 23 March 2009, Nadifa, a twenty-four year-old Somali woman, and her husband Hakim, went to sleep for the night at their home in an apartment block on a busy London high street. Nadifa's nineteen year old brother, Yusuf, who had been staying with the couple for the previous few weeks, was sleeping in the next room. In the early hours of the following morning, at around 5am, Nadifa and her husband were awoken by the sound of a door being kicked open and loud screams coming from a nearby flat. Moments later, the couple became aware that someone had broken down their own front door and heard footsteps coming up the stairs towards their bedroom. Nadifa and her husband began to scream and heard the screams of Yusuf coming from the nearby room. The couple then saw their bedroom door fly open and around ten to fifteen men, some in plain clothes and some in police uniform, burst into the room. The couple were pulled from their bed, dragged to the floor and handcuffed. Nadifa described what happened next:

> I was in shock, we didn't know what to do because we didn't know who they were, so we were just screaming .. I asked them why they were there and they said, 'we can't tell you at this point'. My husband was saying 'how can you not tell us?', and they said 'we can't tell you in case you try to hide any kind of evidence', we said, 'how can we hide anything if you're keeping us handcuffed?', but they just ignored us. I asked them whether I could be covered

---

1   This chapter is based on an extensive ethnographic study of the protests and their aftermath, including interviews with protest organisers, stewards, protesters, family members, lawyers, probation officers and religious leaders; participant observation at protests, court hearings and defence campaign meetings and an analysis of administrative data including legal case-files, Freedom of Information Act disclosures, press releases, newspaper reports, defence campaign documents including film and photograph material and witness statements. All fieldwork was carried out by the author between January 2009 and February 2011. All names appearing in the chapter are pseudonyms.

because I felt uncomfortable with all these men in the house. I was in my night clothes and I wanted to wear something longer. I'm a Muslim and I usually wear a scarf, so I felt even more uncomfortable. But when I asked them they said, 'not now, not now, you might be a threat, you might be hiding something'. I didn't know my rights. Eventually one of the police officers gave me an old piece of cloth he had found in the house and I used it to cover my head. Most of the police were in the living room with my brother, but I couldn't speak to him and they didn't tell us what was going on ... eventually they said that they were there for my brother but they didn't tell us until an hour afterwards, after they had finished searching the house. I assumed it was something really, really big (Interview, 15 July 2009).

This whole episode lasted around two and a half hours, during which time the police thoroughly searched the couple's home, seizing shoes, clothing, paperwork and mobile phones belonging to Nadifa and her brother. When the police eventually found Nadifa's laptop computer they demanded to know whether her brother had ever used it. Nadifa explained that the laptop was hers and she only used it for her university work. She asked why they were interested in her computer and was shocked by the response:

They said they wanted to know whether my brother had been looking at any terrorist material, or whether he was part of any terrorist network. That was bizarre because [Yusuf] has nothing to do with terrorism, my brother doesn't even know his own religion very well.

After the search had finished, the police arrested Yusuf who had been handcuffed in the next room, leaving Nadifa and her husband in their badly damaged home. Yusuf was taken to a police station, where he was questioned by police officers, in the absence of a solicitor, about his political and religious beliefs. The arrest has had a lasting effect on Nadifa and her family:

I don't feel that I have a private life at all after that, it was really embarrassing, especially not wearing anything as a woman with many men being there, it was an awful experience. And the way they came into the house, not telling us what was going on, handcuffing people who had nothing to do with it, was even worse. I feel like I was assaulted.

Unbeknown to the family at the time, and indeed until many months later, the experience of Nadifa, Hakim and Yusuf was being repeated in the homes of Muslim families across the UK. During the following months, a total of 169 people were arrested in a series of these aggressive dawn raids, as part of a policing operation codenamed 'Operation Ute' (FOI 2011). The arrests followed the publication of police press releases containing CCTV images of 'wanted' men, most of Asian appearance, together with a large-scale police surveillance operation which involved tracking the movements and associations of suspects over a number of days and weeks. Another of those pursued by police was 37-year-old Mohammed, who became aware that the police were pursuing him when his photograph was printed on the front page of his local newspaper. Mohammed later discovered that his image had been included in Scotland Yard's 'Top 10 Most Wanted' list, prompting one national tabloid newspaper to label him an 'Islam convert' and 'suspected Muslim fanatic' who was 'wanted by cops'. The newspaper claimed he had made 'chilling references to death' on the social networking website Facebook, declaring himself 'Muslim first before anything' and expressing 'support for the Palestinians' (Hughes 2009). Mohammed, who has suffered mental health problems since his arrest, described his reaction when he discovered the police were pursuing him:

> I was in shock, I was really, really scared, they'd made me look like a fanatic, a lunatic, I was thinking, 'what's going to happen to me?', I was absolutely terrified' (Interview, 28 May 2010).

The experiences of these families mirror those of many of the over 1,800 people arrested in connection with terrorism offences in Britain since 11 September 2001, an overwhelming 92 percent of which have failed to result in successful prosecution under counter-terrorism legislation (Carlile 2010). Unbelievably, however, none of those arrested in this series of dawn raids were arrested in connection with involvement in domestic or international terrorism. Nor were they accused of inciting, glorifying, financing or conspiring to commit any of the wide-ranging terrorist-related offences that have been introduced in Britain during the last decade. Instead, what united those arrested as part of this policing operation, in addition to being young and Muslim, was that they had attended at least one of a series of political demonstrations in response to the Israeli state's devastating military assault on the Gaza strip earlier that year.

From Operation Cast Lead to Operation Ute

On 27 December 2008, Israeli forces launched 'Operation Cast Lead', a three-week military incursion on the Gaza Strip, which resulted in the death of over 1,400 Palestinians and injured thousands more (Goldstone 2009). This attack by the world's fourth largest military power on a largely defenceless civilian population triggered a wave of protests, vigils and occupations throughout the world and in the UK culminated in the largest demonstration in support of the Palestinian people in British history. Despite the majority of British Muslims having little or no connection to the occupied territories (Peach 2005), the three weeks of conflict in Gaza provoked tens of thousands of people, with a large representation of Muslims, to take to the streets, voicing their opposition to both the Israeli incursion and the British Government's apparent complacency at the suffering of the Palestinian people. From the day Israel launched its first air strike on the Gaza Strip, pro-Palestinian protesters held a nightly vigil outside the Israeli Embassy in London (Gillan 2008). Organized by a coalition of groups in opposition to the conflict[2] and beginning with a few hundred people, as the strength of public opposition to the Israeli offensive intensified the protests rapidly grew in size, forcing the closure of a number of streets surrounding the Embassy by the start of the New Year (Bowcott 2009). At the same time, a wave of student protests began to spread across the UK, with students at 16 universities occupying management buildings and lecture theatres, demanding university divestment from companies that support arms to Israel and a boycott of Israeli goods (Lipsett and Benjamin 2009). At the forefront of many of the protests and campaigns were young Muslim women, many of whom had not attended a political demonstration in the past, taking a central role in organizing, stewarding and speaking at demonstrations. There they were joined by thousands of trade unionists, faith groups and peace campaigners, representing the biggest surge in the anti-war movement since the mass protests against the prospect of a US-led invasion of Iraq in 2003.

The police responded to these protests with violent policing on a scale that had not been seen in the UK for over a decade (Gilmore 2010). While pro-Palestinian protesters in Egypt, Jordan and Syria were beaten back with batons and tear gas (Jordan 2008), protesters in London were greeted at the Israeli Embassy by scores of riot police fully equipped with dogs, horses, batons and long shields. As the protests grew in size the level of policing intensified dramatically. During the first national demonstration in London on 3 January 2009, a group of around 5,000 protesters en route to the Israeli Embassy were diverted by police into an underpass near Hyde Park. Once inside, hidden from the view of the world's media, the march was brought to a standstill and lines of police officers were ordered to charge into the crowd. Scores of protesters were injured as those inside the tunnel tried desperately to escape:

> There was a stampede of people walking towards the back of the tunnel, trying to get out ... people were panicking, screaming, falling over, there were people who fell over and were buried under three or four people, it was really scary ... it was absolutely sickening, you just thought, 'this isn't going to end until someone dies' (Interview with protester injured during demonstrations on 3 January 2009, 7 July 2009).

The following week, as the Palestinian death toll continued to rise, an estimated 100,000 people took part in a mass demonstration in central London (Quinn and Smith 2009).[3] As the march surged past the Israeli Embassy protesters threw shoes

---

2   Stop the War (STW), Palestinian Solidarity Campaign (PSC), British Muslim Initiative (BMI), Palestinian Forum in Britain (PFB) and Campaign for Nuclear Disarmament (CND).

3   The author attended the march and rally as a participant observer.

at the gates, in a symbolic echo of the Iraqi journalist who threw his shoes at former US-President George W. Bush (Pilkington 2008). Suddenly and without warning, scores of riot and mounted police who had assembled inside the Embassy grounds charged into the crowd. Protesters described fears of meeting a 'Hillsborough-style death'[4] as police tried to hold up metal barriers to prevent people escaping onto the side streets:

> There was a sudden panic, a big swell, all the crash barriers got knocked over, people fell to the floor. People began to panic, especially people with children ... The police did a charge and then pulled back, and then did another charge and pulled back, just intimidating people. People were just standing around, totally disorientated and worried for their safety (Interview with Muslim Safety Forum steward, 22 July 2009).

As the closing rally came to an end, thousands of men, women and children were held indiscriminately in freezing temperatures inside police cordons, where they were subject to periodic baton charges by police. In response, some protesters began to throw placards and bottles towards the gates of the Embassy and the windows of a Starbucks café were broken. Protesters were eventually released on the condition that they provide their name, address, date of birth and have their photograph taken by police intelligence gatherers. Protesters and journalists attempting to film police actions were detained under counter-terrorism powers. Those of 'Asian' (i.e South Asian) appearance were searched and questioned in greater numbers than their white counterparts. Twenty people were arrested by teams of police 'snatch squads'. Jalil, a British-born Muslim, was arrested while attempting to leave the demonstration on suspicion of assaulting a police officer – an alleged crime for which he was subsequently acquitted:

> I was jumped on, kicked, punched, thrown on the floor and handcuffed. I was in complete shock...[The police officer] was pulling the handcuffs to make me feel pain and when I complained about the pain he said, 'I'll teach you about pain, I'll teach you a lesson you prick, I know your kind' ... One of the police officers started taunting me and asking me questions like, 'Where were you born?' and I said, 'I'm British', but he said, 'you're not British, you don't have respect for this country, you don't understand the laws of this country'. I said, 'I told you I'm British', and he said 'this is the Queen's country and you should obey our rules' (Interview, 23 February 2010).

---

4   On 15 April 1989, 96 men, women and children were killed and hundreds injured during a crush at the Hillsborough football stadium in Sheffield, England. The 1989 Taylor Report identified police mismanagement of the crowd as the main reason for the disaster. See Scraton (2009).

This notion that Muslims are antithetical to 'British' cultural practices echoed much of the racist hysteria surrounding Islamic sharia law that had featured heavily in media and political commentary for much of the previous year. In February 2008, the fiercely anti-Muslim *Daily Express* newspaper called on Muslims who wish to be regarded as 'true Britons' to reject their 'unpatriotic' practices and 'accept the law of the land': 'Muslims who don't should go and find another country with a culture more to their taste.' (*Daily Express* 2009).

'Saddamites' and 'Wannabe Jihadists'

Constructions of Muslims as alien 'others' characterized the media's response to the Gaza war protests, with increasingly lurid stories of 'chaos and bloodshed' on the streets of London as thousands of protesters 'battled with riot police' outside the Israeli Embassy (Silvester 2009). Although some of the broadsheet newspapers reported allegations of brutality on the part of the police (see e.g. Dodd 2009a, McVeigh and Quinn 2009, Dugan, Miles and Osley 2009), the indignation of tabloid journalists was reserved exclusively for the 'illegitimate' actions of protesters, often repeating verbatim the official police account of the demonstrations. The *Daily Mail* blamed the disorder on 'extremists', consisting of 'coachloads of Muslim youths with Pakistani origins' who had been 'driven from Yorkshire and the Midlands' to cause 'anarchist mayhem' (Wright and Drake 2009), while the *Evening Standard* described a violent 'rampage' by an 'angry mob' who had 'ransacked businesses' causing 'hundreds of thousands of pounds of damage' (Blunden and Razaq 2009). As Jonathan Evans, head of MI5, warned that anger over the Israeli incursion could have repercussions for national security by giving extremists in Britain 'more ideological ammunition' (Norton-Taylor 2009), the *Sun* predicted a 'violent Islamic backlash in Britain' as a direct result of the conflict (Phillips 2009). According to *Daily Mail* columnist Richard Littlejohn, the protests represented an attempt by 'the hard-Left and militant Islamists' to 'bring the Gaza war to the streets of London'. Contrasting the 'mayhem' outside the Israeli Embassy with the 'restrained, dignified pro-Israeli rally' taking place at Trafalgar Square, Littlejohn claimed:

> This has less to do with the Palestinian cause and everything to do with the global jihad and Iranian-sponsored terrorism aimed at wiping Israel off the face of the Earth … It's the usual crowd of Trotskyite boot boys, Saddamites and bussed-in wannabe jihadists, spoiling for a fight and an excuse to kick a few coppers. (Littlejohn 2009).

On 22 January 2009 London's Metropolitan Police Service (MPS) issued a press release appealing for information to help trace over forty people suspected of involvement in 'violence and aggression' during the Gaza demonstrations (MPS 2009). According to Commander Bob Broadhurst, head of the force's public order unit[5], those wanted by police consisted of a 'small hardcore' who acted as 'antagonists' during the demonstrations, 'attacking police and smashing shop windows' and 'stirring up others within the crowd'. In stark contrast to the account given by those attending the protests, Broadhurst claimed that his officers had 'worked hard to facilitate to the march to keep participants safe [*sic*]' while the embassy and police officers came under 'sustained attack' from an unruly crowd: 'The Met will not tolerate attacks on officers under the guise of protest. Our right to protest is an important one and should never be undermined by thugs and louts who simply want to cause trouble' (MPS 2009). Included in the press release were a number of CCTV snapshots of those who were 'wanted' in connection with the police investigation. These images were given wide-scale publicity when they were printed on the front pages of a number of local and national newspapers, which reproduced without question the police account of the protesters as violent and the police response as proportionate (see e.g. Davenport 2009, *Hackney Gazette* 2009).

The publicity led to the arrest of 169 people and the start of what was to become one of the most significant series of political criminal cases in over a decade. Of the 148 offences charged, 126 were for 'Violent Disorder', a broadly-drafted public order offence introduced in the wake of the 1984 miners' strike carrying a maximum sentence of five years imprisonment (FOI 2010, 2011a, 2011b)[6]. In contrast to the very mixed demographic of the protests, almost all of those selected for prosecution were from Muslim backgrounds. Some 67 per cent were aged 21 or under at the time of the demonstrations (the youngest was only 12) and all but four were male. The majority had no previous convictions and had been attending their first ever political demonstration. Having been warned by police that a request for legal advice would substantially increase their time held in custody, some of those arrested agreed to be interviewed in the absence of a solicitor. Although none were formally arrested in connection with terrorism offences, many were questioned extensively on their political and religious beliefs. The police demanded the names of any friends and family members who had accompanied them to the demonstrations, some of whom went on to be arrested in subsequent raids. In February 2009, the Association of Chief Police Officers confirmed that groups involved in the Gaza war protests had been targeted by the secretive 'Confidential Intelligence Unit', established in 1999 to coordinate surveillance and infiltration of 'domestic extremists' (Milne 2009).

---

5   In January 2011, Commander Broadhurst was forced to apologise to MPs for giving false information to a Parliamentary inquiry into the policing of the G20 protests in London, during which a 47-year old man was killed after being struck from behind by a police officer operating under his command (Woodcock 2011).

6   Public Order Act 1986, s2.

The Bradford Effect: 'Muslim Riots' and 'Deterrent' Sentencing

For the vast majority of the arrested protesters and their lawyers, it was not until the cases finally reached the packed West London courthouse in October 2009 and defendants were one at a time called before the District Judge to enter their plea that the scale of the policing operation became apparent. In a troubling parallel to the Bradford riot cases of 2001, the majority of those charged appeared individually and were represented by separate lawyers, only a small minority of whom had significant experience of handling serious charges of public disorder. Acting on the advice from lawyers that an early guilty plea would be likely to result in a non-custodial sentence, a staggering 72 per cent of those charged pleaded guilty to the serious indictments against them, denying the opportunity to mount a collective defence or to contest the police account in court. When lawyers were eventually granted access to the footage relevant to their client's case, they were asked to sign an undertaking that they would not disclose any of the footage to anyone other than their client. This initial segregation of protesters, who were arrested and charged individually following night-time raids and represented by over thirty different law firms, undoubtedly contributed to the reluctance of defendants to take their cases to trial, leading some defence solicitors to conclude that this was a deliberate strategy on the part of the police:

> People were raided individually, it was very isolating, and it was kept quiet ... Normally the police are very proud of the number of arrests they make and are shouting out about it, but they were very clever here, it was a very planned operation of individual arrests ... There were individuals who were young, Muslim, and who did not have a clear connection with an organization being picked off, often not represented [by a lawyer]. This leads to confessions through fear and isolation in the courts (Interview with criminal defence solicitor, 6 July 2010).

As the hearings came to an end, the judge took the unprecedented step of concluding that these cases had an 'international element' (a term with no legal meaning) and imposed bail conditions which required protesters to surrender passports and not apply for travel documents without the leave of the Court. Although almost all of those charged were British citizens, protesters were indiscriminately served with immigration notices stating that they could be deported depending on the outcome of the criminal proceedings. When those convicted of offences eventually returned to court to receive their punishment[7], friends and family who had packed into the court's public gallery broke down in tears as the judge announced that he had decided to pass lengthy sentences of imprisonment that would serve as a 'deterrent' to others, citing as authority the precedent set in the Bradford riot

---

7   Cases took on average one year and two months from the protest date to conclude with some protesters having to wait over two years to discover their fate.

cases of 2001.[8] Relying almost exclusively on the carefully edited CCTV footage presented by police, the judge disregarded the advice of the Probation Service in their Pre-Sentence Reports, which had recommended without exception a non-custodial sentence as an appropriate level of punishment. In a carefully worded judgment that echoed much of Judge Gullick's infamous 'tariff setting' statement in the Bradford cases, Judge Denniss concluded:

> Although the Court must have regard to the individual defendant's personal characteristics and actual involvement, the sentence must also reflect the effect of the violent disorder on the public who would have been caused real anxiety and distress. It is not just the individual conduct of a single offender which is important, it is the nature of the offending as a whole. Every individual who takes part by their deed or encouragement is guilty of an offence. Everyone who takes part does so at their peril a deterrent sentence is necessary. The public are entitled to look to the law for protection.

Those wearing over their faces the Palestinian 'Keffiyeh' scarf, a powerful symbol of resistance for opponents of the conflict, were handed down increased sentences as punishment for their attempts to 'conceal their identity'. Two boys, both aged 16 when the protests took place, received 12-month sentences for their part in causing damage to a Starbucks café while two women aged 18 and 19 were sent to prison for 15 months. A 21-year-old student was given a 12-month jail term for throwing a single bottle towards the gates of the Israeli Embassy, while a 17-year-old boy was sentenced to 30 months in a Young Offenders Institution for throwing 'missiles' (wooden placards and plastic bottles) towards police lines. In total, 54 people were convicted and 29 sent to prison for between two months and two and a half years. Almost all had entered guilty pleas at the earliest available opportunity and most had no previous convictions. None were alleged to have caused any direct injury to a police officer or member of the public. An overwhelming 94 per cent were from black and minority ethnic groups.[9]

The rigour with which those singled out by the police as criminal suspects were pursued was in stark contrast to the way allegations of criminal wrongdoing on the

---

8   Following the Bradford riots of 2001, 307 people were arrested and 256 charged with offences. Of these, 231 people were convicted and 187 sent to prison for an average of 4 years and 6 months. Most were charged with the more serious offence of Riot (Public Order Act 1986, s1). For a detailed analysis of criminal charges brought following the Bradford riots see Carling et al. (2004). For an account of the racialized moral panic around the Bradford riots, see Chapter 9 in this volume, by Joanne Massey and Rajinder Singh Tatla.

9   According to Crown Prosecution Service figures based on self-defined ethnicity, 32 of those convicted were recorded as 'Any Other Asian Background', 9 were recorded as 'Pakistani', 4 as 'Any Other Ethnic Group', 3 as 'White British', 3 as 'African', 1 as 'Caribbean' and 1 as 'Any Other White Background' (FOI 2001b).

part of the police were handled by the authorities. Despite the severity of the 33 official complaints about the policing of the demonstrations, none have been fully investigated by the Independent Police Complaints Commission and all of those referred back to the Metropolitan Police for local investigation were subsequently dismissed (FOI 2009a, 2009b). At least two of the most serious complaints were dismissed after the officer who assaulted the protester could not be identified as they had deliberately concealed their ID number. Dissatisfied with the police's handling of the official complaints, a small number of injured protesters decided to pursue civil actions against the police and in July 2010, the Metropolitan Police finally agreed an out of court settlement of £25,000 with two brothers struck on the head by police truncheons outside the Israeli Embassy on the 3 January 2009. Despite an admission from the Metropolitan Police of unjustified use of force, however, no police officer has faced criminal charges as a result of their behaviour at the Gaza demonstrations. Ray, a 79-year-old veteran peace campaigner knocked unconscious outside the Israeli Embassy after being struck on the head by a police shield, described those responsible as 'absolutely vicious, totally irresponsible, arrogant and racist' (Interview, 4 August 2009).

Shoe Throwing and 'Political Correctness'

For much of the media, the severity of sentences legitimized the earlier hysteria surrounding the protests, reinforcing the racialized construction of the protesters as dangerous 'others' who pose a volatile threat to the security of the state. Although many of the news reports highlighted that the majority of those convicted were from Muslim backgrounds, they did so without reference to the controversy surrounding the police's decision to target young Muslims out of the very diverse group of people who took part in the demonstrations or the exceptional way the cases were handled by the courts. This portrayal of defendants as Muslim 'extremists' rather than legitimate protesters intensified following the revelation that one of those singled out for arrest happened to be the son of infamous jailed Muslim cleric Abu Hamza – a consistent figure of tabloid hate for much of the last decade (see Chapter 10 in this volume, by Anneke Meyer). Although the connection between the hook-handed folk devil and student protester predictably attracted significant media attention, the court remarkably refused to grant anonymity to the defendant, dismissing submissions from his defence lawyers that his relationship with his father could prejudice his case. Unconstrained by reporting restrictions, the 20-year-old's name, address and photograph were published in the press alongside photographs of his 'hate preacher' father. Following his predictable conviction, a lengthy article published in the *Daily Mail*, headed 'Hate Cleric's Son Locked Up for Riot Attacks on Police', described in detail the prosecution's account of the part he played in the 'violent clashes' at the 'anti-Israel riots' (Camber 2010). The article was accompanied by a series of unrelated claims about the level of 'huge benefit payments' Hamza's family have enjoyed whilst 'living off the state' at the expense of the taxpayer. In April 2010, another remarkable story published on the front page of the *Sunday Times* claimed that London's Metropolitan Police had 'bowed to Islamic sensitivities' by allowing Muslims 'to throw shoes in ritual protest – which could have the unintended consequence of politicians or the police being hit'. The article referred to the case of a 21-year-old student charged in relation to the Gaza protests who, it maintained, was 'almost certain to avoid a prison sentence' as a result of the police's 'concession' towards Muslim protesters. In reality, the prosecution's decision not to include an alleged incident of shoe throwing in a charge of violent disorder was based entirely on the quality of the CCTV evidence, rather than any exceptional 'concession' towards Muslim protesters. Nevertheless, familiar populist attacks on multiculturalism and 'political correctness' continued to dominate over any sober analysis of the exceptional way these cases were being handled by the authorities.

Resisting Deviant Identities

Hall et al.'s (1978) 'spiral of signification' analysis presents a reciprocal relationship between the media and other institutions of social control such as the police and the courts, whereby particular events constructed by the media as signifying wider problems of social crisis justify a disproportionate response from the state, which in turn serves to expand repressive mechanisms of social control and reinforce existing social and political order. From the repressive protest policing tactics and exceptional counter-terrorism measures, though to the public 'man-hunt', mass dawn raid arrests, severe criminal charges, onerous bail conditions and lengthy prison sentences, all of those selected for punishment for their involvement in the Gaza war protests were subjected to a disproportionate response from the state at every stage of the criminal justice process. This was a response fuelled by media constructions of Muslims as an inherently 'suspect' community and legitimized by a political discourse which presents 'Islamic fundamentalism' as the predominant threat to the Western liberal democracies (Fekete 2004, Pantazis and Pemberton 2009). Far from being exclusively repressive, however, Garland notes the mobilizing and politicizing effects moral panics can have on their 'deviant' subjects, causing the basis of panic 'to be halted, amplified or altogether transformed' (2008: 14, see also McRobbie and Thornton 1995). In January 2009, a packed public meeting in Parliament called by the protest organizers and attended by hundreds of activists, lawyers, defendants and their families demanded the immediate release of all convicted protesters from prison and that the charges be dropped against those still facing trial. The following week, a national defence campaign was formed to coordinate liaison between lawyers, offer support for defendants and their families and generate public awareness of the disproportionate treatment of the arrested protesters. The campaign launched a public petition that went on to receive over 2,000 signatures and organized protests outside of some of the remaining court hearings. The response generated considerable media attention (see e.g. Taylor

2010, Hattenstone and Taylor 2010, Alibhai-Brown 2010), significantly shifting the debate away from the initial moral panic which focused on the dominant police narrative towards the disproportionate response from the state. Those protesters that were supported by their lawyers to challenge the evidence against them were remarkably successful. At the time of writing, a staggering 14 out of the 16 cases where not guilty pleas have been maintained have resulted in acquittal. Many of the cases collapsed following persistent requests from lawyers for the disclosure of police material. In March 2010 a 23-year-old protester was acquitted after his lawyer discovered undisclosed police footage which clearly showed him beaten to the ground by police officers in an unprovoked attack. The case raised serious questions about the validity of the police's account of protesters as the instigators of violence and the reliability of the testimony of individual officers. Between March and July 2010, 14 of the 29 cases where custodial sentences had been imposed were taken to the Court of Appeal. The first appeal saw a 19-year-old woman immediately released from prison in the 'interests of justice and mercy'.[10] During the following hearings, one 12 month sentence was quashed while two others were reduced to the time already served in custody. The remainder of the sentences were reduced by between three and 18 months.[11] The Court, however, steadfastly refused to condemn the trial judge's decision to impose 'deterrent' sentences and the majority of the protesters remained in prison.

Criminalizing Dissent in the 'War on 'Terror'

The Gaza war triggered a level of political mobilization from within Britain's Muslim communities not seen since the mass demonstrations over the US-led invasion of Iraq in 2003, when united action between Muslims and non-Muslims provided a powerful antidote to the 'clash of civilizations' rhetoric that had come to characterize the dominate discourse surrounding the globalized 'War on Terror' and the imperialist military intervention that became its defining feature (Poynting and Mason 2007, Bonnett 2004). Yaqoob (2003) has further argued that the collaboration of Muslims with the wider anti-war movement played an important role in 'helping Muslims to move away from the confining and further marginalizing position of constantly being on the defensive', as well serving to isolate 'extreme' Islamic groups who opposed working with non-Muslims (see also Alam 2003). The racist backlash against Muslims provoked by the London bombings of 7 July 2005, however, placed Muslim groups working within the wider anti-war movement under increasing pressure to retreat from an 'over-politicized' position. In December 2005 the leadership of the Muslim Association of Britain, one of the key groups involved in organizing the mass mobilizations against the

---

    10   R v Lahouidek [2010] EWCA Crim 738 at 13.
    11   R v Alhaddad and others [2010] EWCA Crim 1760; R v Kalaf and McPherson [2010] EWCA Crim 2525.

Iraq war in 2003, lost control of the organization in response to growing internal fears that the group's anti-war activities 'had pitted it too publicly and forcefully against the British establishment' (Phillips 2008: 107). At the same time, student Islamic Societies and Palestinian solidarity groups have come under increasingly intrusive levels of surveillance from the authorities (Mohammed 2010). In March 2009, as the police were busy tracking down young Muslim men and women who had attended protests outside the Israeli Embassy, the British government suspended links with Britain's largest Muslim organization, the Muslim Council of Britain, when it refused government demands to sack one of its leading members after he signed a statement calling upon Muslims to resist Israeli aggression in the Middle East (Dodd 2009b). Indeed, as the British state's overreaction to the Gaza war protests demonstrates, where critique is directed towards Israel, a key ally in the US-led 'War on Terror', the response has been particularly authoritarian – a pattern consistent with state crackdowns following anti-Israel protests across the globe. As protesters in Britain were rounded up by police, 180 people were arrested following a rally of over 30,000 people in Paris while police in Norway used tear gas to disperse protesters outside the Israeli Embassy in Oslo (Rising 2009).The ferocity with which those singled out for their part in the Gaza war protests were pursued and punished by the state was thus fuelled by a continuous cycle of moral panic constructing Muslims as a pervasive 'threat' to the West and legitimized by an establishment political discourse that presents the engagement of Muslims within broader political movements as illegitimate. Whilst those Muslim groups who support government practices are labeled as 'moderate' and rewarded with significant financial gain, those who criticize it are isolated as 'extremist' and subject to intrusive levels of state surveillance and criminalization (Kundnani 2009). In an attempt to depoliticize Muslims and restrict radical dissent, Muslims are constructed as dangerous 'outsiders', to be excluded from political engagement other than that which is proscribed to them by the state. An Imam from a mosque where three of the imprisoned protesters attended described the frustration of young men and women in his community following the arrests:

> We noticed how angry they were, they don't trust the police, they feel that police are not fair with them, not cooperating with them, they feel the media is not giving the right picture about them, and what is happening with the massacres in Gaza. So that makes them boil from inside, and the reaction of the people who are boiling from inside, without giving them the right and facilitating their right to demonstrate, can be very dangerous (Interview, 21 July 2009).

'Is It Because He Is Muslim'?

Although some of those targeted by the police under Operation Ute were undoubtedly politicized by their experiences, this has not been a universal effect. Some have instead become intensely withdrawn, finding it difficult to leave the house or speak to anyone outside of their immediate family. Those attempting to secure jobs and university places on release from prison have predictably found a conviction for violent disorder and lengthy jail sentence to be a significant barrier. Many have sworn never to attend a political demonstration again. What is clear, however, is that the impact has gone far beyond those arrested and incarcerated. Speaking following the release from prison of his son, Kabir, a father described the devastating impact the case has had on his entire family:

> The atmosphere changed in the house completely. My wife was crying all the time, depressed all the time … it was so stressful. She didn't want to cry in front of him but at night she cried .. I used to smile a lot but not now. People at work asked me what was wrong, but at first I was ashamed to say that my son had been to court and put in prison, so I didn't tell anybody at the beginning. The stress affected my daughters also – my eldest daughter had to take a year out of her studies because she couldn't sleep. There were a lot of arguments in the family because of the stress. You can see that there is a sense of unhappiness in the family, a sense that a disaster has happened, a disaster that needs settling. And although [Kabir] is out now, still not everything is settled, we are still thinking about the future. Of course we are not used to this so it upset us a lot. Also for me, it was the sense of injustice hurting me, I feel a lot this sense of injustice, about why this should happen to him. Usually you would not be put in prison for this – why was he? Is it because he is Muslim? That is hurting me a lot (Interview, 11 June 2010).

References

Alam, F. 2003. Battle for Iraq: How war has brought hope to British Muslims. *The Observer*, 23 March 2003, 19.

Alibhai-Brown, Y. 2010. British Muslims are running out of friends, *The Independent*, 8 March 2010, 28.

Bonnett, A. 2004. *The Idea of the West: Culture, Politics and History*. Basingstoke: Palgrave Macmillan.

Bowcott, O. 2009. Protesters to converge on central London to demand Gaza ceasefire. *The Guardian* [Online, 2 January] Available at: http://www.guardian.co.uk/world/2009/jan/02/israelandthepalestinians-middleeast1 [accessed: 6 January 2011].

Blunden, M. and Razaq, R. 2009. Rioters attack Starbucks and loot shops in anti-Israel demo, *The Evening Standard*, 12 January 2009, 24.

Camber, R. 2010. Hate Cleric's son locked up for riot attack on police, *The Daily Mail*, 1 July 2010, 9.

Carlile, A. 2010, *Report on the Operation in 2009 of the Terrorism Act 2000*. London: Home Office.

Carling, A., Davies, D., Fernandes-Bakshi, A., Jarman, N. and Nias, P. 2004. *Fair Justice for All?: The Response of the Criminal Justice System to the Bradford Disturbances of July 2001*. Bradford: University of Bradford, Programme for a Peaceful City, in association with The Joseph Rowntree Charitable Trust.

Daily Express 2009. Sharia law cannot take place of British justice, 9 February 2009, 14.

Davenport, J. 2009. Wanted: The hard core in Israeli Embassy riots, *The Evening Standard*, 22 January 2009, 22.

Dodd, V. 2009a. London clashes: Israel protesters tell of fear and panic, *The Guardian*, 5 January 2009, 6.

Dodd, V. 2009b. UK government suspends links with Muslim Council of Britain. *The Guardian* [Online, 23 March] Available at: http://www.guardian.co.uk/politics/2009/mar/23/muslim-council-britain-gaza [accessed 6 January 2011].

Doward, J. Asthana, A., Smith, D. and Hinsliff, G. 2008. Sharia row: How law and faith war swept the UK, *The Observer*, 10 February 2008, 28.

Dugan, E., Miles, K. and Osley, R. 2009. Riot police called out in London as protest ends in skirmishes, suffering and anger, *The Independent on Sunday*, 4 January 2009, 8.

Fekete, L. 2004. Anti-Muslim racism and the European security state. *Race and Class*, 46(1), 3-29.

FOI 2009a. Figures derived from Freedom of Information responses to Joanna Gilmore from the Metropolitan Police Service, 24 November 2009.

FOI 2009b. Figures derived from Freedom of Information responses to Joanna Gilmore from the Independent Police Complaints Commission, 10 November 2009.

FOI 2010. Figures derived from Freedom of Information Act response from the Metropolitan Police Service to Joanna Gilmore, 17 February 2010.

FOI 2011a. Figures derived from Freedom of Information Act response from the Metropolitan Police Service to Joanna Gilmore, 17 January 2011.

FOI 2011b. Figures derived from Freedom of Information Act response from the C Service to Joanna Gilmore, 14 February 2011.

Garland, D. 2008. On the concept of moral panic. *Crime Media Culture*, 4(1), 9-30.

Gillan, A. 2008. Protests against Gaza attacks planned across UK this weekend, *The Guardian*, 31 December 2008, 4.

Gilmore, J. 2010. Protest policing: an authoritarian consensus. *Criminal Justice Matters*, 82(1), 21-23.

Goldstone, R. 2009. *Human Rights in Palestine and Other Occupied Arab Territories: Report of the United Nations Fact Finding Mission on the Gaza Conflict*, (A/HRC/12/48). UN General Assembly, Human Rights Council, 12th session.

Hall, S., Critcher, C., Jefferson, T., Clarke, J. and Roberts, B. 1978. *Policing the Crisis: Mugging, the State, and Law and Order*. London: Macmillan.

Hackney Gazette 2009. Police hunt Gaza protest suspects, 29 January 2009, 4.

Hattenstone, S. and Taylor, M. 2010. Sent to jail for throwing a single bottle, *The Guardian*, 13 March 2010, 34-5.

Hughes, S. 2009. Guy's Movie Aide is Muslim Riot Suspect. *The Sun*, 13 May 2009, 21.

Jordan, J. 2008. Thousands of protesters in streets, *The Guardian*, 29 December 2008, 5.

Kundnani, A. 2009. *Spooked: How not to prevent violent extremism*, London: Institute of Race Relations.

Lipsett, A. and Benjamin, A. 2009. Storm of student protest over Gaza gathers force. *The Guardian* [Online, 23 January] Available at: http://www.guardian. co.uk/education/2009/jan/23/student-protests-gaza [accessed: 23 January 2009].

Littlejohn, R. 2009. Don't bring Gaza war to the streets of London, *Daily Mail*, 13 January 2009, 15.

McRobbie, A. and Thornton, S. 1995. Rethinking 'moral panic' for multi-mediated social worlds. *British Journal of Sociology*, 46(4), 559-574.

McVeigh, T. and Quinn, B. 2009. London's Gaza protest march ends in violence, *The Observer*, 4 January 2009, 5.

Metropolitan Police Service 2009. *Appeal to trace demonstration crime suspects*. [Online]. Available at: http://cms.met.police.uk/news/appeals/appeal_to_ trace_demonstration_crime_suspects [accessed: 4 February 2009].

Mohammed, S. and Verkaik, R. 2010. CIA given details of British Muslim students, *The Independent*, 1 April 2010, 1.

Norton-Taylor, R. 2009. MI5 chief: al-Qaida threat diminished, but not yet over, *The Guardian*, 7 January 2009, 1.

Pantazis, C. and Pemberton, S. 2009. From the 'old' to the 'new' suspect community: examining the impacts of recent UK counter-terrorist legislation. *British Journal of Criminology*, 49(5), 646-666.

Peach, C. 2005. Muslims in the UK, in *Muslim Britain: Communities Under Pressure*, edited by T. Abbas. London: Zed Books, 18-30.

Phillips, M. 2009. Brit Muslims: Gaza Backlash to hit UK, *The Sun*, 9 January 2009, 13.

Phillips, R. 2008. Standing together: the Muslim Association of Britain and the anti-war movement. *Race and Class*, 50(2), 101-113.

Pilkington, E. 2008. Shoes and insults hurled at Bush on Iraq visit, *The Guardian*, 15 December 2008, 19.

Poynting, S. and Mason, V. 2007. The resistible rise of Islamophobia. *Journal of Sociology*, 43(1), 61-86.

Rising, D. 2009. Thousands in Europe, Lebanon protest Gaza violence, *Associated Press* [Online, 10 January] Available at: http://www.ap.org [accessed 28 February 2011].

Scraton, P. 2009. *Hillsborough: The Truth*. Edinburgh: Mainstream.

Silvester, N. 2009. Police attacked by rioters as anti-war protests erupt in London, *Sunday Mail*, 11 January 2009, 6.

Taylor, M. 2010. MPs step up campaign over jail terms for Gaza protesters, *The Guardian*, 6 March 2010, 17.

Taylor, Rt Hon. Lord Justice, *The Hillsbrough Stadium Disaster: 15 April 1989. Interim Report*, Home Office Cmnd 765, HMSO: London, August 1989.

Quinn, B. and Smith, D. 2009. Tens of thousands join London Gaza protest. *The Guardian* [Online, 10 January] Available at: http://www.guardian.co.uk/world/2009/jan/10/gaza-london-protest-march [accessed: 6 January 2011].

Woodcock, A. 2011. Met misled commons about G20 protests, *The Independent*, 20 January 2011, 16.

Wright, S. and Drake, M. 2009. Bill for keeping control of anti-Israel mobs hits £1m, *Daily Mail*, 12 January 2009, 12.

Yaqoob, S. 2003. Global and local echoes of the anti-war movement: a British Muslim perspective. *International Socialism*, 100, 39-63.

Chapter 12

Where's the Moral in Moral Panic?
Islam, Evil and Moral Turbulence[1]

Greg Noble

Introduction

A highly moralized rhetoric of good and evil has become increasingly strident in Western political discourse in the last decade or so, not just as a result of the 'war on terror' but also in the wake of the resurgence of social and political conservatisms and their critique of the moral relativism of liberalism and multiculturalism. It has asserted a hardening of boundaries between good and bad, between law-abiding citizens and wrongdoers, endemic to a global culture of fear. The emergence of what is often referred to as 'Islamophobia' has become inextricably bound to this rhetoric. Islamophobia, as the intensification of long-standing anti-Muslim prejudice amounting to a widespread hostility in the west, is a complex and dynamic phenomenon. As the Runnymede Trust (1997) report in the UK indicated, it comprises quite diverse elements: 'closed' perceptions of Islam as monolithic, static, radically different, inferior, aggressive, manipulative, anti-Western, and so on. Yet this significant report says little about the decidedly moral dimensions of this hostility. Similarly, even though, as Gottschalk and Greenberg (2008: 106-7) suggest, 'morality' is central to the dominant Western depiction of Islam and Muslims today – in particular the dual focus on Islam as morally militant and Muslims as sexually insatiable – there has been surprisingly little discussion of this aspect. Indeed, Said (1978: 166) showed many years ago that the assumption of the 'seemingly perverse morality' of 'Oriental life' was fundamental to Western colonial discourses.

While a full-scale consideration of the moral dimensions of Islamophobia is beyond the scope of this chapter, I wish to make some contribution towards this by reframing the discussion of the moral panic around Islam in terms of an exploration of 'moral turbulence', the complexities of meaning, value and scale which render moral frameworks necessary but inadequate, and which foster the imperative towards the stabilizing of moral categories. This is evidenced particularly in the

---

1   An earlier version of this paper was published as Noble, G. 2008. Faces of Evil: Demonising the Arab Other in Contemporary Australia. *Cultural Studies Review.* 14(2), 14-33.

symbolization of the 'Muslim' 'face of evil', which functions to 'fix' evil as an identifiable physicality that is seen to reflect a deeper 'truth' of evil.

The Moral in Moral Panic

The idea of the 'moral panic' has been a key frame for the analysis of anti-Muslim hostility, and the link between morality, crime, the state, the media, social anxieties and cultural identities (Werbner, 2002; Poynting et al. 2004, Humphrey 2007, Fekete 2009). Moral panic theory draws especially on the work of Cohen (1972/1980) and Hall et al. (1978) to focus on the process whereby particular groups are identified as threats to social values – a process which fosters intense feelings of disquiet, public debate about the 'problem', and legal responses from the relevant authorities. Central to Cohen's model is the emphasis on the role moral panics – and especially the creation of a folk 'devil' – play in clarifying 'normative contours' and 'moral boundaries' in periods of social strain and ambiguity (1972/1980: 192-3). In the social construction of deviancy, those whom Cohen, following Becker, calls 'moral entrepreneurs' have an especially significant role to play as they make competing claims about the nature of the social problem and its causes. Cohen, again following Becker, focuses especially on the moral entrepreneur who seeks 'to eradicate the evil which disturbs him' (1972/1980: 127). However, for all the evocation of morality, little is said about it. Cohen (1972/1980: 17, 159) refers in passing to the normative 'moral directives' of the media, and to the ceremony of a moral panic as a 'morality play' between good (police, courts) and evil (the delinquent); in the introduction to the second edition he refers to 'bourgeois morality' (1972/1980: vii); and in the introduction to the third edition he refers to 'old morality' and 'political morality', the 'drawing and reinforcement of moral boundaries' (Cohen, 1972/2002: xxv, xxvi). Similarly, Hall et al. (1987: 163-164) refer to 'moral indignation and outrage' and the 'petty-bourgeois voice' of 'public morality'. Neither key text actually unpacks what these terms mean. This does not invalidate moral panic theory, but it does raise the question of what it is that is being talked about when the 'rhetoric of moral panics' is employed (Cohen, 1972/1980: 197). Despite its talk of moral entrepreneurs and 'folk devils', and despite the strong sense of the social construction of deviance as social, legal and moral transgression, it lacks a sustained discussion of the 'moral' dimensions of panic (Garland, 2008: 11). This is not to deny the productive nature of the model, but moral panic theory is primarily interested in considering the processes of labelling and social control at work in constructing folk devils, the ideological representation of 'deviance' and the ways this performs a normative function in sustaining dominant social values, class relations and state institutions of power. Significantly, moral panic theory avoids, rightly or wrongly, engaging with the traditions of moral philosophy (just as moral philosophy ignores the concept of moral panic). But such an engagement is not the issue here – rather, I would suggest that both moral panic theory and moral philosophy, given their focus on the reductive nature of moral order and judgement, avoid the inescapable heterogenous and conflictual nature of moral complexity (Larmore, 1987). It is to this complexity that I wish to return because, as I hope this chapter suggests, the eruption of moral panic works specifically because of its relation to moral complexity.

From Moral Panic to Moral Turbulence

At one level the lack of engagement with the idea of morality in moral panic theory is entirely understandable: it is a notoriously hard notion to define. Morality is typically glossed as the principles of right and wrong that guide human conduct but, while there is a tendency to see these as coherent systems of values grounded in religious or other 'universals', they can of course be quite culturally relativist and often contradictory (Heintz, 2009: 3). As Howell (1997: 2) suggests, morality is something of an 'odd-job word' that covers many things and explains little, yet it is constitutive of human sociality, making human relationality possible (Howell, 1997: 9). This is the crucial insight of ethnomethodology, which explores how people experience social order as moral order (Garfinkel, 1984). It often does this through judgements and sanctions which enforce a localized, group identity by excluding others (Rapport, 1997). But it is the 'plurality of moralities' that I want to give attention to here: as Heintz (2009: 5) argues, the accelerated globalization of recent decades has increasingly forced different value systems into dialogue, especially around human rights. This occurs not just on the international stage, but within nations, cities and neighbourhoods. But this plurality is not simply the result of large-scale migration or technological mediation of world events; it also results from a century (or more) of radical transformation in the West around social values around, for example, gender, sexuality, consumerism and popular culture, producing high levels of complexity, divergence and instability between and within moral systems. Indeed, Waiton (2008) has argued that such changes indicate that there are no coherent moral systems any more, and thus challenge the very sustainability of the existing model of moral panic. Goode and Ben-Yehuda (2009: 86) quite rightly point out that the increasing complexity of the moral order does not negate the idea of a moral panic: folk devils continue to be named and the dynamics of hostility, denunciation and disproportion remain, especially in relation to Islam.

I want to foreground this complexity through the notion of 'moral turbulence' (Cahir and Noble, 2007: 137). This turbulence refers to the ambivalences around the social meanings of an object of moral concern; a complexity which reflects what Cohen (1972/2002: xxvii) refers to as the 'contested terrain' underlying moral panic. Moral turbulence entails constant and sometimes paradoxical re-articulations of a 'social problem' which unsettle social meanings and moral values. These ambivalences foster the imperative towards moral judgement which 'stabilizes' the 'problem' and the imperative towards state intervention for solving the 'problem' but rest ultimately upon the reproduction of moral ambiguity. Islam has become subject to such issues: numerous websites and media organizations around the world increasingly pose questions such as 'Is Islam Immoral?' or 'Is Islam Evil?': these sometimes come from conservative Christians (Pappas, n.d.), and sometimes liberal Christians who discuss it as though it is a legitimate issue (Debating Christianity, n.d.), and sometimes it is posed by journalists reporting other people's words, including those of Muslims (Kerbaj, 2007). There is no single position within these 'debates', and there is no single judgement; nevertheless, the posing of these questions as legitimate questions combined with the plurality of positions captures something of the 'turbulence' around Islam.

This turbulence entails a number of dimensions or complexities, each of which can be seen in relation to what is called 'Islamophobia'. As the Runnymede Trust definition implies, Islamophobia is no single thing: it is a complex of different groups, discourses, anxieties, affects, and so on. Yet, as Goldberg argues, the public imagination has come to fix upon 'the *idea* of the Muslim', a singularity which manages to represent the 'threat of death', fanaticism, female oppression, irrationality (Goldberg 2009: 165-6). This is similar to the earlier argument regarding what was called the 'Arab Other' in contemporary Australian society, a figure that was becoming the folk devil of our times (Poynting et al., 2004: 251). The Arab Other, it was argued, was a useful fiction to describe the ways processes of demonization had conflated people of different cultural, religious, national and generational backgrounds and geo-political regions; it also conflated performance of youthful machismo with the acts of criminal gangs, rapists, refugees and terrorists; and it was built upon the *historical* complexity of an accumulation of moral panics and ideological representations of the Arab Other. Whatever this singularity is called, it creates, out of an array of 'materials', an 'enemy' that articulates a range of social anxieties. The Arab (and now Muslim) Other is portrayed as animal, barbaric, uncivilized, inhuman and the 'essence' of evil.

This *semiotic* complexity is thus matched by the conflation of *categorical* complexity: the moral, the social, the criminal, the affective, and so on. Something may be judged criminal but it may not be immoral, and vice versa, something may be deemed morally unpalatable but it may not be a threat to social order. Yet the function of the process of *symbolization* in the construction of deviance in moral panic theory is a recognition that these categories are simplified (Cohen, 1972/1980: 76) and equated (Humphrey, 2007). There is a tendency in uses of moral panic theory to collapse the complex process of symbolization into a singular, dominant, ideological representation of the folk devil; in fact, however, a key but often undeveloped aspect of moral panic theory is exactly the 'contested' nature of representation that Cohen refers to. A moral panic always entails an ensemble of social actors who compete in the definition of the 'problem', it is not just a cabal of conservative politicians, religious spokespeople and outraged citizens. It is worth remembering that alongside stories of the Lebanese criminal and the Muslim terrorist there was media coverage and public discussion of 'the other side of the story', symbols of hope that undermine dominant stereotypes: Muslim girls who were learning to play football or train as lifesavers, young Lebanese boys who were becoming voices for their generation, Muslims who were victims of racism not perpetrators, friendships across ethnic barriers, and so on (Chandab, 2008; Fenely, 2010). This *value* complexity – or how the 'Other' is esteemed and appraised in contrast to ideological portrayals of evil – further complicates the semiotic complexity of the idea of the Muslim. It also complicates the complexity of *scale* through which the 'problem' of the Muslim is conceptualized. This is not just because global events frame and resignify domestic events, as important as this is (Poynting and Mason, 2007; Fekete, 2009). More importantly, the personal and the local are infused with the provincial, the national, the regional and the transnational: the various scales are experienced as of the same order. Moral panics around international Islamic terrorism, particularly through the intertextual 'reference archive' of mainstream media (Ibrahim, 2007), are experienced as in ontological proximity with people-smuggling from our regional neighbours, state police management of crime gangs and troublesome youth in suburban streets, and local kindergartens banning Christmas celebrations because of cultural sensitivities (Poynting et al., 2004: 224-5).

The point of foregrounding these modalities is not simply to insist that 'things are complex', but to suggest that such complexity is unsettling. These forms of complexity are irritants, because how people experience and feel about key social, political and moral issues around cultural difference are thrown together in turbulent relations. Within this tumult, humans desire moral clarification and certainty, as foundations of a larger sense of security. Being able to 'see' your enemy thus plays a crucial function in stabilizing this turbulence.

Symbolizing Evil

The 'face of evil' has become a common figure in the moralized rhetoric of global Islamophobia. Most typically evoked in representations of international terrorism – the events of September 11, 2001, the Bali and London bombings and so on – the 'face of evil' has also become a motif in local representations of crime and social incivility when specific cultural and religious backgrounds are seen to be involved. Media reportage of 'race rape' [see the chapter by Selda Dagistanli and Kiran Grewal in this volume] and 'ethnic crime' amongst young Arab and Muslim men are often accompanied by graphic images of alleged wrongdoers who are seen to embody evil. 'Evil' has, of course, long been a feature of political and moral discourse. Hitler and Nazism, for example, are used to represent the worst of human behaviour. They have been extensively discussed in the analysis of the nature of evil in the twentieth century, most famously by Arendt (1994) to explore the 'banality of evil': the transformation of atrocities into bureaucratic procedure devoid of human responsibility (Bauman, 1989; Vetlesen, 2005). A crucial insight has been to stress that, despite the perception of 'evil' as primordial in moral discourse, fundamental to law, politics and religion, it is a social construct

central to the regulation of moral behaviour and social order. 'Evil' is central to
these domains because, even though it is analytically loose, it sustains the social
dichotomy of moral good and bad (Parkin, 1985: 2,5). In elevating some acts to a
category of evil beyond 'normal' wrongdoing there is more, however, at stake than
universalistic attributions of good and bad. As Badiou (Cox and Whalen, 2001/2)
argues,

> There is no natural definition of Evil; Evil is always that which, in a particular
> situation, tends to weaken or destroy a subject. And the conception of Evil is
> thus entirely dependent on the events from which a subject constitutes itself ...
> there is no general form of evil because evil does not exist except as a judgement
> made by a subject on a situation.

Third, while much attention has been given to particular historical figures in
discussing events seen to represent evil, little academic literature has focused on
the consequences of seeing those figures as actually *embodying* evil, capturing
its essence in their very being. I am particularly interested in the significance of
the visual images of *faces* of evil because this *faciality* stands out for the very
intimacy and physicality that abstract discussions of notions of evil and fear in
moral philosophy often overlook, and contrasts with assumptions about Otherness
found in the recent take-up of the work of Levinas. The face is important because it
conjoins questions of morality, affect, cultural difference and humanity. Philpott's
(2005) analysis of the smiling faces of Bali bombers and Abu Ghraib torturers is a
powerful reminder of the importance of this conjunction, as well as its complexity,
because it symbolizes relations of domination and resistance.

To reassert the social constructedness of moral categories is not, however,
enough for a sustained interrogation of the moral dimensions of cultural
representation and social regulation. Nor is it enough to emphasize the ideological
function of images of good and evil: we need to think about their sensual and
affective charge, the kinds of moral investments that such representations invite,
the racialized positions of those invoking and those subject to such categories, and
the 'invitations' to emotion and action they present. As Grossberg (1986) argues,
the 'ideological' is most powerful if grounded in the affective. Within a turbulent
moment something more primordial, more emotive than mere representation, is
needed to secure a sense of moral certainty. The 'face of evil', I suggest, works
within the formation called Islamophobia to 'fix' evil as an identifiable entity in
terms of certain physiognomies and demeanours that are seen to reflect a deeper
'truth' of evil. The imagining of evil moves between a necessary abstraction, which
helps constitute evil as a general moral category, and a remarkable specificity
which grounds our fears in everyday realities—a movement that seems central
to the production of cultural panic around men of Arab and Muslim background.
This imagining of evil moves from the idea of a specific act being evil, to the
perpetrator being evil, to a cultural community being evil. Such moves constitute

a kind of 'permission' to indulge in affectively charged social acts that target those identified as social demons.

The visibility of difference has long been an issue in Australia, but this has centred on those, such as Indigenous or Asian Australians, whose difference is characterized as racial. The preoccupation with young men of 'Middle Eastern appearance' seen in the use of ethnic descriptors by police has been hotly debated (Jabbour, 2001), but has amounted to a new form of racialization of crime and the criminalization of ethnicity (Collins et al., 2000). More importantly, it is the specific facialization of evil which is significant here. The face, as scholars as diverse as Goffman and Ekman demonstrate, is central not just to interpersonal encounters but to larger questions of social order. 'Face' here is not simply the medium for the expression of universal human emotions (Ekman, 2004), for it operates within social systems of meaning. Yet nor is it just a symbolic entity, the 'positive social value' people claim for themselves (Goffman, 1972: 5), for it is linked intimately to the physicality of an actual face.

Tomkins (1962: 204) argues that the face is the primary site of affective communication and feedback. We read faces to make judgements about whether we should treat someone as a threat or see them as sincere and truthful. As Gibbs (2001) argues, in an analysis of representations of Pauline Hanson, the face is a rapid, largely unconscious yet social communicative medium that fosters forms of affective mimicry and resonance (smiles beget smiles, distress begets distress) which characterize the 'contagious' force of affect. The meshing of social and interpersonal dimensions of 'facework' is of great import in the work of Levinas (1994; 1985). For him, being face-to-face with radical difference is the basis of the development of a responsibility for the Other. The face of the Other calls forth an ethical response that is elemental to our experience of sociality and our desire to communicate with others. However, there is a problematic humanistic universalism in Levinas' work and, as Butler (2004) suggests, especially in a global climate shaped by a 'clash of civilizations', the demands the face of the Other makes upon us aren't always that clear, or can't be decided outside the context. Bauman (1990) argues that throughout human history, physical and moral proximity largely overlapped, as did distance and estrangement. The world was divided, he argued, into neighbours—with faces—and aliens, who were faceless. Modernity ruptured this link, requiring that people increasingly live with strangers who refuse to go away. The face, as a signifier of familiarity or strangeness, is crucial in the management of moral proximity. Despite Bauman's desire to sustain Levinas' claim that the encounter with the Other makes ethical demands upon us, his analysis shows that forms of civil inattention reproduce an indifference to otherness, a denial of the stranger as morally significant.

The truth of the face is, therefore, more complicated than the ethical claims Levinas makes, especially in the wake of the rise of Islamophobia. The debates around ethnic profiling and the portrayal of criminals of 'Middle Eastern appearance' point to the ideological work accomplished through the fetishization of cultural and physical attributes. This entails a boundedness of identities, a fixing of social categories of difference which delimit, rather than foster, interaction (Markell, 2003).

Relations between social order and face become more complex in the context of globalization. In such societies strangers dominate both our cityscapes and mediascapes: our sense of others is shaped by the mediations of communications technologies: *virtual* encounters of a kind that Goffman, Levinas and Bauman don't examine, but which play increasingly important roles in the production and management of pervasive anxieties in the west. Tester (1994, 2001) argues that the media are especially significant in the mediation of moral relations in a transnational world, foregrounding moral concerns and our obligations to others as well as global fears.

Such processes mean that emotions are mediatized as are moral concerns. Gibbs (2005) describes the illusion of intimacy sustained by television that seems to mimic the proximity of face-to-face encounters but instead enables the *avoidance* of physical contact with real bodies. She argues that the media act as vectors in affective epidemics which 'smuggle in' cultural meanings. Such meanings include the *negative* affect attributed to faces of evil.

The Faces of Many Evils as One

Let us turn to images of Islamic terrorism and the young Muslim men involved in gangs and rape. The central element of many of the stories involving such young men is that the perpetrators and their acts are framed as evil. Osama bin Laden was frequently framed this way–as 'Evil Close to Home' (*Bulletin*, 2002), 'Evil Speaks' and the 'Mastermind of Evil' (*Daily Telegraph*, 2002c) —but so too are other terrorists. Photofit images of three of the Bali bombers adorned the front page of the *Daily Telegraph*, described as 'the faces of evil behind the bombs' (Clifton, 2002). The photo of Al-Qaeda's Abu Faraj al-Libbi was captioned 'The face of a killer', while the beheading of an American civilian by 'terrorist psychopaths' in Iraq was dubbed 'PURE EVIL' (Jawad, 2005; Coorey, 2004). The *Telegraph* described the 'fear and courage' of survivors of the London bombings 'in the face of pure evil' (English, 2005). At the same time, 'ethnic' criminal gangs were said to have Sydney in 'their evil grip' (Lawrence and Miranda, 2003). The Skaf brothers, described as two gang rapists of Muslim background whose 'evil crimes shocked NSW', received record prison sentences (Miranda and Casella, 2005).

The characterization of these crimes as 'evil' is only part of the story; a significant symbolization of the folk devil occurs when the perpetrators themselves are portrayed as embodying evil. Butler (2004) describes what she calls the hyperbolic absorption of evil into the faces of Bin Laden and Saddam Hussein. There is something of a paradox here: on the one hand these faces represent specific cases of criminal behaviour perpetrated by individuals while on the other they work to constitute a universal moral category of evil—yet this universal category is culturally-inflected *through* their specific faciality. This paradox exists because notions of evil must offer both abstraction and specificity.

These events may be distinct but they share a figurative language and run together in terms of what Hartley and McKee (2000) call 'narrative accrual', the building up of an arsenal of meanings and images over time and through parallel narratives. Newspaper reports of terrorists and rapists make use of many images of the alleged perpetrators. Large images of the face of Osama bin Laden, for example, appeared in major magazines such as *Time*, *The Bulletin* and *Newsweek*. There have also been repeated images of those involved in the bombings in Bali and of gang rapists.

The temporal dimensions of this accrual are complemented by the connections between different events made through media reportage and commentary; the role of recurring military metaphors, for example, in juxtaposing gangs of Lebanese male youths as similar to militarily-trained international terrorists (Poynting et al., 2004). Sometimes the connections are explicit—claims, for example, that young Muslim men were trained by terrorists. These links were fanciful, but had purchase. The youthfulness of the bombers was emphasized and linked to local youth. Devine (2001) claimed in a piece on the 'triumph of evil':

> The perpetrators of the September 11 attacks were young Middle-Eastern Muslim men. Bin Laden's followers are young Middle-Eastern Muslim men. So it is young men of Middle-Eastern Muslim background who will be targeted in Sydney, many of them Australian citizens.

Within the paradox of the specificity of the face and the generality of evil, a number of themes emerge. Foremost, there is a reduction of the humanity of the perpetrators both visually and in the text. This dehumanization is demonstrated in several, often contrasting, ways. One common image is a conventional portrait of the 'criminal type': a man of sinister demeanour staring at you with knitted brow, missing tooth and unshaven face. This large computer-enhanced image of an alleged perpetrator was captioned, 'Face of a rapist' (Birch, 2001). This image has a menacing but unspecified quality to it: the expression is almost blank and not easily defined. The downcast eyes of Mohammed Skaf in his 'mug shot' suggests a drug-induced reverie; a kind of blankness (Miranda and Casella, 2005). A frequent image of Bin Laden is a close-up that conveys an unnervingly blank expression. This image can be dressed up in darkened tones or framed through the lens and target hairs of a rifle to add menace, but the expression is still blank (*Time* 2001; 2002. Absence of affect is also seen in the computer images of the Bali bombers, framed as a 'wanted' poster and with the anonymity of generic labels – 'suspect one' (Clifton, 2002). These images are sinister *because* of the absence of emotion. The face reflects a capacity for criminal behaviour, moral transgression or incivility because of the absence of remorse, guilt or shame.

'Humanity' is expressed through emotions; drain the emotion, and you erase the humanity. These images are in contrast to the humanity of victims, whose lives are represented in their emotional fullness, as in the case of the rape victims and in the family photos of the bomb victims. After the London bombings one of the victims was dubbed the 'face of innocence' (Gysin and Levy, 2005). The *Daily Telegraph* ran a front page of the faces of the Bali victims, and many pages to their stories. The images are first denoted as 'the faces of our dead', then 'faces of tragedy', 'faces missing', and the 'face of broken humanity'. This faciality is accompanied by the vast range of human emotion. Alongside the happy faces are faces of mourning, agony, despair, distress, horror and grief: 'raw emotion' in the midst of which 'hardened professionals cry' (*Daily Telegraph*, 2002b). A moral opposition is being constructed which aligns humanity, emotion and morality on one side, and their absence with evil.

In contrast, there are examples where the perpetrator is shown with positive emotions, yet these images are also read as exemplifying lack of humanity. The mug shot of Bilal Skaf grinning broadly was reprinted several times over several years as was an infamous shot of the 'evil' Skaf smiling proudly while resting a gun on his lap (Casella, 2005). He was condemned as 'a menace to any civilized society', and his lack of remorse and apparent joy in his actions were taken as demonstrations of his lack of feeling (Miranda and Casella, 2005). Bali bomber Amrozi, the 'smiling assassin', was decried for his lack of compassion: 'Suspect Amrozi was 'delighted' when his Bali bomb exploded, laughing so hard his wife asked him what had happened' (Callinan, 2002).

Attention was given to Amrozi's behaviour in court; acting like a 'clown' was taken as evidence of his being 'evil' and a 'madman' (Wockner, 2006). For many commentators this behaviour personified evil because it defied easy cultural categorization. This *excess* of affect, like the absences of emotion in other images, contravenes conventions of appropriate behaviours and is taken to be illustrative of a lack of moral feeling —the elemental condition of evil (Philpott, 2005). The absence and excess of emotion are inscrutable within the normative terms of human behaviour. This anxious lack of certainty about the meaning of outrageous acts is central to their characterization as evil. The response after the London bombings, as after the events of September 11 and the Bali bombings, was to first acknowledge the images of the young men responsible as 'the face of evil', then to ask, 'Why did they do it?' (Good Morning America, 2005).

This enigmatic quality of evil is seen in stories of terrorist ontogenesis which ask how a 'normal' young citizen becomes a terrorist (*Daily Telegraph*, 2004). It is also seen in the anxieties concerning the elusive identity of the terrorist: Al Qaeda's network was described a 'the enemy with a thousand faces' (Kamiya, 2001); one Al Qaeda figure was dubbed 'a man of many faces' (Rizk, 2004). This elusive quality is not just reserved for terrorists: a criminal 'master of disguise', Ramon Youmaran, was characterized as having 'six faces' (Lawrence and Jones, 2006). Despite this, the accumulated effect of these images of wrongdoers is their distillation into a singularity—an abstraction that represents an essence of evil.

The Work of Evil

Evil here functions in two significant ways within globalized Islamophobia: it offers broad confirmation of a moral worldview that guarantees the possibility of good by posing the necessity of evil, but it does that by attaching evil to whole religiously and ethnically defined 'communities' through an affectively charged threat of action outside 'normal' human morality. There is a double movement— we are shown the face of a perpetrator who is cast as an evil person and this face is taken as the embodiment of a larger evil, one aligned with a cultural pathology. This movement is premised on a fundamental moral code of good and evil, and locates this 'incomprehensible' evil elsewhere. It doesn't matter, in a sense, that these 'communities' are ideological fictions which conjoin geo-political regions, ethnicities, national backgrounds, faiths and languages, because the function is to provide evil with a recognizable physiognomy of difference. The capacity for evil is perceived as a cultural trait of a religious worldview, whose reception is affectively charged. One journalist was concerned about the existence of 'evil families of hate' whose young men were 'bonded in name and culture' (Casella, 2005). Devine (2002) argued that 'the powerful tool of shame' needs to be 'applied to the families and communities that nurtured the rapists, gave them succour and brought them up with such a hatred of Australia's dominant culture and contempt for its women'.

The 'face of evil' works in several, contradictory, ways. It allows us to identify evil, to recognize it as a material entity. It provides us with a physiognomy of evil where a face is a reflection of the character of evil, personified in particular humans but representative of a certain moral universality, much like phrenology. This allows us to recognize evil as type—uncaring, sadistic, animalistic, violent, unemotional. Yet this type is grounded in the abhorrent behaviour attributed to particular groups—Middle Eastern, Lebanese or Muslim. The face becomes the metonym for the cultural pathology of evil, while evil becomes the pathology of a 'culture'. This allows us to fix in our sights a sense of evil as both present and removed—it is near, but someone else.

This double movement is an act of 'defacement' (Goffman, 1972) whereby the individual face becomes the symbol of something other. In the process whereby faces of perpetrators become *the* face of a racialized evil, not only the perpetrator but a whole community loses face. This is not just a process of identarian *reduction* but also processes of *intensification*, the affectively charged dimensions of recognition. As Bauman suggests, when media reduces strangers to surfaces, they remove them of their moral integrity, their humanity. Garland (2008) and Irvine (2007) point to the need to examine affective role of moral panic, the mobilization of emotions and anxieties and not just the ideological representation of otherness. Nussbaum (2004: 166-7) has shown how disgust directed at an Other is central to the enactment of law as it is in everyday life, and produces a sense of stability by creating clear boundaries.

This fixing of evil via defacement is especially significant in a world of moral turbulence; it is an affectively charged symbolization that provides a sense of certainty and security in an increasingly 'fluid' world, marked by economic and social instabilities and transformations, as well as cultural difference (Bauman, 2005). It addresses the need for an abiding sense of moral truth and the identification of the social manifestation of evil amidst complexities of meaning, scale and value. It allays our anxieties around loss of cultural harmony and moral decency by identifying and condensing wider processes of cultural decay in the Other: our disgust with the Other allows us to transcend our own vulnerability (Nussbaum, 2004: 254-9, 109). It locates moral certainty in the social order even as it identifies the sources of threat there too. As Badiou (Cox and Whalen, 2001/2) argues, 'the idea of Evil has become essential' in the West, but with the rider that 'real Evil is elsewhere': 'Under the pretext of not accepting Evil, we end up making believe that we have, if not the Good, at least the best possible state of affairs—even if this best is not so great'. We accept as ideal, therefore, the inequalities of capitalism— we may have problems, we say, but we aren't evil like foreign dictatorships. This turns, he suggests, on a universalizing of evil: 'political regimes that have fought against liberalism and democracy all share the same face of Evil'.

Evil is typically linked to the threat of social disorder; folk devils are central to the ideological diagnoses of a society's ills. As an 'explanation' they work because they speak to popular anxieties—about social, economic and technological change, loss of community, cultural disharmony and so forth—and because they work through affectively charged social perceptions. Ironically, however, the pervasive nature of evil disrupts the certainty and security it offers. There are moments when the fixing of evil in the face of an Other falls apart. The very nature of a panic, Cohen (1972, 2002) reminds us, is its short-lived volatility. The 'fixing' of evil is momentary: the anxieties contained by the easy recognition of the face of evil are never far from the surface. We oscillate between the stability offered by naming evil and the turbulence around us.

The identification of evil, therefore, becomes an increasingly anxious task of the dominant, especially in a globalized world where social order cannot be contained by national boundaries . As a *Daily Telegraph* editorial reminds us, 'images of evil serve a vital role', they 'remind us that evil exists, and must be overcome if freedom is to be sustained' (*Daily Telegraph*, 2002a). Note that evil here is contrasted with freedom, as well as with good, and it is presented as something that must be fought. In this discourse, evil has a totalizing quality—it turns wrongdoing into absolute categories of self-evident right and wrong, shorn of context and causality. It also essentializes moral and social transgression, and, in the end, turns evil into a pathology which is translated into cultural terms as well as being deemed a flaw of individual psyche. As Baumeister (1997) has argued, we hold on to the 'myth of pure evil' as an intentional, pleasurable, egotistical act conducted on an innocent victim. In this myth, evil is Other, the antithesis to social order, and eternal. This myth, however, conceals the complex social, political and economic causes of crime, terrorism and violence. It is a process of *depoliticization*, turning history into universals, and the *moralization* of social problems, whereby complex processes are translated into moral terms: such moralization not only aids the erasure of social explanation, it substitutes our global anxieties with a reassurance of someone else's moral culpability.

Conclusion: Stabilizing Turbulence

It is not surprising that much effort has been made to 'discover the face of Muslim Australia' (*Sydney Morning Herald* 2007). To give a 'Muslim' face to evil paradoxically produces it as concrete and abstract, knowable but elusive. The face of evil fosters the racialization of crime through the suturing together of disparate events and is ultimately an act of defacement. It involves reduction, displacement and intensification. It decontextualizes social acts and yet renders them more amenable to 'explanations' drawing on cultural pathologies. The face of evil is therefore very powerful. Indeed, Latour (2005) argues that a 'society' is unified less by a shared set of values than a dominant set of 'worries', each of which 'generates a different pattern of emotions and disruptions, of disagreements and agreements'. Such 'matters of concern' are not simply symbolic entities, but are also magnets for social emotions and actions.

At heart, however, is a certain anxiety about ourselves. As one media report put it: 'Face it. We've changed'. The report went on to ask, 'what does an Australian look like? How have our faces changed over the decades?' before concluding that 'gone is the open, weather-beaten Australian visage' (Smith, 2006). Identifying a face of evil doesn't solve this anxiety—at best it offers us a 'virtuous paranoia': we remain insecure about what we are but we have a kind of working explanation that at least reassures us of an overriding moral unity (Morton, 2004). The transcendence of our own vulnerability through disgust with the Other is then only ever provisional. The oscillation between turbulence and fixity underlies the condition of 'neurotic citizenship' (Isin, 2004), where the relation between nation and cultural diversity is structured by fragile concerns around security and safety, and the obsession with moral boundaries and their transgression.

I might argue, rephrasing Vetlesen (2005: 5, 289), that *naming* evil offers the foregoing of responsibility (deferring to a higher moral order) but it also offers the reclamation of agency, in so far as it provides an object and a means for action. Like *doing* evil, the *naming* of evil entails a protest against vulnerability and a recuperation of social power under threat by the named evil. But this action is deeply problematic: it licenses racial vilification directed towards Muslim and Arab Australians across every social space as an 'affective regulation of belonging' which endorses belonging for the perpetrators, and steals it from the victim (Noble and Poynting, 2008). Defining evil as a type marked by cultural difference is an 'invitation' to legitimately act on that affective motivation. It licenses hate crime, which has real consequences in the lives of Muslims though everyday acts of harassment because it treats victims as representatives of threatening communities.

An emphasis on the moral and the affective allows us to see how the immediacy of the local is conjoined with the administrative functions of the nation-state and the circulation of global fears: Muslims have become not just objects of national governance, but a focus for the transnational coordination of security and the management of cultural diversity in a globalized world (Humphrey, 2010: 199). Yet, as Philpott (2005: 251) argues, the 'fixing' of meaning around images of evil not only evades a deeper understanding of what is at stake in the war on terror, crime and social disorganization, it encourages complicity in the erosion of civil rights.

References

Angel, M. and A. Gibbs 2006. Media, Affect and the Face. *Southern Review.* 38(2), 24–39.

Arendt, H. 1994. *Eichmann in Jerusalem*. New York: Penguin.

Bauman, Z. 1989. *Modernity and the Holocaust*. Oxford: Polity Press.

Bauman, Z. 2005. *Liquid Life*. Cambridge: Polity Press.

Birch, S. 2991. PUT ON HOLD: Face of a rapist. *Daily Telegraph*, 15 August, 1.

Bulletin 2002. Evil Close to Home, 19 February, 1.

Butler, J. 2004. *Precarious Life*. Verso, London.

Cahir, J. and Noble, G. 2007. It's a Security Thing: Mobile Phones and Moral Regulation, in S. Poynting and G. Morgan eds. *Outrageous: Moral Panics in Australia*. Hobart: ACYS Publishing.

Callinan, R. 2002. Bali Bomber Laughed When Told of Carnage. *Daily Telegraph*. 14 November, 5.

Casella, N. 2005. Why are We Breeding Evil Families of Hate? *Daily Telegraph*. 1 August, 21.

Chandab, T. 2008. Fears, dream and racism in a rural paddock. *The Sun-Herald*. 6 January: 9.

Clifton, B. 2002. WANTED. *Daily Telegraph*. 31 October, 1.

Cohen, S 1972/1980. *Folk Devils and Moral Panics*. 2nd edition, Oxford: Basil Blackwell.

Cohen, S 1972/2002. *Folk Devils and Moral Panics*. 3rd edition, Oxford: Routledge.

Cox, C. and M. Whalen 2001/2. On Evil: An Interview with Alain Badiou. *Cabinet Magazine Online* 5, <http://www.cabinetmagazine.org/issues/5/alainbadiou.php>

Coorey, P. 2004. Pure Evil. *Daily Telegraph*. 13 May, 1.

Daily Telegraph 2002a. Images of Evil Serve a Vital Role. *Daily Telegraph*, 9 September, 16.

Daily Telegraph 2002b. Terror in Bali. *Daily Telegraph*, 15 October, 1–13.

Daily Telegraph 2002c. Evil Speaks. *Daily Telegraph*, 14 November, 1.

Daily Telegraph 2004. One Boy's Journey from Suburban Australia to World Terrorism. *Daily Telegraph*, Inside Edition, 12 June, 27–9.

DebatingChristianity. N.D. Is Islam Immoral? http://debatingchristianity.com/forum/pda/thread.php?topic_id=8772

Devine, M. 2002. Racist Rapes: Finally the Truth Comes Out. *Sun-Herald*. 14 July, 15.

Devine, M. 2001. Triumph of Evil in Dancing on American Graves, *Daily Telegraph*, 11 November, 28.

Ekman, P. 2004. *Emotions Revealed*. London: Phoenix.

English, B. 2005. Fear and Courage in the Face of Pure Evil. *Daily Telegraph*. 8 July, 4.

Fekete, L. 2009. *A Suitable Enemy: Racism, Migration and Islamophobia in Europe.*

London: Pluto Press.

Fenely, R. 2010. A nation's line in the sand. *Sydney Morning Herald News Review.* January 23-24: 1.

Gottschalk, P. and Greenberg, G. 2008. *Islamophobia: Making Muslims the Enemy.* Maryland: Rowman & Littlefield.

Garfinkel, H. 1984. *Studies in Ethnomethodology*. Cambridge: Polity Press.

Garland, D. 2008. On the concept of moral panic. *Crime, Media, Culture.* 4(1): 9-30.

Gibbs, A. 2991. Contagious Feelings: Pauline Hanson and the Epidemiology of Affect. *Australian Humanities Review.* 24, 2001 <http://www.lib.latrobe.edu.au/AHR/archive/Issue-December-2001/gibbs.html>.

Gibbs, A. 2005. In Thrall: Affect Contagion and the Bio-Energetics of Media. *M/C Journal*, 8, 6, <http://journal.media-culture.org.au/0512/10-gibbs.php>;

Goffman, E. 1972. *Interaction Order*. Harmondsworth: Penguin.

Goldberg, D. 2009. *The Threat of Race: Reflections on Racial Neoliberalism.* London: Wiley Blackwell

Good Morning America 2005. NBC, 13 July broadcast on Channel 9, Sydney, 4.30am, 14 July.

Goode, E., and Ben-Yehuda, N. 2009. *Moral panics: The social construction of deviance*. Oxford: Wiley-Blackwell.

Grossberg, L. 1986. History, Politics and Postmodernism: Stuart Hall and Cultural Studies. *Journal of Communication Inquiry.* 10(2) 61-77.

Gysin, C. and A. Levy 2005. Face of Innocence. *Daily Telegraph.* 12 July, 5.

Hall, S, Critcher, C, Jefferson, T, Clarke, J & Roberts, B 1978. *Policing the Crisis: Mugging, the State, and Law and Order*. London: Macmillan.

Hartley, J. and Alan McKee 2000. *The Indigenous Public Sphere*. Oxford: Oxford University Press.

Heintz, M. 2009. Introduction, in M. Heintz ed. *The Anthropology of Moralities*. New York: Berghahn. 1-19.

Howell, S. 1997. Introduction, in S. Howell ed. T*he Ethnography of Moralities*. London: Routledge. 1-24.

Humphrey, M. 2007. Culturalising the abject: Islam, law and moral panic in the West. *Australian Journal of Social Issues*. 42(1) 9-25.

Humphrey, M. 2010. Conditional Multiculturalism: Islam in Liberal Democratic States, in D. Ivison ed. *Ashgate Research Companion to Multiculturalism*. Farnham: Ashgate. 199-216.

Ibrahim, Y. 2007. 9/11 as a new temporal phase for Islam: The narrative and temporal framing of Islam in crisis. *Contemporary Islam*. 1, 37-51

Irvine, J. 2007. Transient Feelings: Sex Panics and the Politics of Emotions. *GLQ: A Journal of Lesbian and Gay Studies*. 14(1), 1-40.

Isin, E. 2004. The Neurotic Citizen, *Citizenship Studies*. 8(3), 217-235.

Jabbour, R. 2001. Policing Partnership in a Multicultural Australia, Australian Arabic Council. <http://www.aac.org.au/media.php?ArtID=6>.

Jawad, R. 2005. Net Closing in on Bin Laden. *Daily Telegraph*. 6 May, 32.

Kamiya, G. 2001. The Enemy With a Thousand Faces. *AlterNet*. posted September 13, <http://www.alternet.org/module/11497 31/10/2005>;

Kerbaj, R. 2007. Warning to West on 'evil of Islam'. *The Australian*. August 21. http://www.theaustralian.com.au/news/nation/warning-to-west-on-evil-of-islam/story-e6frg6nf-1111114230210

Larmore, C. 1987. *Patterns of Moral Complexity*. Cambridge: University of Cambridge Press.

Latour, B. 2995. From Realpolitik to Dingpolitik, or How to Make Things Public. <http://www.bruno-latour.fr/articles/article/96-MTP-DING.pdf>.

Lawrence, K. and C. Miranda 2003. Outlaw Generation. *Daily Telegraph*. 23 October, 1.

Lawrence, G. and G. Jones. 2006. Six Faces of a Fugitive. *Daily Telegraph*. 11 April, 3.

Levinas, W. 1994. *Outside the Subject*. trans. M. Smith, Stanford: Stanford University Press.

Levinas, E. 1985. *Ethics and Infinity*. trans. R.A. Cohen, Pittsburgh: Duquesne University Press.

Miranda, C. and N. Casella 2005. NO JUSTICE. *Daily Telegraph*. 4 February, 1.

Morton,A. 2004. *On Evil*. New York: Routledge.

Noble, G. and Scott Poynting 2008. Neither Relaxed nor Comfortable: The Affective Regulation of Migrant Belonging in Australia, in R. Pain and S. Smith eds. *Fear: Critical Geopolitics and Everyday Life*. London: Routledge. 129-138.

Nussbaum, M. 2004. *Hiding from Humanity*. Princeton: Princeton University Press.

Pappas, J. N.D. Is Islam Evil? FaithFreedom.org http://www.faithfreedom.org/oped/JasonPappas40401.htm

Parkin, D. 1985. Introduction, in D. Parkin ed. *The Anthropology of Evil*. Oxford: Basil Blackwell. 1-25.

Philpott, S 2005. A Controversy of Faces: Images from Bali and Abu Ghraib. *Journal of Cultural Research*. 9, 3, 227–44.

Poynting, S., Noble, G., Tabar, P. and Collins, J. 2004. Bin Laden in the Suburbs: Criminalising the Arab Other Sydney: Institute of Criminology.

Poynting, S. and Mason, V. 2007. The resistible rise of Islamophobia: Anti-Muslim racism in the UK and Australia before 11 September 2001. *Journal of Sociology.* 43, 1: 61-86.

Rapport, N. 1997. The morality of locality, in S. Howell ed. T*he Ethnography of Moralities.* London: Routledge. 75-98.

Rizk, G. 2004. A Man of Many Faces. *Sunday Telegraph.* 6 June, 87.

Runnymede Trust 1997. *Islamophobia: a challenge for us all.* London: Runnymede Trust.

Said, E 1978. *Orientalism.* London: Penguin.

Smith, D. 2006. Face It. We've Changed. *Sydney Morning Herald.* 7–8 January, 15.

Sydney Morning Herald 2007. Islam in Australia. 28–29 April, 1, 8, 25, 31.

Time Magazine 2002. 25 November.

Time Magazine 2001. 26 November.

Tomkins, S. 1962. *Affect, Imagery, Consciousness.* vol.1, New York: Springer.

Vetlesen, A. 2005. *Evil and Human Agency.* Cambridge: Cambridge University Press.

Waiton, S. 2008. *The Politics of Antisocial Behaviour: Amoral Panics.* London: Routledge.

Werbner, P. 2002. *Imagined Diasporas among Manchester Muslims: The Public Performance of Pakistani Transnational Identity Politics.* Oxford: James Currey.

Wockner, C. 2006. Amrozi Sings for his Evil Mate. *Daily Telegraph.* 20 April, 11.

Index